Ivor A. Stevens:

Soldier, Politician, Businessman, and Family Man

Ivor A. Stevens:

Soldier, Politician, Businessman, and Family Man

The Man, His Times, and the Politics of St. Kitts-Nevis

Whitman T. Browne, PhD

iUniverse LLC
Bloomington

IVOR A. STEVENS:
SOLDIER, POLITICIAN, BUSINESSMAN, AND FAMILY MAN
THE MAN, HIS TIMES, AND THE POLITICS OF ST. KITTS-NEVIS

iUniverse books may be ordered through booksellers or by contacting:

iUniverse LLC
1663 Liberty Drive
Bloomington, IN 47403
www.iuniverse.com
1-800-Authors (1-800-288-4677)

ISBN: 978-1-4759-2825-9 (sc)
ISBN: 978-1-4759-2826-6 (hc)
ISBN: 978-1-4759-2827-3 (ebk)

Library of Congress Control Number: 2012909275

Printed in the United States of America

iUniverse rev. date: 07/16/2013

Contents

ACKNOWLEDGEMENTS

This book was written back in 2001, but there was a problem with its editing. Thanks to Sue and John Morris of Editide for their suggestions, the presentation is now much more creative. Meanwhile, the observations, thoughts, and ideas that came together to fashion this book, are not all mine. Mr. Stevens, his wife, sister, and other members of his family, along with close friends, political colleagues, and many other persons in St. Kitts-Nevis talked with me, shared written material, and worked with me in a variety of ways to help, as I compiled the manuscript. To all those many persons who gave of their time and ideas, some named in the book, others not, I am profoundly grateful for your help.

There are some friends who read the original draft and suggested further editing. It took almost ten years to get it completed, but thank you! Now that the production process is over, I hope it was worth the wait. Also, what can I do but to be eternally grateful to a wife, children, grandchildren, and other family members who have been there for me through it all!

While others provided ideas and perspectives for the documentation, all the conclusive statements and arguments are mine. If anything I said irritates your sensibilities, I accept the blame. As a human being, I do not possess complete knowledge. Neither do I see the world perfectly. However, I do endeavor to see clearly and speak honestly, in the information shared. Thanks to iUniverse for helping to make the book available.

Whitman T. Browne, Ph. D.

Introduction

It is a truism that history and cultural experiences shape human lives. Generally, people become who they are because of the times in which they live, and how they interact with those times. Sometimes, however, there are people who help shape history, fashioning the now and helping to create that future, beyond the now. Even after such people are long gone, because of death, there can be agreement among those still alive, that society is different and at times better, because such persons lived. In that inevitable historical postmortem, social and political, it will not matter much who asks the questions to write the annals for the islands, Nevis and St. Kitts. The evidence is permanent. The unique markings of that legacy can be seen everywhere on Nevis. They show and speak to the fact that Nevisians' lives and destiny were transformed because of the uncommon life and politics of the Kittitian, Ivor Algernon Stevens.

Many people who knew Ivor Stevens well agree that he committed himself to the improvement of Nevis. That challenge he accepted from the time he returned to the island in 1953, and before he entered the island's politics in 1957. Mr. Stevens' nephew Maurice noted that long before Uncle Ivor entered politics, he, his brother Garnet, and Esmond Williams worked together and used scrap metal to build a plough to aid farmers on Nevis. Seemingly, Ivor maintained a special commitment to the island and its people, from that early time until he died in June 1997.

Although Ivor was born on St. Kitts, many of his formative years were spent in Nevis. He could not claim the island through birth, but whenever Ivor had to choose one island over the other, he claimed Nevis because of his long residence there. In 1997, shortly before his death, he wrote, "Not being a Nevisian by birth and considering myself to be one on account of my many years spent here, I consider it my home."

Such was the thinking and commitment demonstrated repeatedly through his actions on the island and on behalf of Nevisians. In 1953, for example, shortly after marrying his beautiful, adorable Dora, Ivor chose to move from their secure jobs in bustling St. Kitts to much uncertainty in underdeveloped, struggling Nevis. That act itself was more than a symbolic returning to the home where he grew up. It was a deliberate choice as to where he wanted to spend the rest, and the best remembered years of his life. Ivor determined at that point to cast his lot with Nevis and Nevisians. He came back to the island, enjoined the political struggle there, to counter domination by St. Kitts and never left or relented until he died. By moving back to Nevis, Stevens also demonstrated a belief and an unusual commitment to the idea that there is the human capacity to achieve change in one's life experiences and circumstances. Mr. Stevens also exhibited a high level of confidence in his ability to lead the change process, and to bring about the quality of change that would empower Nevisians.

Today, Stevens is best remembered in Nevis as a committed politician, and for his varied accomplishments through politics. However, that road to his success was strewn with blind curves, deep valleys, and some rugged mountains. But, he remained committed and persisted through it all, finally realizing a fair measure of political success on the island. This is still a powerful testimony to the fortitude and tenacity of the man. Stevens believed in himself. Neither time nor difficulties changed his vision for Nevis, or the confidence with which he envisioned change in the future of the island—an island he had come to love and call home.

BOOK I

LIFE AND TIMES

CHAPTER 1

LIFE

Because Ivor was neither the first child nor the first boy in the family, the occasion of his birth must not have been too momentous or stressful for his parents, Ethelinda and James Stevens. Accordingly, Ivor Algernon Stevens was born unceremoniously at Downing Street in Sandy Point, St. Kitts, on August 23, 1911. As fate had it, that birth occurred just 3 short years before the beginning of the First Great War (1914-1918). However, since that war did not end all wars, as was promised, after the First World War, European domination and thrust in the area continued, despite the Monroe Doctrine, placing Caribbean islanders in line for an increased role in the Second World War (1939-1945). In time, these events also set the stage for more involvement in the Caribbean area by the United States of America. Ivor Stevens lived to become an important player in that ensuing scenario of dramatic social and political changes in the Caribbean. New developments in technology, ideas about democracy, and global politics also affected the Caribbean scene, bringing to the area unprecedented economic, social, and political transformations. One of the earliest factors to cause great change in the St. Kitts, Nevis, and Anguilla colony at the turn of the 1900s was the establishment of a central sugar factory in Basseterre, St. Kitts, in 1912—at that time a new and innovative attempt to invigorate the dominant, but failing sugar plantation economy in the islands.

Family

That was the economic, social, and global political milieu into which Ivor Algernon Stevens was born in 1911. His mother, Ethelinda Leonora Penn-Stevens was from the British Virgin Islands, and his father, James Henry Stevens, hailed from St. Kitts. While the event of Ivor's birth took place without much pomp or ceremony, his life was to be more momentous. Shortly after he was born, the child was christened at the Methodist Church at Sandy Point, not far from his home.

As fate would have it, 2 months after his son's birth, Ivor's father, who had worked as a schoolteacher on St. Kitts, was transferred to Nevis by the government and given a new assignment. James Henry Stevens became the new Superintendent of Public Works on the island. Ironically, many years later, while his son, Ivor, served as a Minister of the People's Action Movement—Nevis Reformation Party (PAM-NRP) coalition government, he, too, supervised the Public Works Department. Through time, Ivor aspired to, and believed in his ability to serve the people of Nevis. That was his overpowering dream even as he was elected to the House of Assembly on St. Kitts, then later as a member of two governments, one on St. Kitts, and one on Nevis. His brothers and sisters, who were alive then, rallied with him and always assured Ivor of their full support. Sister May, who outlived him, remained a best friend and ardent supporter of her brother. She died in 2006, some 9 years after him.

Ivor had 4 brothers and 2 sisters; these 7 survived of the 11 children conceived from the union of Ethelinda and James Stevens. At the turn of the century, families in St. Kitts and Nevis were much larger than 2 or 3 children, as is now common in the islands. However, a more primitive era of medicine, poor nutrition, and high poverty rates resulted in high levels of infant mortality on the islands. Since contraception was uncommon in all classes of society, there were high birth rates. Notwithstanding, it was also a time when miscarriages and early death from diseases were common to the poor as well as the wealthy in plantation-driven societies. For example, despite the success of sugar on the island, St. Kitts was once noted as one of the British Caribbean islands with an unusually high incidence of infant deaths. Although the focus here is on Ivor, brief comments and glimpses of his siblings can help to locate him and broaden understanding about his story, the society, and the time in which he lived.

Cardigan MacArthur was the oldest of the 7 children. At one time he worked as a civil servant for the colonial governments of Antigua, St. Lucia, and in time, also the government of St. Kitts, Nevis, and Anguilla. Many older persons in St. Kitts and Nevis remember Cardigan as a government enforcer, working against importers and transporters of illegal liquor. He was authorized to capture persons who smuggled liquor into St. Kitts, Nevis, and Anguilla from the neighboring French territories of St. Barth's and French St. Martin. The oral history from that time claims Cardigan Stevens was very serious about his assignment. At times he also became an arbiter of justice and an executioner on the high seas. A son, Maurice, was born to Cardigan in St. Lucia. When Maurice became rebellious, Ivor brought Maurice to St. Kitts-Nevis to assist in raising him "to be a Stevens." Even today Maurice comments on the memories and praises his uncle, but says little about his father.

Garnet Hughes, another older brother, managed the early telephone system on Nevis during the late 1940s and early 1950s. Garnet is also remembered as one of the earliest motor mechanics on the island. He trained a number of other Nevisians, many to carry on the trade later. Although Ivor took pride in, and boasted about his skills as a fisherman, Nevisians who know about fishing suggest that Garnet was the successful fisherman in the Stevens' family.

Hope Renolph was born in Tortola, the British Virgin Islands. As a young man, Hope worked in St. Kitts and in Tortola. For a while he was among the anticolonial voices in the British Virgin Islands. In time, however, Hope joined the mass Eastern Caribbean migration to the Dominican Republic, during the early 1900s. Eventually, he too emigrated to the United States, where, through sheer determination, commitment to personal development, and belief in social change, he became a successful labor lawyer. Hope Stevens was also active in the Harlem Renaissance movement for

Caribbean political evolution and independence. He became a lawyer and a staunch supporter of labor unionism in New York and the Caribbean. Horne[1] mentioned Hope Stevens in his discussion of Caribbean expatriates and their exploits during the Harlem Renaissance era. Hope Stevens also became a significant person in the civil rights and anticolonial movement that started to blossom in Harlem, New York. During the Nevis Reformation Party's struggle for political development and autonomy in Nevis, like the other members of the family, Hope demonstrated his solidarity with Ivor. From time to time, he visited Nevis to show support for his younger brother.

Hope's success in New York and his contributions to movements for Caribbean political development earned him honorable mention in the writings by a number of authors. New York City Schools ensured that Hope Ellerton Stevens was included with other famous New York personalities in a series of books, *Call Them Heroes*, published by Silver Burdett. He is also highlighted in a book about outstanding Caribbean persons in New York.[2]

An older sister to Ivor, Marian Agatha, worked in the Department of Agriculture, and then for a much longer period at the post office in St. Kitts, but she too retired in Nevis. During the 1970s, when Nevisians were searching for independent, authentic, cultural expressions different from those seen in St. Kitts, Ms. Stevens was among the innovators. Her expertise in handicraft contributed to the development of local offerings for tourists, to a revival of the local crafts, and the cultural activities associated with Culturama on Nevis.[3] After her retirement, this member of the Stevens' clan was involved in a tireless promotion of crafts on the island. Her work was displayed in a modest building on the site of the present Nevis electoral office building.

---

[1] Horne, G. (2007). *Cold War in a Hot Zone: The United States Confronts Labor and Independence Struggles in the British West Indies.* Philadelphia, PA: Temple University Press.

[2] Burdett, S. (1965). *Call Them Heroes.* New York, NY: Board of Education.

[3] For a description of Culturama, see Sports and Recreation.

Yvonne May (always called May on Nevis) studied nursing in England from 1935 to 1942. She became the first non-White person to serve as a matron at a hospital in St. Kitts and Nevis. Yvonne May's tenure as head nurse lasted from 1942 until 1961. After retirement, May resettled in Nevis where she lived as a vibrant and seemingly very happy senior citizen. Although May was interviewed for this book about her brother, she died before the book was published. May remembered Ivor at school, and talked about receiving a letter from him while Ivor served oversees with the Canadian forces in Europe and North Africa.

Cecil Ellerton was the last of the 7 children to be born. He went on to become a Howard University-trained dentist. Dr. Stevens worked for many years as one of the first native-born dentists in St. Kitts-Nevis. Seemingly, despite the outward show of conflict between them, Ivor and Premier Bradshaw were never real enemies. With his brother Cecil as dentist and intermediary, Ivor maintained a cordial family relationship and friendship with Bradshaw that was never obvious from the political barbs exchanged during the House of Assembly debates. The same was true of Steven's relationship with Lee L. Moore, another stalwart in the Labor Party, and in the Labor government during the 1970s. Moore also served as Cecil Ellerton's lawyer. During their encounters outside of politics, Ivor and Moore interacted with each other from a stance of civility and an understanding that each belonged to a different political organization. There were occasions when Stevens did acknowledge his respect for Mr. Moore as a politician and attorney.

Education

Ivor grew up as a Methodist, but later in life lost interest in organized religion. At one point he was schooled by his mother at home, but Ivor was exposed to formal, public elementary education by 1916 at the Charlestown Boys' School, located in the Methodists' building at the top of Chapel Street. He later attended the private Excelsior School, started in 1921, by Miss Helen Bridgewater, at Charlestown, the capital of Nevis. Ivor also attended the elite St.

Kitts Grammar School until about the late 1930s. That school was located at Basseterre, the capital of St. Kitts, in the same area where the Basseterre High School now stands. According to his sister May, Ivor found school to be an inconvenience and probably never took the school's terminal Cambridge exam, set in England.

Ivor's parents were not wealthy compared with members of the landowning plantocracy in either St. Kitts or Nevis. However, members of the Stevens' family were of fairer complexion than the average Nevisian and Kittitian; and at that time color mattered on the islands. The father's long-term prestigious employment with the government also ensured the family some high social status. These parents understood the power of education as an avenue to social mobility. They were determined to educate their children well, despite the barriers to a good education in Nevis at that time. Consequently, Mr. and Mrs. Stevens grasped every available opportunity to ensure that their children received the best education available to them on Nevis, St. Kitts, or elsewhere.

Prior to 1915, churches were in charge of elementary education on the islands. After 1915, church buildings remained a fixture in elementary education on St. Kitts, Nevis, and Anguilla. However, because the British government finally agreed to pay a share of the cost for education in the colonies, there was a movement away from church schools as the prime mover in education on the islands. At that time, secondary education was available only to the rich, the almost rich, those who were White, and those who were almost White. Higher education was restricted and too costly for the working class. It was in that social and academic atmosphere that Ma and Pa Stevens encouraged their children to reach beyond the primary education, offered as the terminal level of education in the public elementary schools on Nevis.

Ivor's siblings spoke about their family as being very ordinary, and like others, victims of the harsh economic times imposed by the economic, social, and political limitations of British colonialism. However, in spite of the existing hard times, they noted that the Stevens' family was a caring family and one well knit together, despite external circumstances. Hope reflected on his schooling and those times:

> Pa's salary was so small it could barely sustain us. We usually had barely enough to eat. Our mother made all our clothes, including those for our father. They found it almost impossible to keep us in shoes. But there were two things we had a lot of: ambition and love for one another. . . . Our father wanted his children to have as much education as possible. He persuaded the headmistress at Excelsior High School (a private school on Nevis, then) to admit his male children, even though it was a registered girls' school.[4]

The school later became a mixed school, admitting both boys and girls. For a number of years it was the only secondary school available on Nevis. The headmistress could decide which children to accept or not to accept. Initially, because of the social mores on the island, children born out of wedlock could not attend the school. At that time having children out of wedlock was considered to be gravely immoral and a bad model for society. Such children were given second-class status, and treated accordingly, in Caribbean societies. Ironically, those most guilty of the immorality charges were the wealthy elite and plantation owners who systematically exploited their poor servants sexually and otherwise. It was the irony inherent in that social situation, which in time undermined the rigid rule barring children born out of wedlock from attending the school. Further, the fact that the Stevens' managed to get their boys into a privately run girls' school also spoke to the power of social status back then. Little wonder that in time wealthy men willing to pay for their "bastard" children got them admitted at Excelsior School, too.

Ma Stevens was consistent about taking the time to encourage positive attitudes toward education in her family. According to daughter, May, no one ever doubted who ran the Stevens' family.

---

4 Burdett, S (1965) *Call Them Heroes*. New York, NY: Board of Education.

Ma Stevens managed the house, determined the dos and don'ts, and would set the tone for the whole family. Pa Stevens understood that and remained resigned to the situation.

School days in Nevis for Ivor, his sisters, and his brothers had challenges and limitations. However, despite drawbacks in the system, life for the Stevens' children gave them more hope for their future than for the mass of young children in Nevis then. Their father had a stable government job and earned about $40.00, per month—back then a government job served as a powerful social-status enhancer. While the Stevens' children could not boast of plantation wealth, their father's job, their skin color, and their education helped them achieve social success, on both Nevis and St. Kitts. The Stevens family was noticed and eventually became numbered among the social elites in the islands. Ivor never denied that reality. Rather, as Lee Moore of the Labor Party was careful to note, Stevens manipulated his social status very skillfully, so that in time he managed to achieve the important personal goal of capturing the attention and confidence of the masses on Nevis. Eventually he experienced both a high level of social acceptance and political success.

James E. Cross was headmaster at Charlestown Boys' School, where Ivor received his primary education. During the early 1900s, headmasters in the colonies were hard taskmasters and quite authoritarian. Back then, attaining a meaningful formal education on Nevis was a daunting, tough, and rigorous endeavor. Notwithstanding, the curriculum and program of education designed for the colonies was quite limited. Despite the limitations, head-teachers such as Cross and Bridgewater were committed to their task and taught for results. Many headmasters from that time also left legacies of enlightenment and hope among the children they taught. For headmasters and teachers of that time, the future of the community was on their shoulders. They knew all their students and all the parents. They knew too, where their students lived and how they struggled. Quite often the educators, the children, and their parents also worshipped together. Schools were seen then for what they really are—extensions of communities. Many of the teachers understood, too, that the dreams of change rested with the schools. In time, limited as the process was, even the downtrodden masses on the island learned to stake their future on education, viewing it as a transformational and liberating force for their lives. However, despite the growing interest and positive attitude toward education, few of those parents really understood its potential as a force for social, economic, and political change. Students such as Ivor were challenged to succeed because of what their parents knew. Over time, they received experiences in empowerment from their parents and other committed educators, including headmaster Mr. Cross and headmistress Bridgewater. The students were taught to read, to understand and reflect, and to appreciate their world. Then they were expected to move and change it in positive ways. Their great challenge was to become agents of social change!

Compared with today, headmistresses and headmasters were respected and revered by their students. The opportunity to attend school and get a good education was something very special. Parents held head-teachers as important role models for their children to emulate. There was the notion that children were like sponges and would readily absorb the "enduring virtues," leading to a culture of survival and success. However, at times, the future was not seen as an experience in dynamism, evolution, and constant change, as we know it today. Rather, there was the perception of a constant reality, forever dominated by the social elites—colonizers, landowners, and some selected others. The colonized could survive only by being prepared to accept such a dominated world. Students who failed to accept that world, or who did not meet the stringent standards set by their teachers, were not expected to become successful men and women. Undoubtedly, such a perception of education was shaped by colonialism. However, with a view toward an eventually changed future, every student who made it inside the school doors was challenged to excellence, to responsible citizenship, and to being ethical human beings in their time.

Ivor's parents wanted all that and more for him. He was expected to emulate the academic commitment of his older brothers and sisters. And, as with all their other children, Ivor's parents nudged, encouraged, and urged him toward academic success. They also demanded piety and discipline. Despite what he might have promised his mother and father, Ivor's sister May observed that, by nature, he was precocious, curious, and independent; he quietly resisted some of the pressure and rigidity he saw around him. May did add that their home was disciplined and God-fearing. Her brother Ivor, she observed, "was always mischievous and in trouble." Reflecting on those growing-up days, Ivor reminisced:

> I was born and raised in a Christian home of the Methodist faith, and I can recall the time when I was a choir member under Miss Helen Bridgewater, and a Sunday school pupil under the late Charles Byron. . . . I also recall the days when we would be sent upstairs at school for 5-minute devotion.

Ivor also commented on another growing-up experience that brought his precociousness and independence to the fore, but got him in trouble with his father. One day Ivor spotted Mr. Thomas Montgomery, who was all dressed up. However, to Ivor, the suit Mr. Montgomery wore was outrageous and clownish. It deserved to be ridiculed. Accordingly, Ivor forgot the lessons taught at home about being respectful to older people. Right in the sight of Mr. Montgomery he stared to laugh haughtily, almost rolling on the ground. Mr. Montgomery knew he was being laughed at, and was not amused. Not even a member of the Stevens' family could get away with that. The matter was duly reported to Ivor's father, who administered the punishment deemed appropriate at that time, for flagrant disrespect to an elder, and for bringing such dishonor to the Stevens' family.

While Ivor and his brothers attended the Charlestown Boys' Elementary School, his sisters attended the Charlestown Girls' Elementary School. May remembered that her headmistress was Miss Ethel Christian. Few headmistresses got married, or had children of their own back then. The moral standards set for female teachers were quite stringent and different from those for male teachers. Generally, women who became school leaders were unmarried; the students they taught became their adopted family. Seemingly, society did not allow female teachers to court, marry, and raise children in the same manner as male teachers did such things. There was that rigid pattern of discrimination against women teachers, securely institutionalized at that time, and no one challenged the status quo. That situation persisted in St. Kitts-Nevis into the 1980s. During all that time only men made laws in the colonies and the colonial laws were clearly discriminatory against women. Unmarried female educators lost their jobs if they became pregnant. The male educators who impregnated them kept theirs. In most cases they were not even reprimanded.

At that time the number of persons in the colonies who could read and write well was small. Families often had to decide whether their children would go to school, work as maids, or work in some type of agriculture to boost their families' earnings. Children were considered privileged if they managed to attend school regularly, particularly during harvest time. However, because the Stevens' family understood the value of education, they grasped every opportunity to have their children attend school in both Nevis and St. Kitts. In time, Ivor, too, began to appreciate and value education as a passport to future success.

Despite the importance of education, the process of attaining it was not always glamorous. Even for very young children, much of the teaching required rote learning. It was the era of "chalk and talk." Most teachers then were taught in an authoritarian manner and passed on education as they experienced it. Those who did not learn readily were punished to influence them to do so. The tamarind rod or leather strap was always ready and waiting for undisciplined and "dunce" children. The headmaster, Mr. Cross, was not known to spare the rod at the Charlestown Boys School. To do that would have set the wrong model for his students. He was careful to challenge them intellectually and physically every day. Ivor must have had reasons to be concerned about the frequent and random application of those carefully selected instruments of torture. Commenting about his former headmaster, Ivor wrote,

"The late Mr. J. E. Cross was headmaster and disciplinarian of no mean order."

In elementary school, Ivor and the other boys were exposed to academic material common throughout the British Caribbean colonies at that time, some of which survived well into the 1960s. Because radio, and later television, came to the area slowly, the popular Brer Nancy stories were told and retold, with varying twists throughout the islands. Books were few and precious. The typical family in Nevis professed some knowledge of Christianity, and in many homes the Holy Bible was standard reading. However, stories about obeah, evil spirits, jack-o-lanterns, Brer Nancy, and various oral-history traditions were part of the socialization process at school and at home.

Hope, May, and Ivor repeatedly commented that family togetherness was important to their parents and to them as children, bonding them closely and allowing for quality time together. Later, in his own household, Ivor treated family time as sacred. His nephew Maurice also spoke about how he grew to love such times when he lived with Uncle Ivor; those experiences, in time, profoundly influenced his own family life.

Children attending school worked at home before and after school. At school, physical activity included running, skipping, playing with marbles, rounders, cricket, and soccer. According to May, Ivor mastered both soccer and cricket, and became good at walking, too. Back then, walking, rather than perceived as a form of exercise, was the chief means of transportation. It was a necessity. Quite often, people walked for many miles, to and from town, church, and school. The horse and donkey were also important forms of transportation. The bicycle was quite a welcome addition when it became available on the islands later on.

In his academic development, Ivor progressed to secondary education and experienced adequate success. In addition to the two schools he attended on Nevis, Ivor worked under the watchful eyes of his dear mother, Ethelinda. When the time came for exposure to higher education than what was available on Nevis, the family decided Ivor should attend school on St. Kitts. It was not until the early 1950s that a public secondary school became available to Nevisians, many years after Miss Helen Bridgewater operated her successful private school, the Excelsior School. At the time, the cost to attend the Excelsior School was 6 shillings and 3 pence. That was about $1.00 to $1.50 U.S. currency per month. However, the poverty and ignorance fostered on the islands by the British government and its colonial system were quite limiting. Few Nevisians understood the power of a good education, or had access to the money that could buy them one.

According to Hope, when the Excelsior first opened its doors, it was a school only for girls, but later came to include boys. All the Stevens children except Cecil spent some time at Excelsior. The cost for admission to the school was quite an excessive sum of money for the average working-class Nevisian to raise on a monthly basis. Consequently, despite the claim of financial difficulties made by the Stevens children, only those in the middle and upper classes of society could have afforded to pay for such schooling. Hope himself noted, "Many of the Negroes on the island did not have a chance to get a good education. The best schools were for children of parents who were well-to-do." Ivor's family did manage to afford such schools for most of its children.

Ivor did win a scholarship to attend the elite St. Kitts-Nevis Grammar School on St. Kitts, a secondary school for boys. While there, Ivor resided with his brother Hope, who worked on the island. For girls, there was the elite girls' high school, known as the Pickard School. In commenting on his experience at the Grammar School, Ivor reflected on the school's rituals and discipline during the 1930s:

> While at the Grammar school, a pupil could be easily identified on the street by virtue of a chip-hat with school band and tie and was not permitted to pass an ex-school-boy, an elderly person, or a person of prominence without raising his hat, as in those days a mere complaint led to a caning at school. This eventually gave authority to a member of the public, in whose opinion, if your action deserved a

> whipping, gave you one on the spot. Another was administered at home for having behaved in such a disrespectful manner in public.

Despite the efforts of the White plantocracy to control and frustrate their progress, a Black middle class was emerging in St. Kitts and Nevis. By 1916, labor unionism was on the verge of transforming the society and its one-sided politics. Meanwhile, with their growing thirst for education, both high schools on St. Kitts eventually began to promise the lower classes some social success and upward mobility. However, because of the stubborn enclave of a lingering elitism in St. Kitts and Nevis, years passed before the children of the working class were allowed easy passage into those two schools. It was even longer before there was impact and change in the culture, so that children of the working class could be comfortable and accepted while attending those schools.

Ivor was comfortable during his time at the Grammar School, partly because his brother Hope lived and worked on St. Kitts as a civil servant. In time, he also became an enthusiastic sportsman. Ivor did take the time to improve his game at both soccer and cricket, becoming an outstanding player. However, his sister May could not recall whether Ivor wrote the terminal Cambridge Exam when he left school. She felt that such an exam would have been considered a nuisance by Ivor; too structured and tedious an exercise for his free spirit. Perhaps the pressure and competition for academic success also overwhelmed and frustrated Ivor. Seemingly, he did not perform at the academic level that would have allowed him to pass the difficult Cambridge General Certificate Examination (GCE).

According to his sister May, Ivor continued to play cricket seriously after he left the Grammar School. While he worked with the firm of S. L. Horsford & Co., Ivor received a call to represent St. Kitts in the Leeward Islands Cricket Tournament. However, the management of S. L. Horsford did not agree that Ivor's participation in that series of cricket matches was in the best interest of the firm. He did not get the time off to participate in the tournament. Such a scenario today, with so much interest in sports, would not have been acceptable to the average Kittitian, but at that time it did not appear to have caused much stir on the island. The plantocracy was too focused on making money, and the poor masses were often too concerned about their day-to-day survival to pay much attention to a cricket series that hardly included them.

Few persons ever heard Ivor boast of his cricketing prowess. However, he became a staunch supporter of the cricket revolution on Nevis during the 1970s. Meanwhile, those who knew Ivor well heard him boast repeatedly about his ability as a fisherman, never about cricket. Victor Martin was a great friend of Ivor, a progeny, and a colleague in the Nevis Reformation Party with Ivor. When Victor eulogized Ivor in June 1997, he spoke humorously about Ivor's fishing limitations. Nothing was said about his cricket.

Although the Stevens family was well accepted among the middle class and social elites of the day, it was challenging for Mr. and Mrs. Stevens to send 7 children to college. A college education then meant traveling to England to study law, medicine, or education at Oxford, London, or Cambridge, a venture far beyond the financial ability of the Stevens family then. Later on, persons who worked closely with Ivor observed there were times when he seemed to have regretted that his formal academic pursuits ended at the St. Kitts-Nevis Grammar School.

Even if Ivor had dreams and aspirations to do more academically, he soon settled for employment with S. L. Horsford in Basseterre. At that time, even for those who attended the Grammar School in Basseterre, job opportunities beyond firms such as S. L. Horsford and the sugar industry were few. In the British-dominated islands, even better educated middle-class children had few opportunities for work and growth. For poor working-class children, tethered to the ups and downs of the declining yet overpowering sugar industry, opportunities for social success were elusive. Their pattern of life was home to school, then the cane fields. For thousands, it was home to the cane fields. Both scenarios led to enduring the rigor of low-level, labor-intensive roles in the sugar industry. On Nevis, however, the early decline of sugar production allowed for the development of some apprenticeship programs, and an independent peasantry.

The War

Ivor's first round of employment with S. L. Horsford did not last long. He left in 1940 to become a soldier with the Canadian Army Signal Corps. It is unclear why Ivor chose to serve with the Canadians, rather than the British forces. However, he saw action in North Africa and in Europe. Ivor was one of the hundreds of young men from the British, French, and U.S. Caribbean colonies, who went to Europe, North Africa, and elsewhere, in defense of democracy during World War II. Ironically, they fought and many died defending freedom in the British Commonwealth and the world, at a time when colonialism limited the freedoms of thousands throughout the Caribbean area. Ivor later suggested that his entry into the military was a result of his commitment to standing with those who stood against Hitler. Few persons on St. Kitts or Nevis were forced to do military service; that choice was usually voluntary. However, despite its dangers, the military always appears to hold an attraction for young men.

This was one of the four major periods in Ivor's adulthood when he was separated from his family. May recalled receiving one letter from Ivor during the war. It came in the second of the 6 years he served in Europe, but she was unable to provide details about what was in the letter. In fact, no one recalled Ivor discussing the war, despite the exaggerated war stories a number of other politicians have used to win popularity. Ivor served successfully and had bragging rights, but refused to keep bringing to mind the horrors of World War II, only for political gain. It was not until he died in 1997 that many Nevisians and Kittitians knew that Ivor was a veteran. While he eulogized Ivor, Sim Daniel, former colleague and leader of the Nevis Reformation Party noted, "Not many of us know that the late Ivor Stevens saw active service in the Second World War, of 1939-1945."

His war experiences appeared to alter Ivor's young, aggressive, selfish dreams, and sobered him. They also left some permanent scars. He was no longer innocent, wholesome Ivor. One of those scars of war, a shrapnel injury to his body, probably contributed to his eventual demise. Based on some of the conversations they shared, like father and son, Ivor's nephew, Maurice recalled that Uncle Ivor did share with him some nuggets from his war experiences: "Uncle Ivor was wounded in his chest by shrapnel during the war. His hearing was also impaired as a result of the experience. Uncle Ivor never boasted about war because he came to hate it." When Ivor was questioned about joining the armed forces, he simply stated, "Here was a job to be done for the good of the world and someone had to do it. Further, Hitler had become a problem for the world, and I am a citizen of the world."

A Methodist preacher Ivor befriended, Rev. Lester Bowers of Antigua, commented about Ivor's war experience. During his final days, those harrowing war experiences came back to Ivor, haunting and terrorizing him. Then, being enfeebled and victimized by time, his body was too weak and his will too fleeting to steel himself and keep forgetting. Thus, Ivor's mind wandered through his lived experiences, including the war. He was in no condition to resist the flows of life, not even in his own mind. Consequently, as he lay in bed, Stevens responded with screams of fear, as he seemingly relived the horror of falling bombs and ricocheting bullets, around his helpless self. Those war years were long gone, but even as Mr. Stevens lay dying, they came back in vivid, horrific scenes and haunting memories.

Sugar and Labor

When Ivor returned to St. Kitts-Nevis, as a civilian, after the war, he was in close touch with his family, but he was also a young man, energetic, worldly wise, very curious, and with a heightened sense of independence. His military years fostered greater independence, but, also, a special yearning for home and family. On returning home, Ivor was confident he could begin to make his own mark on the world. He was able to get his job back at S. L. Horsford, but Ivor returned to the Caribbean with skills that prepared him for leadership. Accordingly, he reached beyond his clerk position at Horsford. His sister May noted that by 1947, Ivor was working at the St. Kitts Sugar Factory as the foreman of one of the shifts, and as an engineer. Ivor and the men he worked with were not responsible for the critical engineering issues that made the factory work. Rather, they ensured that sugarcane flowed through the factory processes necessary to produce molasses and sugar for export. Ivor and the men worked well together and the group was awarded special recognition for outstanding performance. However, Ivor did express concern that at times his men were treated as second-class people at the factory.

Stanley Franks, Jr., who once served as secretary to the St. Kitts, Nevis, and Anguilla Trades and Labor Union, recalled seeing a letter in the union archives from Ivor. The letter, addressed to the first secretary of the union, sought support for Ivor's desire to organize a branch of the St. Kitts, Nevis, and Anguilla Trades and Labor Union on Nevis. A variety of factors could have been critical in Ivor's decision to quietly take the workers' side, as they struggled against the arrogant planters. Growing up on Nevis, coupled with his military experience, allowed Ivor to take an independent position in the conflict on St. Kitts. He noticed that the men on his team always worked hard, but were constantly the victims of discrimination and their hard work taken for granted. Further, no matter how capable Black workers were, important leadership positions were held only by White men. In the broader society, bankers, lawyers, doctors, and preachers in the dominant churches were all White men. They dominated all the positions of power and leadership on the islands—sending messages of subservience to the Black majority. Notwithstanding, since there were few plantations operating in Nevis, Stevens would have had problems organizing the more independent peasantry on Nevis to support the labor union on St. Kitts, very despised in Nevis. At that time, neither Nevisians nor Anguillans saw meaning in labor unionism.

Courtship, Marriage, and Move to Nevis

Ivor's nephew, Maurice, and Ivor's friend, Rev. Bowers, spoke repeatedly of his commitment to family, and how their personal association with Ivor helped them in their own family life. Above all, Rev. Bowers and Maurice acknowledged that there was a very special bond of love between Ivor and his wife Dora. On a number of occasions Ivor said to close friends, "I am the man of my house, but my wife Dora is in charge."

Dora Harper and Ivor Stevens met at her 21st birthday party, not long after he returned to St. Kitts from the war. At age 21, Dora was a beautiful debutante looking for a partner. Mrs. Stevens admitted that they both experienced some level of attraction during their first meeting. Neither Dora nor Ivor was brave or candid enough to discuss what they were experiencing. Within a short time, however, they both confessed their growing attraction and special feelings for each other. Not long after the revelation, Dora and Ivor began to date each other regularly.

Despite Ivor's middle-class family background and his hero image as a returning soldier, Dora's mother, Rosanna Edwards, was cautious about the match. However, the dashing, daring, and persuasive Ivor was not daunted; he was always chivalrous and gentlemanly. One ritual of that time was the letter written to the woman's parent(s) expressing interest and the intent to marry her. Accordingly, love-struck Ivor performed the usual ritual. He wrote to Dora's mother, stating his romantic interest in her daughter. Although Ms. Edwards approved of Ivor as an acceptable suitor for her daughter, she did set some guidelines: Ivor had to make certain Dora returned home by 11 pm, when they were out on dates. During the 1940s and 1950s, mothers were much more afraid than now about their unwed daughters becoming pregnant. Family status mattered greatly, and unmarried pregnancies were considered a disgrace.

It was a boon to Ivor that an Anglican priest, Bishop Hand, moved to St. Kitts from Antigua, and started drama programs there. When he staged the *Sun Bonnet Sue Operetta*, in St. Kitts, Dora Harper was one of the performers. She spent many hours after work practicing her roles. At first, Ivor took Dora to practice on his motorcycle, then in his car, a Morris Oxford. Later, Ivor taught Dora to drive, and when she received her license, Dora was allowed to chauffeur herself, and even to keep the car, from time to time. Ms. Edwards' distrust of Ivor disappeared eventually. Soon, talk about marriage blossomed between Dora and Ivor.

On a Tuesday, November 29, 1949, at 4:00 pm, Ivor and Dora were joined in holy matrimony at the Basseterre Methodist Church. Dora Harper, now Dora Stevens, worked as a mathematics teacher at the prestigious Girls' High School. Four years later, Ivor decided to move back to Nevis. Mrs. Stevens had to remain at her job in St. Kitts during the first year after her husband moved back to Nevis. In 1953, there was no arrangement in the government's organizational structure to facilitate an easy, quick transfer of a teacher from St. Kitts to Nevis. The transfers were usually in the other direction, from Nevis to St. Kitts. There was no public high school on Nevis until the Charlestown High School opened in 1950. In 1954, Mrs. Stevens received her transfer to teach on Nevis. She still remembers the year when Ivor lived on Nevis, while she lived and taught on St. Kitts: "It was an awkward period for the family," she mused.

Ivor's move from St. Kitts to Nevis in 1953 was permanent. Despite being born on St. Kitts, and having lived there for part of his adult life, Ivor never lived on St. Kitts again, after 1953. Actually, at a time when he was still weighing his next move in life, Ivor's father took ill on Nevis. The family lost its patriarch later that year. Because the Stevens' family was held together in a close bond, the death of Mr. Stevens was a severe blow to all. However, with Dora at his side, Ivor was better prepared to weather such a storm. He also needed the love and support of his wife as he returned to Nevis and began to dream about investing in, and initiating a new politics that would change the island forever. In time, Ivor started a search for new beginnings. He also began to dream of other directions for Nevis and its politics. When Stevens entered politics on Nevis, neither he nor his wife understood where the journey would take them, or how it would impact their lives.

Ivor understood that he could live in Nevis enjoying the secure togetherness and reduced stress his family circle provided. At the same time, he could also take stock and lay some groundwork for a position of prominence in the political future of the island. According to Mrs. Stevens, "While at the factory Ivor always wanted to come back to Nevis and help Nevisians." When his father fell ill, it was not difficult for him to return to the island and start preparing for his new beginning.

However, on his return to Nevis, Ivor encountered an unexpected reality. All that he hoped for did not fall into place readily. He was back home with his mother and father. But, his wife was working in St. Kitts and it was not because she or Ivor wished it. Mrs. Stevens was a new bride longing to be with her husband who had moved 11 miles across the sea to Nevis, but there was no structure in place to facilitate her move from a school on St. Kitts to one on Nevis. She saw her husband occasionally while she waited a full year for her transfer to Nevis. Meanwhile, Ivor was waiting on Nevis, caring for his parents and surveying the possibilities for politics. He was also beginning to envision himself as part of the political process on the island. Probably, that period of traveling between St. Kitts and Nevis also helped Ivor develop his unusual appreciation for lighters (sailboats) and for the sea. Eventually, Mrs. Stevens received the transfer to Nevis. However, shortly after she arrived there, Ivor had to be separated from his family again as he traveled to Barbados to oversee and help with the repairs on one of his sailboats, *Patricia Ann*. Later, he owned a number of other boats and was involved in personal and family businesses, including trucking and boating on the island.

Family Man

Ivor Stevens was a family man. The well-being of his family was always dear to his heart. His parents had been careful to pass on to all their children the importance of family bonding and other positive family values. The instructions of his parents and his memories of growing up with his brothers and sisters stayed with Ivor throughout his life. His nephew Maurice also commented that good family values were passed by Ivor to a second generation of the Stevens' family. For Ivor, those values helped shape the vision he held for his immediate family and also the relationships he forged with other relatives. Each one of Ivor's brothers and sisters appeared to have held the other siblings, particularly Ivor, in high regard. His nieces and nephews also loved and felt comfortable with Uncle Ivor. Most business and problems in the family were handled by Ivor.

Mother, Ethelinda Stevens, was in charge of things in the home where Ivor grew up. She was never an afterthought to the man of the house, James Stevens. Consequently, Ivor learned early to see women as important persons in the management of the home and family. Further, his father, mother, and the children always came together as a team whenever that was required. Many years later Ivor could be heard talking about the cooperation and team play that he found so supportive and useful in his own family.

Many of Ivor's friends, and enemies also, knew about his attachment to family. It was that knowledge that enticed Fitzroy Bryant to bring up the matter of Ivor's child, Effe Jeffers (now Effe Jeffers-Collins), fathered out of wedlock; a child Ivor at one time refused to acknowledge as his own. Ivor appeared to have become a participant in that historical interplay of power and sexual favors that occurred between maids and "massas," a phenomenon rampant throughout Caribbean colonial history. Despite his moral declarations, Stevens was human, tempted like other men, and not immune to what Fitzroy Bryant captioned, "the joys of the flesh." However, to Bryant, because of Ivor's legendary declarations about dedication to his family and claims of wholesome family values, here was one matter he could not overlook as a chink and weakness in Ivor's seemingly shining character. It was a matter of clear ethical conflict and one that could cause Ivor and persons of his ilk to become frazzled and very concerned. Bryant hoped that sharing the matter with the public would humiliate Stevens.

That public revelation of the child and the identity of her father helped force a permanent wedge between the two men. The accusation eventually brought the matter back to Ivor's wife and family, leading to some public humiliation. Psychologically, Mrs. Stevens avoided the issue. However, the fact that the child was born to someone else, after their marriage, must have, at some time, resulted in painful, difficult discussions about the matter with her husband. Undoubtedly, Ivor, the model husband and knight in shining ethical armor, must have had some awkward times, finding ways to assuage his wife's doubts, and to answer her many "why" questions. None of the opposition politicians on Nevis made the matter a campaign issue. It remained a whispered, but known matter on Nevis. Those of his family who knew about the child chose at first to become stoic about it. In time, some accepted the reality. For example, during the funeral of Ivor's brother, Cecil, eyebrows must have been raised, when Effe Jeffers had the honor of laying the wreath for the Stevens' family. It was also a subtle message to Ms. Jeffers that she was accepted as part of the Stevens' clan.

Seemingly, Ivor was consumed by two obsessions: Nevis politics and his family. Other matters, designed to limit or sidetrack him, were unsuccessful. His attention always returned to Nevis politics and to his family. He boasted frequently that his wife was the brain in his home, his measuring rod, and his computer. Everything Ivor did was passed through and checked by his "darling computer" for validity and reliability. Once his Dora approved, then Ivor was certain he had an issue that could comfortably be taken to the public for political debate or for action.

There was a special relationship between Ivor and his family, and between Ivor, Nevis, and the politics of change. When he was overwhelmed by the ongoing island politics, Ivor found consolation and solace in his family. Maurice claimed he always knew from afar when his uncle was upset because his hair would be untidy and at times flying in the wind: an early indicator to the family that something was amiss. However, Ivor never used the stresses and strains of politics as an excuse to abuse or disrespect his wife or other members of his family. During the many years he lived with his uncle, Maurice claimed he never once heard Uncle Ivor speak loudly or abusively to his wife. That model, Maurice suggested, continues as a powerful instructive force to his own life and marriage relationship.

Every member of the Stevens family stood with Ivor and supported his political endeavors. His wife was not often an open, active campaigner; she was more subtle. But his sister, May, was always visible in Charlestown, chatting with the people, being pleasant to them, and making them feel comfortable about the Stevens' family. His sister Marion was involved with the creation of local crafts for tourists, even as Culturama evolved to be an annual celebration on Nevis. Such contributions to society were important at a time when their brother was seeking to broaden his political base and as he was vying to gather new votes. Generally, the masses in Nevis came to know the Stevens family well, during the 1960s. And, through those years, the Stevens increasingly came to be held in high regard on the islands. From time to time, Hope, the brother who lived in New York, would visit Nevis to lend his knowledge and aura to his brother's campaign, and also took time to appear publicly with the rest of the family. Whenever nephew, Maurice, visits from Florida, he is still hailed pleasantly by his former schoolmates and friends. He also talks about the political successes of Uncle Ivor, openly and unashamedly. It was subtle campaign politics, but Ivor's family was there showing solidarity with him at crucial political times. Ivor's family was also there when he needed rest, diversion from politics, or financial support. Since his family was there from early times, when Ivor had little political clout, he found in their support the fortitude to survive through the 1950s, the 1960s, and into the 1970s. Hundreds of Ivor's friends, farmers, fishermen, and his turn-hand merchant friends, were there for him too.

In time, Ivor's vast store of experience, his growing political savvy, and his business acumen, made him the ideal person in his clan, to manage the family's affairs. When Maurice needed to be disciplined and brought up like a Stevens, he was assigned to Ivor's charge. Later, securing the family's right to property belonging to his mother's family, the Penns' in Tortola, was assigned to Ivor. This was many acres of ancestral land, including estates located in the British Virgin Islands, which over time had its ownership disputed. The issue became quite contentious, pitting descendants of the Penn's clan against one another. It was finally resolved in a real property case heard in the British Virgin Islands by the Court of Appeal of the Eastern Caribbean States, in 1984: *Pickering v Stevens.* Ivor's side prevailed in the matter. His case was led by the St. Kitts born attorney, Joseph Archibald, QC, and supported by G. Farrara. Success in that case returned unprecedented wealth to Ivor, despite his frugal lifestyle. It was observed by a friend, "Ivor died being one of the wealthiest men on Nevis, probably much wealthier than his nemesis, Sim Daniel."

After the passing of his brother Cecil, the dentist, Ivor also served as executor of his brother's last will and testament. By that time, such a task was no longer bothersome to Ivor; it had become routine. And so it was, over the years, other family members repeatedly turned to Ivor to manage personal or family matters. In the process, he became quite adept at managing the family's affairs. It did not matter whether the issue was a small thing, as in arranging for family members to visit Nevis, or a larger matter such as overseeing the mandates of a will. Ivor was the family member first approached by the others, and they expected him to get it done. Despite his ranking in the birth order, Ivor became virtual leader of the Stevens' clan. Meanwhile, being trusted repeatedly with such responsibilities was quite an honor, since others in the family could have managed the special roles they gave to Ivor.

Through the years, Ivor had become so caught up in his family and with the meaning of family that whenever he lectured to others about politics and other aspects of life, he talked family. Lester Bowers, Ivor's Methodist preacher friend, still remembers Ivor's advice to him about how to live with a wife. Bowers recalled that Ivor told him he should never forget the words, "Yes, darling." According to Ivor, "They cover a multitude of sins." "Those two words," Ivor mused, "saved my marriage."

Maurice talked about family activities he shared and enjoyed with his Uncle Ivor. Bowers added more light in explaining and giving meaning to those activities. He noted that Ivor insisted that mealtime should be a sacred time for families: time to reflect, share advice, help build character, and strengthen family bonds. However, while having good family values is important to the survival and well-being of a people, everyone in Nevis, then, as now, does not share the family gatherings suggested by Ivor. Unfortunately, the growing incidents of breakdown in family relations at this time, may well be the painful result of Nevisians rejecting the practices of family bonding that Ivor learned first hand, as a boy growing up on the island.

Seemingly, Ivor's instructions about family values, family harmony, family sacredness, and the critical role of family in human societies, had a profound impact on the young preacher. Bowers continues to lament that Ivor died before Bowers' son was born. However, Bowers suggested that his son shares a very special connection with Ivor. Mrs. Bowers played the organ at Ivor's funeral, while she was pregnant with that son. As Bowers saw it, "My wife and my son played at Ivor's funeral."

The saga between Ivor and his nephew, Maurice, provides a useful illustration of how Ivor saw the family unit in society. Ivor demonstrated, in his relationship with his nephew, that traditional values and peculiar family aspirations should be important. It was such thinking that forced Ivor to enter the life of the rebellious Maurice. Ivor thought that the attitudes and actions in which Maurice was engaged, on his early arrival in St. Kitts-Nevis, were not appropriate for a member of the Stevens' family. Further, since education should be valued by all the Stevens family, it was not acceptable for a young Stevens to wander around St. Kitts as a truant. Ivor held this belief very strongly. It was therefore little wonder that he threatened Maurice with "breaking him." Maurice soon understood that his uncle meant what he said. For Ivor, any child who is called by the name Stevens, and related to him, is expected to behave as a good citizen, showing respect to his mother, and having interest in a good education. Because Maurice did not understand and respect these unwritten laws, he had to be shown how to live by them. Ivor was therefore committed to ensuring a change in Maurice's behavior.

Maurice learned quickly and very well during the years he spent growing up on Nevis. When his Uncle Ivor died, Maurice admitted that he had lost an important teacher, a true role model, a friend, and a father. Uncle Ivor was the man who provided him a home; the man who took him fishing; and the man who cared and made him feel loved. His uncle also taught Maurice how to love and share his life with a woman. Maurice admits readily that the success in his own marriage of now almost 50 years can be attributed directly to his Uncle Ivor's excellent example. Maurice noted that Ivor showed him how to turn his life around, how to be a real man, and how to act as a responsible citizen. "What would have happened to my life if Uncle Ivor had not stepped in when he did?" Maurice asked reflectively. Then, after a dramatic pause he said, "I really do not know." Maurice admitted that the relationship between him and his father, Cardigan Stevens, was a poor one. "Uncle Ivor was the real father that I knew," he concluded.

As Maurice recalled, his uncle did not compromise or mend bridges on certain matters readily, particularly when issues were related to his personal life. For example, Mrs. Stevens said of that characteristic about her husband, "He never forgave you if you double crossed him." However, when matters related to Nevis or his family, Ivor would do whatever was necessary to achieve some measure of resolution to problems, and to attain eventual success, even when it demanded going the extra mile. Ivor's wife and other members of his family still have many wonderful memories of him doing little things, and also some bigger things, to help families in need on Nevis.

Politics

The most demanding experience that impinged on Ivor's family life was his involvement with politics. The demands on Ivor's time were constant and pervasive. However, he was so committed to making a difference in the life and politics on Nevis that he immersed himself in the process for some 30 years. During the entire period, Ivor managed to keep his family together. To the extent that he could, Ivor kept his wife interested, and aware of what he did in politics. There were those times too, when campaigning, strategizing, and other political activities took him away from his family. Ivor remained attuned to the politics He did what it took to keep abreast and win the people's favor.

When Ivor tried to combine politics and family matters, quite frequently, he learned, like other dedicated politicians, that politics and family do not mix well. Quite often the demands of politics can become an overwhelming force larger and more powerful than any individual. That invasiveness of politics was one of the reasons his wife hesitated over her husband's entry into politics, back in 1957. At times, the challenges and trials of politics did get to be harsh and painful. There were even times when the wrangling reached a point that both Ivor's personal and family life came under attack. In one instance during the early 1960s, Eugene Walwyn said painful things about Ivor's family. In another attack during the 1970s, Fred Parris, challenged Ivor that the bulls on his farm were more fertile than Ivor was. The classic attack against Ivor Stevens occurred in a *Labor Spokesman* guest-editorial column written during the 1980s by Fitzroy Bryant, a political nemesis of Stevens from the Labor Party on St. Kitts. Bryant attacked Ivor on the matter of marital infidelity, reminding everyone that Ivor fathered a daughter, but not with his wife.

Such personal and cleverly directed attacks were painful to Ivor and his family. Notwithstanding, Ivor, in his turn, fought back, giving as good as he got. Unfortunately, those early political campaigns on Nevis often dealt with melee, not the real economic, social and political issues at hand. As Archibald (2010, p. 16) saw it,

> There was little the Nevisians could do about the neglected infrastructure of their homeland. They had to rely on the government to fix the roads, provide electricity, water and the other amenities on which to build a modern economy. But the government was not in Nevis, it was in St. Kitts and decisions to fix the roads to provide and maintain electricity and water, and to lay the infrastructure for a modern economy in Nevis could not be taken by any other than the government in St. Kitts.

There is also another view of the situation. Through the colonial years, the British government buried its head in the sand of a very inglorious history of exploitation in the Caribbean. They washed their hands, sat back in feigned ignorance, and allowed it all to happen. That reality of the political situation between Nevis and St. Kitts was what forced an early disagreement between Nicholls and Walwyn, during the early 1960s. They wrestled over whether it was possible to achieve legislative success without joining with Labor Party politicians. Ironically, even as Nevisians went to the polls in 2011, the relationship between some Nevis politicians and those of the Labor Party on St. Kitts was still very much an issue for discussion.

There was interest in real change on Nevis, however, because of the ineffectiveness of Nevis legislators in the House of Assembly on St. Kitts, personal criticisms and melee were more exciting to listeners during political campaigns. That was a sad situation, but because the islands' politics was totally controlled and driven from St. Kitts by the Labor Party, there were very few policies or developmental goals that Nevis politicians could have initiated or promised in sincerity. After the campaign's dust cleared, often the winners of the election were the persons who found and spread the most dirt or the person who had the biggest bag of campaign tricks. It was not necessarily the one best qualified to confront the islands' social, economic, and infrastructural problems. But, Nevisians were willing to accept and live on promises from their politicians for many years before the 1980s.

According to Maurice and Mrs. Stevens, by the mid 1980s Ivor's family advised him to quit politics. To them, politics had worn him out. They wanted him to walk away from politicking while he was still sane and healthy. Further, by the early 1980s, politics was changing for the worse on Nevis. During conversations with Ivor, his family noted he was becoming increasingly disillusioned with trends in the islands' politics. The naivety and innocence he saw during the 1950s and 1960s were gone.

One day in 1987, whether due to tiredness, his growing disillusionment with politics on Nevis, or because he was finally sensing a need to spend more time with his family, Ivor Stevens announced he was leaving politics and returning to civilian life on Nevis. On that morning, Ivor quietly said to his wife, "I do not think I am going to offer myself for election again this year." Mrs. Stevens recalled, "I was surprised but overjoyed." She had waited 30 years to hear that statement from her husband.

Mr. Stevens' role as a politician on Nevis did not allow him the time or focus that his wife wanted from family life. Ivor, too, did not see his family experience then as being all what he wanted it to be. Meanwhile, Ivor's position in politics made it possible for him to see and hear varied stories about other families on the island. Even back then, some of those stories bewildered him. As could be expected, being the committed family person that he was, the stories of problems and rifts in families were disturbing. Ivor also lamented the way children were being raised at the time, lacking discipline and respect. During his childhood, Ivor grew up believing "Good manners can take you around the world." Before he died in 1997, Ivor noted:

> Sufficient to say the modern generation has never been taught; therefore it does not know the merits, or demerits of the old time system. It is time that the parents be taught how to raise a family along refined and decent ways, as parental control does not exist today. I will go further and say that if my father and a colleague's father were at variance over an incident which brought about a breakdown in the social status of these two men, the children of these two men could not pass one of the men in the street without raising his hand in deference to the gentleman; otherwise he would be told that what happened between the two fathers was between men, and boys have no business in that. This takes me further down the road when I say that an elderly man finding that you were rude in some way could hold you and give you a licking for such misbehavior. Today, teachers and elders are totally ignored by the youth, particularly the school children. Of all the discipline known to me the most important one

> deals with the grandchildren of today's child-bearing women, that is, youthful respect. When the youth of today can put a value to himself in this regard, he automatically respects himself, others, property, government, and his country. We, meaning the elders, and the government, will recognize our responsibility to the youth, and act accordingly, government included. In other words, I feel that the great grandchildren to whom I refer should get the maximum care and protection bearing in mind that whereas a woman has very much control over the child in her womb, but less after it is born. To be more explicit, the mothers to be have to be taken care of by the government in similar manner, all leading up to a future generation of substance.

Much of his thinking on child development and education was innovative. It was far ahead of his time. As we surge into the 21st century, the themes in education increasingly focus on total development. There is also a growing trend toward pre-kindergarten education. Meanwhile, there is also the need to help older children and youths understand the folly of dropping out of school. However, the ascendency of rapid cultural shifts and the inability of Caribbean societies to manage all the culture changes are tearing the islands and their societies apart. Now that there is such a tendency toward social instability in the Caribbean, this may be a good time for governments to reemphasize the importance of education in the area. A failure in this matter can lead to stymied, all-around development and an undermining of the quality of life for all citizens. Ivor believed the government should ensure that traditional family values are preserved, while heeding new research findings about human development.

Although the matter of a child being born out of wedlock brought a discordant note into Ivor's family and its relations, by the time of his death in 1997, that irresponsible act by Ivor had become less of an issue among some members of his family. His wife still dealt with the matter through denial. Even if he hesitated to discuss the child with his wife, Ivor admitted to others that Effe Jeffers was his daughter. Reliable sources claimed she shared his physique, complexion, and aggressive approach to life—she looked and acted like him. Later, on more than one occasion, Stevens used his influence to intervene and secure employment for Effe. Attorney Henry Browne also recalled that he was once charged by Ivor to obtain housing in St. Peter's area for Effe. Also, Franklyn Brand, at one time a close associate of Ivor, noted that Ivor introduced Effe to him as, "my daughter." Effe Jeffers-Collins now resides in the United States and was interviewed by phone, during the early 2000s. She appeared not to hold any lingering animosity toward her father; she was surprised that Mrs. Stevens' denied knowing her. She claimed to have visited the home many times, while her father lived, and that she spoke with Mrs. Stevens on numerous occasions, including, during the period when her father was ill and dying.

Once Ivor left politics, he turned inward to his family, and appeared to live life with an unusual zest. For the next 10 years, according to Mrs. Stevens, "Life was at a slower pace. They were lovely years. Ivor and I traveled together a lot more." Ivor, his wife, and sister May became a tight threesome, often seen travelling or attending functions together. Seemingly, Ivor tried to make up to his family for all the stress and loneliness he brought to their lives during his 32 years of politicking (1957-1989). While Ivor left Nevis local politics in 1987, he served for an additional 2 years in St. Kitts as a representative from Nevis. Mrs. Stevens noted repeatedly that those last 10 years of her life with Ivor, after he walked away from politics, were some of their most wonderful years together.

Today, Mrs. Stevens misses their discussions, their togetherness, and the security he provided in her life. The memories from those warm and wonderful final years, with no active politicking, and with Ivor totally hers, Mrs. Stevens promised, will remain with her forever. She prefers to remember Ivor as a loving husband rather than a frustrated, burdened politician. The people of St. Kitts-Nevis, too, remember Ivor Stevens. He was a man of both St. Kitts and Nevis. Undoubtedly, Ivor Stevens was an imperfect human being, but a committed family man, and a trusted, innovative political leader on Nevis.

Secession or Divisionism

Ivor Stevens was born on St. Kitts, but on the secession issue one would have believed he hailed from Nevis. His frequent diatribes against the "mother colony," St. Kitts, were loud, caustic, and vitriolic (see Appendix A). As a minister in the St. Kitts-Nevis coalition government (1980-1989) Stevens' outbursts were heard whenever he suspected any Kittitian, who was a coalition colleague, of thwarting the development of Nevis. Even 10 years after he retired from active politics, Stevens declared: "I wish it known that I am a firm believer in Nevisians directing their own affairs and not be directed by St. Kitts . . . . In fact, I am forced to consider myself a Divisionist."

Despite his position on matters related to Nevis, Ivor never hid the fact that he was a born Kittitian. He simply wanted parity between the two islands. Stevens was caught between two loves—St. Kitts, the land of his birth, and Nevis, the land of his adoption. Over time, Stevens became a master at playing the two roles, even in times of crisis. Some people believed Ivor would have loved being leader of Nevis, but he always insisted: "I want it to be known that a person whose umbilical cord is buried on Nevis becomes the leader of the country." This viewpoint probably mitigated the subtle battles between Daniel and Stevens over leadership of the island.

Although not raised on St. Kitts, Ivor spent some of his growing years on the island, allowing him scope for higher education, early work experiences, and an initial exposure to St. Kitts-Nevis politics. It might have been Stevens' life experiences on the two islands that pushed him toward his unusual Divisionist politics. He had a firsthand view of populist politics on St. Kitts during the emergence of labor unionism. It was probably during those years of early development in his political thought that Ivor adopted the political ideal: "The use of political power should have moral justification and that it should always promote and enhance human dignity."

Generally, he was a proponent of the idea that acts in politics should be ethical and, as much as possible, beneficial to the mass of the islands' citizenry. During his years at the Grammar School, during the 1930s, Stevens must certainly have grasped that there are social and political differences between the two islands. Because of their systems of production, more intense class divisions existed on St. Kitts than on Nevis. There was also little doubt that the sugar industry on St. Kitts fashioned the social, economic, and political relations on the island.

It was that time too, when global economics, new political aspirations in the colonies, and the resultant social realities, were pushing British colonies around the world toward transformation and a new synthesis. From the start of the 20th century, political and social revolutions were unfolding on St. Kitts-Nevis and in the other sugar-producing colonies of the Caribbean. Toward the end of the 1800s there was evidence that the sugar industry on Nevis had failed. Most plantations on the island were abandoned as early as the 1930s. So, unlike Kittitians, few Nevisians on Nevis were at the direct mercy of the sugar-plantation system during the 1900s. Many were engaged in peasant farming, or involved in numerous trades including tailoring, shoemaking, carpentry, and masonry. Emigration is always a factor in the lives of Nevisians, too.

If Ivor had been limited only to the economic, political, and social happenings in Nevis of that time, he would have slept through an important period in his political education. While political struggles were fueled by labor protests on St. Kitts, and raged throughout much of the rest of the Caribbean in the 1930s and '40s, the citizens who remained on Nevis appeared unaffected and largely disinterested. The Anguillans also had no commitment to sugar or to labor unionism. In time, the differences among the islands became a useful political tool, used effectively by the planter-class and by the working class; each to spread its brand of politics. "Why would Bradshaw the labor leader on St. Kitts try to control the politics in Anguilla and Nevis, when the people of these islands have no commitment to the labor union?" The planters must have asked.

Two Nevisians who became deeply involved in the labor-protest politics developing on St. Kitts while Ivor was there were J. N. France and Charles Halbert. Halbert owned a library and bookshop on Fort and Central Streets and was a participant observer in the emerging radical society. Over the years he became a close confidant of Premier Bradshaw, but remained a proud Nevisian until his death in 1971. France served as the first secretary of the labor union and remained a stalwart for the masses' cause throughout his life. He was a very active participant observer in the labor-union process. Later, he ensured that his experiences with the process were documented in a book being edited by Mrs. Victoria Borg-O'Flaherty. There were also hundreds of less well-known men and women from Nevis, living on St. Kitts, who fought in those battles for economic, social, and political justice against colonialism and planter exploitation. It was a slow process, but eventually some of the political awareness growing in the Caribbean, and that had emerged on St. Kitts, did get to Nevis. Ivor resided on St. Kitts as a young adult. That placed him in the arena of the working-class revolt at a critical point in the islands' political evolution. Further, Ivor attended the elite Grammar School at a time when vulgar capitalists were in charge. He must have heard the planter-class viewpoint espoused among his schoolmates, who were generally of the elites. It was also a time shaped by false consciousness, under colonial rule.

Ivor also saw the misery and heard the painful, piercing cries of those who labored for inconsequential rewards in the sugar industry. Perhaps, that shaped Ivor's decision to enter politics, albeit on Nevis. His populist approach left observers certain that Ivor learned lessons from the St. Kitts labor union experience. Those experiences became useful to him as he campaigned, throughout his political career. However, what has never been fully explained was Ivor's supposed overtures toward the Labor Party, back in the 1950s, and his promise to run as a Labor Party candidate on Nevis, then.

Undoubtedly, Stevens' first job assignment at S. L. Horsford in Basseterre must have also provided valuable instruction for him. While he worked at Horsford, through its shipping department, Ivor was exposed to a much wider world of trade and world events.

For the Caribbean, even at that time, there was globalization based on sugar production and trade. The islands produced sugar, but they imported almost everything else from Britain, during a time when, "Britannia ruled the waves."

At Horsford, Ivor also met people from all walks of life. Of Kittitians and Nevisians who managed to raise enough money to build wooden houses, some would probably have purchased materials from S. L. Horsford, one of the hardware stores then. Thus, there were opportunities for Ivor to witness the intricacies of commerce as he talked and mingled with clients, particularly those from Nevis. What Ivor saw and heard helped provide him with critical growth experiences and prepared him for a future of involvement with the people, and in the islands' politics. The firm, S. L. Horsford, was also a major player in the management of sugar estates on St. Kitts at a time when globalism was already the idea driving the economic system in the Caribbean.

Many plantation owners opted to live in England rather than deal directly with the day-to-day drudgery of managing their estates in the islands. Consequently, firms such as S. L. Horsford provided that service. Thus, for a number of years, including the labor-revolution years, S. L. Horsford, served as one of the agents for a large percentage of the absentee owners of sugar estates on St. Kitts. Particularly during the 1930s and 1940s, that was an unenviable position for any firm on St. Kitts. Its management was constantly battling with leaders of the local labor union. Such firms were in a position to actively assist in dwarfing the socioeconomic and political development of the working class on the islands. For example, during that time of labor crises, firms such as S. L. Horsford found they were on the opposite side and standing in for those who oppressed the working class on the islands. In time, the resulting conflicts and festering animosities left bitter feelings between the two warring sides for years to come. Although Ivor was not there throughout the entire period of conflict, he served with S. L. Horsford, and at the sugar factory, long enough to see and understand the peculiar role of these businesses in the emerging drama.

All for Nevis

Few persons born on Nevis demonstrated their love for, and commitment to, their island in the manner that Ivor Stevens did. He pursued every avenue possible in his desire to change the stagnant social and economic condition on the island. He wanted to create some sense of innovation and progress there. Stevens was determined to help Nevisians see change, feel success, and experience prosperity. They needed to know contentment on their island.

Stevens could have chosen to live in St. Kitts, where he was born, in the British Virgin Islands because of his mother's connection there, or Canada, where he served as a soldier during World War II. But he had grown up on Nevis. Over time Ivor appeared to have fallen in love with the island, then appeared to become intrigued by the possibility of political participation there. In 1953 Stevens did not return to Nevis in search of a handout. He was quite aware of the economic and infrastructural backwardness that pervaded the island. At that time, Nevis had little more than "hard knocks" to offer its residents; even those born on the island were leaving in large numbers, searching for a better life elsewhere in the world. Between 1962 and 1977, over 100,000 citizens emigrated from St. Kitts-Nevis to England, the United States, Canada, the U.S. and British Virgin Islands, and the Netherland Antilles. Migration from St. Kitts-Nevis started in the 1840s and continued in large numbers into the 1950s, 1960s, and 1970s.[5]

Despite economic and other challenges, Stevens' goal was to change the existing conditions on the island, in whatever way he could. To achieve that goal, he intended to use every avenue and endure every hardship. The physical and emotional costs did not matter to him. Further, it was easier for Ivor to challenge the less

---

[5] Frucht, R. (1967). *Community and Context in a Colonial Society: Social and Economic Change in Nevis British West Indies*. Ann Arbor, MI: Ann Arbor University Microfilm; Richardson, B. C. (1983). *Caribbean Migrants: Environment and Human Survival on St. Kitts and Nevis*. Knoxville: University of Tennessee Press.

organized politics on Nevis than the more organized, bruising labor vs. planter politics emerging on St. Kitts. Ivor also showed himself to be fully committed to bringing new ideas to the islands' politics. He was not given to wavering, talk, and no action. In retrospect, Ivor seemed to have ranked his loves in the following order: his wife Dora, his big sister May and other family members, then Nevis politics. Arthur Evelyn made the point, "Ivor had to be satisfied that what he did was in the interest of Nevis. He had a genuine interest in Nevis. . . . Things had to get better for Nevis. There was too much dependence on St. Kitts."

The annals of Nevis are still being written. However, the island's oral history is replete with stories of how Ivor Stevens went beyond the normal call of duty to help struggling Nevisians. Long before he had the force of political rank and status behind him, Ivor showed concern for Nevisians, especially those who were poor and downtrodden: fishermen, farmers, and hucksters (peddlers). At times, Ivor even attempted to empathize, internalize, and act out the roles of the persons he was trying to help. After 1980, Stevens simply received governmental authority and legitimization to continue what he had already been doing on Nevis for many years.

There was some prestige and status in being a political representative for Nevis, particularly since Ivor was a Kittitian, not a Nevisian. Numerous stories are told on St. Kitts-Nevis about how politicians abused the elective privilege and trust to enhance personal fortune and fame, while forgetting their promises and commitments, once they ascended to office. That type of criticism could not be directed toward Ivor. He placed the good of Nevis above his personal ambitions. Few Nevisians speak of times when Stevens was callous, aloof, or uncaring about the people, or the affairs of Nevis. Rather, he was perceived as always contending with problems and searching for real solutions. Stevens was steadfast in his ultimate goal: to make a creative and discernable difference in the lives of Nevisians. He was committed to changing those things that made life in Nevis a miserable drudgery, caused frustration, early onset of depression, and at times premature death.

Many stories have been told about the continuous migration from Nevis since the 1840s. That pattern of migration reflects how some people felt about their future on the island. From time to time, there were Nevisians who saw living on Nevis as leading to hopelessness. Others seemed ashamed to be born on the island. As a number of them moved away, some claimed birth on St. Kitts or elsewhere. Enterprising and adventurous Nevisians also adopted strange accents. Meanwhile, there were thousands who migrated to Britain, preferring to die in the "mother country." Even the island's cricket program appeared to have suffered from that malaise. Throughout the 1950s and '60s, Nevis had outstanding cricketers: Orville Morton, Ed Arthurton, David Parry, Livingstone Sergeant, Alford Howell, Ira Hobson, Theodore Hobson, Bobo Webbe, Harold Walters, Egbert "Timmix" Halliday, and others. However, Nevis often took last place in the annual Leeward Islands Cricket Tournament, losing repeatedly to Antigua, St. Kitts, and Montserrat. Somehow, year after year, Nevis cricketers did not appear to have the commitment to personal dignity. They seemed to lack the will that could make them win for Nevis. Psychologically, they seemed to exist in a hazy, unreal world created by their double colonial experience. They were dominated and oppressed, first by Britain, then by St. Kitts. Even the cricket on Nevis was in need of a revolutionary experience fostering ideological decolonization and the sense that its cricketers were on par with those on St. Kitts.

That reality started to change drastically, during the early 1970s. The period following the loss of the *Christena* (see Chapter 5) saw the birth of the Nevis Reformation Party and a rediscovery that the objective interests of Nevisians are different from those of Kittitians, often requiring fundamental changes on the island. Meanwhile, as Culturama became institutionalized, also during the 1970s, a great political, social, and psychological awakening started to occur on Nevis. Many Nevisians began to believe they could remake their life and world, and then started to act on the idea.

Sugar and Politics

When labor unionism came of age, during the 1940s, the St. Kitts Sugar Factory was still the focal point of life, economics, and power on St. Kitts. Even the governor paid homage to its manager. However, the powerful landowning sector of a very class-conscious society depended on the powerless and landless working-class to perform the very difficult task of keeping the factory supplied with sugarcane, in a labor-intensive production system.

Yet, those sugar workers were barely welcomed at the factory. Few worked there in any capacity, and even fewer found leading positions at the factory because of their skin color, class, and limited education. As late as the 1950s, a former governor of the Leeward Islands, Sir Kenneth Blackburn, noted with concern that a high level of racism persisted on St. Kitts. He described the society there as being more intensely class conscious than Barbados, the most British of the Caribbean colonies.[6]

The labor movement on St. Kitts goes back as early as 1916-1917, but not until 1940 did the British government allow workers in its Caribbean colonies to organize into legitimate labor unions. Then, the workers on St. Kitts became united in a powerful and radical advocacy union led first by Edgar Challenger, then by Matthew Sebastian. The leadership passed to Robert Bradshaw in 1944. Through intense labor activism, wars of words, and union-designed guerrilla tactics, there was the birth and emergence of a new politics on St. Kitts. The coming of labor unionism to St. Kitts remade the world for the working-class on St. Kitts, and eventually for those in Nevis and Anguilla. The union fought a relentless class war for many years to win equal rights, political participation, education, and empowerment for all on the islands, particularly the despised, poor, and exploited working masses.

Stevens was there in St. Kitts during some of those battles. He might have avoided direct involvement, but he could not have

---

6 Blackburne, K. (1976). *Lasting Legacy: A Story of British Colonialism.* London, UK: Johnson.

missed the general and intense fray: nobody did. Stevens' wife claimed he was distressed that all the managers at the factory were White or near White and none Black. At that time the working-class had few avenues to success and little encouragement toward social mobility. Very little education and few opportunities for leadership were afforded the working-class. Although he led one of the best performing work teams at the factory, Ivor observed that his men got few tangible rewards.

However, he dared not challenge the powerful sugar industry openly. Instead, Ivor quietly voiced discontent with the social structure engendered by the system. While working the third shift, Ivor endeavored to show that Black workers were as capable as any other group of workers at the factory. He also wanted to show that color was never the limiting factor the wealthy and powerful planter class tried to suggest and teach. Sadly though, even when they saw the truth, factory management opted to continue believing carefully contrived myths. Notwithstanding, leaders did exist among the working-class. Ivor's education at the St. Kitts Sugar Factory heightened his sensibilities to the social and labor inequalities there. The factory also provided him another view of the class-driven struggle between the labor union and the planters.

It was commonly believed that Ivor was once connected and committed to the Labor Party in some way, when he came to Nevis in 1953. Seemingly, Ivor took the plunge and became obligated to the workers' union before he left St. Kitts to live on Nevis. Over on Nevis, Ralph Harris had no doubt that Ivor Stevens was the "labor-man" whom Bradshaw claimed he had on Nevis during the 1957 election campaign. As recently as 2006, Stanley Franks Jr., a former secretary of the St. Kitts-Nevis Trades and Labor Union, reiterated that he saw a letter from Mr. Stevens in the union archives, written during the 1950s to J. N. France, then secretary of the union. It declared Stevens' willingness to be Bradshaw's man on Nevis. Seemingly, Stevens acted on his conviction that the sugar industry was dealing unjustly with the working-class. He was willing to challenge the system, fighting on the side of the oppressed. It has also been suggested that Ivor understood what it took to enter, and then remain in the politics of the time. Nevisians were hostile to the labor union; Stevens, being the pragmatist that he was, avoided any frank discussion of labor unionism on Nevis.

In time, the labor movement did foster a social and political revolution that eventually benefitted St. Kitts, Nevis, and Anguilla. The working-class entered the politics of the islands, and this shift in leadership led to unprecedented, far-reaching, and remarkable changes.[7] Those early transformations left indelible marks on the impressionable mind of Stevens. Years after, his strategy to achieve political success on Nevis mirrored and incorporated many of those very tactics that brought success to the efforts of labor-union agitators during the 1940s.

Long before Ivor Stevens became known for his oratorical skills, there were Edgar Challenger, Thomas Manchester, Robert Bradshaw, Paul Southwell and others, all practitioners of the art of dramatic oratory. Stevens may have learned from them that it was important to have an effective, appealing, oratory style, a strategy that could make or break political leaders. Each took care and pride in his ability to speak in a convincing style. In the Mutual Improvement Society (MIS) and the labor union, not surprisingly, good elocution with style became a prized art and an envied trademark. British politicians, such as Winston Churchill, were imitated in presentation style and diction. Many West Indian politicians emulated Englishmen and took pride in crafting their speaking rhythm and style to sound British. Robert Bradshaw of St. Kitts-Nevis and Lavity Stout of the British Virgin Islands became masters of the British accent and speaking style. However, such acceptance of colonial indoctrination and false consciousness never seemed to have appeal for better educated leaders such as Dr. Eric Williams of Trinidad and Tobago or Norman Manley of Jamaica. Even while they led their islands, they kept the speaking accent and style common to everyone in the culture.

---

7 Browne, W. T. (1992). *From Commoner to King.* Lanham, MD: University of America Press.

Another very important political-success strategy used by the labor union and then by Stevens was the skillful use of the power of numbers, particularly the masses—the working poor. Stevens did not befriend the poor and the downtrodden by accident. In the matter of elective politics, these are the people who hold the winning card in a game that depends on numbers. When Ivor entered politics on Nevis he did not have to learn that strategy. It had been demonstrated to him by labor-union politicians before. If he built a symbiotic relationship with the mass of poor voters on Nevis, then, like Bradshaw, he could be sure to be elected for the duration of his political life. After two false starts, Stevens did just that, and managed his politics very well. In time too, Nevisians became aware that he worked relentlessly to ensure equal rights, social involvement, empowerment, and the "good life" for Nevisians of every class, race, and creed. Stevens went out of his way to court everyone's friendship, thereby ensuring a relatively safe seat and numerous reelections.

Stevens' struggle on Nevis reminded him of the working-class battles he saw on St. Kitts. He attacked many of the social myths and sacred cows seen in Nevis. They were similar to those he had seen the planter class use in St. Kitts to protect their interests while he was there. The labor union victories on St. Kitts eventually helped to foster success for the masses' cause in both Anguilla and Nevis. Accordingly, the transformation on Nevis was never a single-handed task for Ivor. There were Nevisians such as Uhral Swanston, Ralph Harris, Fred Parris, Sim Daniel, and others, who shared the vision of transformation, and who labored alongside Ivor to move life and society in Nevis in new and unprecedented directions. At that time, the pioneers became champions to many Nevisians, because of their ideals and their will to reshape political and social realities on the island. Many who observed the process recall that Stevens was never at the back waiting on others for ideas. Quite often he was the point-man, filled with ideas of his own, but he listened to others—always poised and ready for action.

Ivor's ideas about change and new directions for Nevis were constant. There were no eternal verities as change began to take place on Nevis. Every area of life was challenged. Most colleagues agreed that Stevens usually saw the ends first. He contrived the means later. For example, it was evident that he learned from the labor union struggles on St. Kitts, as he secured the trust and friendship of the lower class on Nevis. However, only cautiously would Stevens have admitted on Nevis that he was a student of labor union politics. Many years later, when the People's Action Movement came on the scene, that party subtly represented and defended the status-quo ideals of the elite against the mass ideals of the Labor Party. Yet, Stevens was willing to join with the People's Action Movement to enhance his politics and to heighten his challenge to the Labor Party government. That strategy was also a part of Ivor's search for a changed politics on Nevis. According to election records, Stevens did stand for the People's Action Movement in the 1966 election.[8]

Hugh Heyliger, a former minister of the People's Action Movement-Nevis Reformation Party coalition government, remembers his first encounter with Stevens at an emergency meeting in 1967, during the Anguilla breakaway crisis. Ivor came to the meeting dressed in his farming outfit, the way he was dressed when he received the call. At that time, every opposition politician in the State criticized the Anguillan policies of Bradshaw and his Labor Party. Ivor was a leading voice among them. He used the Anguilla situation to bolster the call for secession on Nevis. It was good political strategy then, that he collaborated with the new People's Action Movement party. They calculated their every political move to frustrate the powerful Labor Party, at that time also severely encumbered by the Anguillans' revolt and the one emerging on Nevis.

By the late 1970s, the call for secession for Nevis had intensified. Some think Stevens never really severed his political relationship with the People's Action Movement, despite his role in the Nevis Reformation Party. However, by the mid 1970s, Stevens had officially changed his allegiance from the PAM to the NRP. Stevens'

---

8 Borg-O'Flaherty, V. M. (2004b). *20th Century Election Results: St. Kitts-Nevis.* Basseterre, St. Kitts: Author. p. 24.

detractors tried to build their case against him so they criticized his willingness to work cooperatively and openly with a St. Kitts political party. Although such a matter may be viewed elsewhere as trivial, on St. Kitts-Nevis, it can have profound political value, as such issues do become significant factors in the lives of politicians. The fact that St. Kitts and Nevis are profoundly connected never escaped Ivor, even if he did not dwell on that reality; he struggled to work with it. Ivor saw himself intricately wrapped, along with all other Kittitians and Nevisians, in a complex mix of blood, birth, history, politics, and persistent conflicts—and he danced to it all! However, doing this well was always a challenge, and never easy.

Retirement

Nephew Maurice recalled that by the mid 1980s, politics had got to Ivor emotionally. The divisiveness that had come to the process pained him. It was with what seemed to have been a yearning for change in his life's direction that Ivor turned to friends, to family, and to home, where his wife had always been waiting for him. He started to catch up with his interest in farm-related activities, including raising rare birds and growing orchids. When Ivor turned to bird farming, he did so with zest, moving beyond chicken farming to include ducks, turkeys, and guinea fowls. During that period, Ivor was probably the only person on Nevis who raised such birds. His wife noted that Ivor became quite adept at making dove and other birds' calls. At times, he even boasted that he was capable of speaking the languages of both birds and bees. Mrs. Stevens highlighted that there were also times when untamed birds were coaxed until they ate from her husband's hands.

Not much detail was given about Ivor's farming of pigs, though he did so during his retirement. Raising birds and pigs was quite an unusual combination of animals in Nevis, during the 1980s and 1990s. However, the diversity of Mr. Steven's entrepreneurial interests, at the latter stage of his life, gives testimony to the complexity of the man.

Ivor also had interest in plants. He enjoyed the challenge of flower gardening. He grew and took great pride in his orchids. Mrs. Stevens recalled that Ivor enjoyed giving their female friends orchids as presents. There were numerous occasions when he made special arrangements of orchids for friends who visited their home. At that time, Nevisians who liked flowers tended to choose roses. Most who kept flower gardens took pride in their varieties of roses. Ivor was a flower gardening innovator with his orchids.

Both Rev. Bowers and Mrs. Stevens spoke about Ivor's love for bridge. He was a dedicated and keen player of the game. Bowers suggested that Ivor used the strategies of that game in dealing with other aspects of his life. Mr. Stevens' preacher friend noted, "Ivor used bridge playing to organize his mind." The group with which Ivor played bridge met every Friday night: Ivor, his wife Dora, his sister May, and family friend, Al Thompson. After Ivor met and took a fancy to Rev. Bowers, he tried to entice the Methodist preacher to appreciate and play the game. However, Bowers recalled, "I could not grasp it."

Ivor's church attendance lagged. His friend Rev. Bowers noted,

> Although Ivor was religious, he did not attend church. He had reverence for God and reverence for life. But he saw little utility in church attendance. During the year I spent on Nevis Ivor attended church only on special occasions, for example, the dedication of the organ at Gingerland, in July 1994. Ivor was a Mason and he seemed to have got more meaning from the meetings at his lodge.

At one time, after he had retired, Ivor was in the St. Kitts-Nevis National Bank, and the line was moving very slowly, but the manager did not appear to notice the long delay. Ivor sat on the floor and dragged himself toward the counter, as the line moved along at a snail's pace. His unusual action soon drew everyone's attention, including the bank's manager. In quick time another teller joined the two already serving the clientele, and the line began to move faster. However, when Ivor got home and shared his strange banking experience with Mrs. Stevens, she reprimanded him. She still remembers that Ivor did not protest. He simply responded with his usual, "Yes, darling."

None of his other activities prevented Ivor from finding time for the activity that was very special and dear to him: fishing. Just as at the height of his political career, during retirement, Ivor continued to spend time fishing with his friends. When Ivor started to sense the approach of death, he became increasingly interested in spending time at sea fishing. Even as he experienced a deterioration of his health, he kept insisting that his friends take him fishing. At least one of his friends, Carlton Tyson, refused to take Ivor to sea as he weakened. Another fisherman friend, Yampee, explained he was so sorry for Mr. Stevens that he did take him on one of those last fishing trips.

When he turned age 86, Ivor understood that time was against him. For Mrs. Stevens, every one of those final days with Ivor was treasured—not endured: "I appreciated the end. Every moment was a joy." When Ivor became too ill to be comfortable in their regular bed, Mrs. Stevens purchased a special bed for him from St. Croix. She reflected, "At that time when he moved to that special bed, I realized it was the end of our sleeping together in the same bed. But I treated him with love." What seemed to have bothered Mrs. Stevens most was the fact that after all those years of knowing a strong, vibrant, and independent Ivor, it was hard for her to accept and comprehend the new reality, "There was ill and broken Ivor in need of help."

He had been stricken with acute emphysema. Mrs. Stevens noted her husband appeared to have become addicted to smoking, while he served in the military. When they dated during the later 1940s Ivor still smoked heavily. For a time he had stopped; but he began to smoke again. It was not until about 1956 that Ivor really overcame his addiction to smoking. Another suggested cause of Ivor's emphysema was a shrapnel wound he received while in action with the Canadian military in North Africa. Pastor Bowers believed that the shrapnel could also have affected Ivor's lungs. A third proposed cause of Ivor's illness was his association with birds. Some people believed that something Ivor inhaled, while he attended the birds, could have caused the onset of his deadly illness. It could also have been caused by a combination of those factors.

Mrs. Stevens continues to hold vivid memories of her husband's last days. She endured them with much difficulty: they were very painful, lonely, and frustrating. Ivor was still the man in the house and she still loved him. However, the Ivor she had known, the Ivor she adored, the Ivor who caused her heart to flutter was no more. He had left long before that fateful morning in June 1997, when the ailing Ivor that remained, breathed heavily 3 times, and then died.

Mrs. Stevens was not at the hospital when Ivor died. She had kept watch all night, then left to go home for an early breakfast, intending to return and continue her vigil. However, Mrs. Stevens' plans changed when friends called her back to the hospital. Doreen Thompson, Monica Tyson, and Eulalie Francis had remained to keep the death vigil. They were all good friends of the Stevens' family and had worked out a system with Mrs. Stevens to spend alternate shifts watching over sick and dying Ivor. His wife recalled, "When I arrived at the hospital and saw Ivor, I thought he was still alive. On realizing he was dead I screamed loudly."

What Mr. Stevens and thousands of Nevisians hated with passion was the constant unfair second-class treatment Nevis and Nevisians received from Kittitians, usually from those who held political power. That practice and the resultant experience were contrary to Stevens' ideal for Nevis. Such actions undermined political success, inter-island harmony, and the good life Ivor dreamed of for Nevisians. He was usually flamboyant about his political presentations, and in his display of chivalry when dealing with women. But Ivor was never known to be extravagant or showy with his material possessions. Further, because of his commitment to populist ideals and politics, Ivor always seemed careful to emulate and depict the poverty and the forbearance of the common people he represented. As one person noted about Ivor, "He lived a simple life, almost miserly; he had become a typical Nevisian." And that was how he died—a committed Nevisian.

The Man and His Style

The first leader of the Nevis Reformation Party was Sim Daniel. He was a quiet man who thought much more than he usually spoke. In contrast, his deputy leader, Ivor Stevens, had a vibrant personality and was very much an actor who had mastered rhetoric and style. Ivor could talk intelligently about most things, and did so with little provocation. His initial frustration in the House of Assembly was caused by a lack of legislative success during the *Christena* period. Ivor was constantly on his soapbox talking about the *Christena*, the roads on Nevis, or other social and political matters that retarded progress on the island. Stevens often reminisced about that time and his tenure as a member of the opposition. He considered that period "some of my best years in the House of Assembly." Stevens had a real cause and a persuasive mission for Nevis. He also knew his opponent. Many of his hours were spent selecting ammunition and preparing to do verbal battle as a champion for Nevis. Accordingly, Mr. Stevens' command of the language became a powerful and useful weapon for launching offensives or rebutting attacks. He was also a man of action. A number of interviews with people who knew Ivor well, revealed him, his ideas, and his politics, as much more complex than just rhetoric and style.

Norman Jones, a Nevisian and former administrator of the Social Security System in Nevis, for the Nevis Reformation Party government, knew Ivor well. Norman concurs that Ivor loved being in the opposition during the *Christena years*. Jones observed that "Ivor was greatest in the role as an opposition member in the House," and that "Ivor's finest moments came when the Labor Party and Bradshaw stood in his way and hindered the dreams he harbored for Nevis. In response Ivor would declare a relentless war by unleashing many verbal attacks on the government."

Jones also observed that few tangible achievements accrued to Nevis during that period, but Stevens derived much personal satisfaction from the fact that he had numerous opportunities to speak for Nevis. Nevisians heard him present and defend their cause in the Assembly, on the radio, and in village meetings. Usually, Stevens' language was vitriolic and scathing, especially when its purpose was to belittle and cut down an enemy. Maurice, his nephew, recalled about Ivor, "He could talk in colorful terms; some of the words do not bear repeating." Another observer recalled that, "Stevens was a skillful and opportunistic politician." He researched his opposition, then used the information to neutralize that person. Ivor was also versed in the art of war; accordingly, his knowledge and use of military strategies boosted his politics, while they undermined that of the opposition.

Franklyn Brand was one of Ivor's friends, and a political protégé. For a number of years, he observed Ivor and his politics at close range. Brand concluded, "Ivor Stevens was an actor." To Lee Moore, "Ivor's rhetoric was profoundly paradoxical." Moore believed that Ivor speaking for the grassroots was a stratagem: "Ivor did not believe thoroughly in the populism he touted throughout his career." In that same vein, Joseph Parry, who served in government with Stevens for many years, noted that, "Ivor was a complex person of many sides."

At times when he spoke, particularly on political issues, Ivor seemed to be energized by his last word and enticed by the next. There was a certain rhythm and finesse that kept him in motion. Words invigorated Ivor, speaking to his self-confidence. Perhaps secretly, Ivor enjoyed the challenges and skill of using words as an essayist, a poet, or a dramatist would. Some thought he was always self-conscious about not being an intellectual, but he was willing to aspire toward such a direction. In retrospect, many observed that Caribbean political leaders, during that era, were fighting difficult battles, locked in an ongoing struggle during an unyielding colonial period, that profoundly shaped the social, political, and economic realities of the Caribbean area.[9]

---

9 Bolland, O. N. (2001). *The Politics of Labour in the British Caribbean: The Social Origins of Authoritarianism and Democracy in the Labour*

Seemingly, Ivor could have had many reasons for choosing to make politics a career, during that period of political awakening in Nevis. Those reasons must have been varied, some being very personal. In retrospect, it seems that one of the reasons was the confidence Ivor had in himself and his ability to harness, command, and direct words well enough to become successful, even in the then relatively new experience of a mass-controlled Caribbean politics. Whatever his other reasons were for choosing that calling, Ivor ignored the odds, gritted his teeth, and stepped head first into Nevis—St. Kitts politics, intending to make a difference.

For the next 34 or more years through his commitment to Nevis, through his dogged tenacity, through his belief that there is something worthwhile in every man, through his vision for Nevis, and through his unique use of language as stratagem, Stevens touched and liberated lives, built relationships, and in a number of instances, opened doors to change. He encouraged a greater sense of happiness, and brought varied measures of success to many Nevisians.

Younger men of Nevis—Victor Martin, Franklyn Brand, Norman Jones, Elmo Liburd and also, the Rev. Lester Bowers from Antigua—continue to speak fondly of their close and cherished friendship with Ivor. All agree that he had a way with words. But, were those words empty rhetoric? Arthur Evelyn, a former member of Nevis local government, noted, "Ivor gave much advice and guidance. His word was his bond." Many young men gravitated toward him as a friend because he took time to reason with them, and they learned from him. Today, Nevisians are a more politically aware people. However, they continue to hold very fond memories of Ivor's genuine, relatively open, and insightful friendship with them.

Movement. Kingston, Jamaica: Ian Randle; Manley, M. (1982). *Jamaica: Struggle in the Periphery*. London, UK: Third World Media; Mitchell, J. (2006). *Beyond the Islands*. Oxford, UK: Macmillan Education; Palmer, C. A. (2006). *Eric Williams and the Making of the Modern Caribbean*. Chapel Hill: University of North Carolina Press.

Even Lee L. Moore, an accomplished orator himself, and at one time a keen political opponent of Ivor, noted he was, "a man who had become well connected to the grass-roots and thought he spoke for them. He pursued his goal to the end, giving the idea of commitment." Moore did not recall oratorical clashes with Stevens, but did admit, as Stevens related to friends, that there were times when Stevens used his oratorical skills to prod and challenge him. In Moore's words, "He did tease and provoke me in the Parliament."

Throughout his career as a politician, Ivor talked frequently with, and listened to, persons from every level of society. In many instances he was searching to find solutions to some problem or simply seeking to know how they saw the world. For Al Thompson, who served many years as a permanent secretary to Ivor in Nevis. "There were many things noteworthy about him, besides his oratory skills." Al Thompson noted,

> Ivor saw politics as a profession rather than just a job. He gave much thinking time to critical things. Even as he walked the streets he made notes and wrote things down. He was always thinking about how he could solve problems by creating change.

At one time Stevens boasted, "I am never always right, but at the same time, I am never always wrong. Even when I am wrong I depend on my permanent secretary to get it done right."

In one exchange, Maurice Stevens spoke about Uncle Ivor with much awe and sincerity. Before he could end the interview, tears were streaming down his face:

> To me, Ivor was an uncle and a friend. He has had a profound impact on my life. Even today there are things I do which I learned from Uncle Ivor. My marriage has lasted these many years because of the example my uncle set me. He always treated his wife with respect, even when they disagreed. He never raised [*sic*] his voice against her. From him I

> learned to appreciate the small things of life—an orchid, a sunset, or a bird. He took time out to share his thoughts on such things, and he taught me to pay attention to detail.

What Maurice became, and the appreciation he developed for his uncle, represented a remarkable turnaround from when they first met. Maurice was brought to St. Kitts-Nevis from St. Lucia because his father was off the island studying, and Maurice had become too rebellious for his mother to manage. Try as she might, she could not control him. When Maurice arrived on St. Kitts he took to the practice of skipping school and hanging out on the wharf with some friends. He soon became known as one of the "wharf rats."

Eventually, Maurice's truancy was reported to his Uncle Ivor, who felt such behavior was not becoming a Stevens. Ivor traveled to St. Kitts and confronted Maurice. This is a part of the conversation that took place, with Ivor speaking to Maurice.

> You are coming to live with me in Nevis. There is a saying that one man cannot break the army. I am the army and you cannot break me. Everyone should have the fear of the Lord in them. If I cannot drive it through your ears, I will drive it into your ass.

Maurice has never forgotten that meeting. According to Maurice, his experiences with Uncle Ivor in Nevis were a mixture of love, caring attention, guidance, and heavy discipline. At times he was beaten with a leather belt, but his uncle would take him fishing half an hour later. In retrospect, Maurice understood that his uncle's discipline was designed to change him completely: "He loved me. I cherish every one of those blows," he commented.

Further, in that association, Uncle Ivor always led by example. Frequently his talks were deep, at times becoming philosophical. Maurice was encouraged to become a critical thinker, as he dealt with the daily challenges of life. Through the years, Ivor also discussed and shared many tidbits of wisdom with his nephew.

From time to time, Ivor shared and examined ideas with friends during his Sunday Morning Club. Members of that club included Arthur (Buggy) Freeman, Victor Martin, and others. The group did not always consist of the same people, changing over time. However, those who participated in the meetings were always handpicked and given a special invitation by Ivor. On several occasions the meetings were held at Freeman's house. According to Victor Martin, some of the ideas discussed and exchanged included the matter of governance, family life, the economy, and other issues. One matter they pondered was the best approach to governing Nevis. On occasions they argued which matters the Nevis government should set as its priorities. Ivor also included discussions about economics and education during those meetings. Historically there have been many limitations to economic development and its success on Nevis. Accordingly, everyone in the group was challenged to work out a best approach to economic success, for all Nevisians. No discussion in which Ivor was involved could have gone on for long without touching his favorite Nevis issue: secession, or some examination of an approach to greater autonomy for the island. These were common topics, and Ivor always referred to them as part of his vision for Nevis.

Victor added other insights about Ivor's love of ideas and willingness to use good ones, no matter their origin. Although they spoke often about independence for Nevis, Ivor believed the island had to be prepared to make a success of any move toward that independence. He once said to Victor, "At present, Nevis is not ready. Independence goes beyond sentiment. We must be able to maintain our sovereignty." Because of the close relationship that grew and blossomed between Ivor and Victor, he was asked to present the eulogy at Ivor's funeral. The manner in which Victor recalled the dimensions of their friendship adds drama, insight, and an understanding of what it had become for Victor:

> Ivor Stevens had a wonderful and endearing capacity for long and rich conversation. It was at his insistence that—no matter the circumstances—he and I met at one special time each week. Ivor put

> it to me that we should get together to chat and to solve the problems of the world. And since it was established that these sessions would best be suited for Sundays it was he who first gave them the name, choir practice.
>
> The first time Ivor Stevens and I spoke of politics we did not speak to politics at all. Ivor Stevens spoke about decency and good order. He told me about his favorite parliament, the Charlestown Iron Shed. We debated the meaning of life and the meaning of death. We ventured into the art of war and the mental dexterity required for the game of bridge. And then it came to be that Ivor waxed poetic about the beauty of orchids and lectured me on the wide yon sea—its potential pleasures, its pitfalls, and of course, its fishing.

Martin noted that Stevens was also a good listener, yet he was really a man of action. "There was no one in government who knew better than him how to get things done. He always sought to attract ideas, and then he used from them for his own purposes."

"Another remarkable characteristic of Ivor," said Victor, "was his capacity to rise above the fray of politics and cross the divide in search of dialogue. Despite the obvious lack of cooperation between them, Stevens always spoke with Bradshaw and did employ Lee Moore once, when he needed a good lawyer." A further observation Victor Martin shared was that Ivor never bypassed an opportunity to meet and chat with the ordinary farmer and fisherman. "He always wanted to visit the ordinary people to share their views. Ivor believed sincerely that the ideas of these people must be heard."

Alvea Sergeant worked with Ivor as a secretary. She too spoke about his interest in sharing the thoughts and ideas of the ordinary Nevisian.

> He was very humorous. Mr. Stevens listened to even Dabby (a well-known intellectually challenged male adult in Nevis). He used to say, "everyone has a story. No one knows what he can learn from others.'" Mr. Stevens also thought constantly; it could have been observed even in his sick-bed. He was a real politician, a politician's politician. The views of others were treated with respect by him. Even when he disagreed with your ideas, he gave you the right to express them. He was no hypocrite; if he did not like what you were saying you would know.

Alvea also noted that he often saved the island from difficulty, because he was always much more willing than Daniel to negotiate and resolve issues with Prime Minister Simmonds. "Mr. Stevens had a way with words, and he could help to solve problems, because he listened." Simmonds corroborated Alvea's statement, agreeing that he and Ivor worked well together to resolve problems between St. Kitts and Nevis. On, the other hand, he often found Daniel elusive and noncommittal.

Al Thompson also commented on his respect for Ivor's creative mind. During Ivor's funeral, Al said the following about his former boss:

> His great belief was in the development of the mind, which, in my estimation, goes beyond the usual definition of the concept of education. I think of Ivor as a philosopher, and I deem it a pity that time did not permit him to complete and publish ideas and theories about the art of living, that he had not only accumulated in his head, but had put together on paper

The late Fitzroy Bryant noted that the April 1974 Nevis Secession Bill was never voted on in the House. Ironically, he blamed Ivor for preventing a timely vote in the House of Assembly. Bryant suggested that when the issue was presented to the legislative body, Ivor outdid himself and everyone else. That was the occasion when Ivor set a record in the House for time spent on the floor presenting an address. Even the usually eloquent Bradshaw and Southwell were outdone. Mrs. Stevens recalls that he spoke for 23 hours on the Nevis Secession Bill. Bryant claimed it was 25 hours. When Ivor finished speaking, no vote was called on the bill. Despite Bryant's claim against Ivor, it was a proper session and the matter should have been voted on. However, those were the years when the Labor Party government ruled the land with an iron fist. It determined which bills lived and which died. And, back in 1974, no one in the Labor government really understood the yearning of Nevisians for more autonomy. Nevisians had no legislative authority except that approved by the Kittitians. Consequently, the bill to ensure more autonomy for Nevis, in 1974, was allowed to die. However, the rigidity and control by the Labor Party then rendered such a request on Nevis far ahead of its time.

Whether it lasted for 23 or 25 hours, that address in April of 1974 was one example of how Ivor Stevens used his oratory skills to dominate, to charm, to agitate, and at times to irritate the St. Kitts-Nevis legislative body. In the process of irritating the Assembly, Stevens was on stage, pleased, confident, and, at his best, while he held the attention of St. Kitts-Nevis citizenry for 3 successive days. The session was being broadcast on the government's broadcasting system, Radio ZIZ, and Nevisians were listening. That record for the length of a presentation in the St. Kitts-Nevis House of Assembly still stands after 39 years.

I had three memorable encounters with Stevens. One occurred on the sailboat *Sakara* on our way to St. Kitts. He was suggesting that it was a good thing that Deryck Parry, a Nevisian cricketer, accepted a contract to play cricket in South Africa. The apartheid system, to which the South African government subscribed, had barred South African cricketers from playing with, or against, non-White cricketers for many years. After the cricketing world excluded South Africa from all official international cricket, the government there devised a plan and started to invite West Indian cricketers, among others, to come and play cricket in South Africa; the visiting cricketers were paid large sums of money. For a time the matter was very disruptive to West Indies cricket and to Caribbean society. Some persons agreed that West Indian cricketers were right to accept the money and play cricket in South Africa. Others, including Viv Richards, then captain of the West Indies team, thought differently. That morning when Stevens agreed that it was ok for a Nevisian to ignore South Africa's history of apartheid and go there to play cricket for money, I opposed him verbally, but aggressively. It is not possible for me to recall all that was said but it was not a pleasant conversation. Later, Stevens and I clashed again when I chose to oppose the Nevis Reformation Party in the 1983 Nevis local election. Stevens did make some uncomplimentary remarks about me in his political meetings. However, I opted out of the politics eventually, then I left Nevis shortly after. The next time I remember seeing Stevens was in 1996, shortly before he died. He was obviously very ill. We spoke freely. I held no animosity toward him, and seemingly, he had none toward me.

For many Nevisians, Ivor Stevens is gone but not forgotten. While he did not lead the Nevis Reformation Party, he did become personally involved with the lives of Nevisians and in the affairs of the island. To that extent, he became a critical catalyst for the transformations that came to the lives of Nevisians and Kittitians, after 1980.

Total Commitment

Former Prime Minister Kennedy Simmonds, and former Minister of Trade and Development, Hugh Heyliger, two Kittitians, spoke glowingly of Stevens' commitment to Nevis and to his Ministry in St. Kitts, when he served as the Minister for Public Utilities, Communications, and Works, in the PAM-NRP coalition government (1980-1989), Mr. Heyliger reflected,

> Ivor took his assignment seriously. And he was very deliberate about how he could help Nevis. Because

> Ivor was so focused on making improvements in Nevis he often got into conflict with Sim, who was Minister of Nevis Affairs, and who felt no one from St. Kitts, not even Ivor, should infringe on his authority in Nevis. However, Stevens seemed to think if he could get more from the government on St. Kitts for Nevis, then the argument for secession would go away. He continuously searched for parity with St. Kitts, for Nevis.

Commenting on the years Stevens spent as a member of his cabinet, Dr. Simmonds provided useful insight into another important facet of Ivor's involvement with the government on St. Kitts. The former Prime Minister reflected,

> I listened to him a lot. Ivor always had his pulse on how the common people saw things. He did not allow small obstacles to stand in his way. Very often, for instance, he came to St. Kitts on fishing boats. At first, he was a very strong secessionist. Later, Ivor suggested that the islands should be kept together. He had become convinced that it could work. But, secession should always be kept as a safety valve. Ivor brought to the government experience and the maturity to deal with conflicts and differences of opinion. He always kept the larger objective in mind. Ivor often intervened between Powell and myself, when we had different opinions. On a number of occasions, he was the one who kept the government together.

Former Prime Minister Simmonds also suggested that Stevens' ability to focus on the big picture and encourage peaceful communication always brought back memories of another critical time and incident, in Caribbean history. The place was Ocho Rios, Jamaica, November 16-18, 1982. A Caribbean Community

(CARICOM) meeting was being held. As the proceedings progressed, Maurice Bishop of Grenada, then the maverick in Caribbean politics, got into an argument with Forbes Burnham of Guyana.

According to Simmonds, had it not been that Vere Bird Sr. intervened as peacemaker, that meeting in Jamaica could have ended on a very sour note for everyone. Simmonds applauded Stevens' ability as the peacemaker between St. Kitts and Nevis. It always reminded him of how Vere Bird stepped between Burnham and Bishop, many years ago in Jamaica. "Ivor's ability to become involved in conflict situations and encourage peaceful resolutions was remarkable. Whenever there was a controversy and Stevens managed to forge a settlement, I remembered Vere Bird Sr. and Jamaica."

During his years as a member of the federal government in St. Kitts, Ivor, like Sim Daniel, was also part of the local government on Nevis. However, Daniel did not trust Stevens, believing he was becoming soft on the secession matter. Daniel also felt that Stevens was interested in taking over leadership of the Nevis Reformation Party. Accordingly, he started to refer to Stevens as, "a St. Kitts-man." At times, Sim even tried to deal with Ivor as an outsider and enemy. However, the mass of Nevisians saw Stevens as a friend of Nevis. Many found him more accessible and more sympathetic to their everyday concern than was Mr. Daniel, the leader of the party.

Both Simmonds and Heyliger agreed that Stevens was much easier to deal with than Daniel, during the coalition years. They suggested that Stevens' willingness to communicate did more to help the cause of Nevis than Sim's aloofness and continuous combativeness. When dealing with Sim, while Ivor served as a go-between for St. Kitts and Nevis, he had to walk a tight rope and maintain good balance. If he was going to benefit Nevis, Ivor understood that he had to cooperate with the members of government on St. Kitts. Equally, he had to deal with Sim, as leader of the Nevis government, although Mr. Daniel was suspicious of everyone born on St. Kitts, including Ivor Stevens. In retrospect, the people should have questioned Mr. Daniel's grasp of the give, take, and compromise required for good politics. Even the statement used by Archibald (2010) as a caption on the back of his book about Daniel's legacy reads in a confusing manner: "If Nevis were to lose its independence, it must not be said that I was the last to jump ship. I never abandoned my country's independence." The proverbial statement is that the captain should be the last to abandon ship. This is not what one reads in Daniel's comment. Maybe, such a statement was demonstrative of the complexity of the man, and of his politics.

A Question of Loyalty

Through it all, including suspicion about his loyalty, Ivor remained faithful to Sim and to Nevis. Over the years, however, he became concerned about having been more loyal to Sim than to Nevis. After he retired from politics, Ivor repeatedly stated with a measure of regret, that he could have done more for Nevis if he had not remained so committed to Sim, the leader of his political party. Long before it became known publicly that the two men held mutual suspicion against each other, there were bad feelings and mistrust between them. They simply managed to hide it well from the general public. Ivor always seemed to have kept a clear vision about Nevis and his dream for the island. Daniel tended to be divided among his law practice, his lucrative real estate business, and his ideas about infrastructural development for the island.

Stevens' last political years in the coalition government appeared to have been very difficult. He moved from being a radical secessionist in the '60s and '70s, to advocating for inter-island harmony during the 1980s. From time to time, Ivor had to maneuver between Sim's mistrust of his St. Kitts connection, and Simmonds' cautious scrutiny of what he was about to do in building Nevis. Further, popular support for the Nevis Reformation Party had also begun to wane, as the Nevis Independent Party (NIP), then, later, the Concerned Citizens Movement (CCM) emerged on the island, in opposition to the Nevis Reformation Party. Numerous sources revealed how Ivor used his years as a Minister in the PAM-NRP government, to reach out and do things that unquestionably improved life and conditions on Nevis. Quite frequently, some of Ivor's approaches to that goal did not meet the ready approval of either Daniel or Simmonds. Seemingly, the leadership role Stevens played was not always comfortable for him or appreciated by others. Accordingly, that situation stressed him psychologically and wore him out.

Stevens kept sending equipment to Nevis whenever he knew there was a need, and when he saw an opportunity. Many times there were unscheduled deliveries to Nevis from his Ministry in St. Kitts. There were also occasions when Ivor invited mechanic Esmond Williams to visit St. Kitts, and together they scrounged among old condemned vehicles in the bushes at Frigate Bay and elsewhere, to get spare parts for government vehicles on Nevis. At that time, there was always difficulty in obtaining spare parts. to repair government-owned vehicles on the island.

When he became a minister of government, Ivor had finally attained the political authority and a unique, unprecedented opportunity to enhance the well-being of Nevis and its citizens. In time, Mr. Stevens achieved goals he could only dream of previously. Prior to attaining that position in government, all he could do for Nevis was talk about the conditions there. During his time as a minister with the government in St. Kitts, Ivor strategized carefully about how he could act to improve the infrastructure, life, and society on Nevis. There was hardly a time when the status or aura of his office caused him to waiver from the early promises he made to Nevisians. In the words of Wendell Huggins, "Ivor saw himself as a Moses, or a Joshua for Nevis." Ivor died viewing his role on Nevis in that manner. He wanted to change perceptions held about the island, and to make it a prosperous land.

Earlier, during the previous era (1952-1970), and even during the Statehood period, there was no champion for Nevis in the hollowed corridors of political power. Consequently, Ivor had few tangible achievements to model, at that time. In Ivor's master plan for the island, and for Nevisians, 1971-1980 were dry wilderness years. They were spent back and forth in St. Kitts, serving as a member of the Assembly, but battling in opposition to the Labor Party government. The Nevis Reformation Party was new on the scene. Sim, Ivor, and all the other lieutenants were combative, impatient, and aggressive. They were all bitter over the lack of meaningful concern and response to the needs of Nevis, coming from the government on St. Kitts. That would all change with an agreement to participate in the 1980 coalition government with the People's Action Movement. Decisions had to be made that would result in the development of the island's infrastructure, and give more political autonomy to Nevisians.

The years before 1980, and the ascendancy of the coalition government, were frustrating years for St. Kitts and for Nevis. Politicians on both islands learned useful short-term lessons, but lessons that were ineffective as future political strategy. The anger, the hatred, and the vindictiveness of the *Christena* years were too costly for the people of the two islands. Too many times, virtually with the blessings of each island's politicians, Nevisians and Kittitians confronted one another on netball courts, cricket fields, and elsewhere, with an attitude of hatred and war. That period of vindictiveness toward Nevis also cost the Labor Party the chance to lead the islands into independence. It might have been Ivor's special leadership in the politics of compromise, during the PAM-NRP era, that encouraged sanity and healing between the islands, as they went through the 1980s. Wendell Huggins reflected that Ivor saw his role as being two-fold: "Bringing his people out of bondage and bringing healing, too."

All was not lost for Ivor during those frustrating years, dealing with the Labor government. He remembered them as growing years. He continued learning about the politics of politics, the hard way. It was also during those difficult, dry years that Ivor, in the company of political stalwarts such as Robert Bradshaw, Fitzroy Bryant, Lee Moore, Paul Southwell, and Joseph France, was challenged to the fullest. In that company of men, he sharpened, polished, tested, and developed much of his legendary oratory skill and political strategizing. During those years, through his constant interaction and wrangling with them, Ivor also developed great respect and admiration for Robert Bradshaw and Lee Moore, but an intense hatred for Fitzroy Bryant. While they both lived, little love was lost between the two men.

Ivor's active years in politics outlasted all the aforementioned combatants. But, the tense situation between St. Kitts and Nevis, after the 1995 general election, led to another aggressive, but indecisive secession vote on Nevis, in August 1998. It would have been interesting to see whether that matter could have boiled to such a critical point, if Ivor was still actively involved in politics. However, Ivor was not there when the People's Action Movement fell from grace in 1995. And, he died before the 1998 secession vote. Had he been there, Ivor would have seen the referendum result as an outcome from his, "healing role" between the islands. That was in conjunction with a certain hesitancy in how Simmonds and the People's Action Movement dealt with the matter of autonomy for Nevis. Daniel was not always wrong in his observations and reactions to the PAM, and to Nevis. The People's Action Movement, too, had its limiting view of what should be allowed for Nevis.

Ivor's other connection with St. Kitts was less dramatic and less political, but began a trend that has now become commonplace and normal: acceptance of a branch-office position in Nevis, with the firm of H. F. Wildy and Co. Ltd., based on St. Kitts. In the late 1950s, early 1960s, such a venture in Nevis from St. Kitts might have been viewed as risky and unwise. Today, there is no such thinking. Rather, there is growing acceptance that the economic prosperity of both islands is inherently tied together. Not even Ivor might have realized how true that is. His early venture with H. F. Wildy made him a further pioneer, not only in politics, but also in cooperative business venture between the two islands.

Ivor claimed to be a citizen of Nevis quite frequently, and also made parity with St. Kitts a major thrust in his politics for Nevis. However, such behaviors should not be accepted as evidence that Ivor cared nothing about St. Kitts. His connection to that island was also intricate, complex, and sacred. It was a linkage he neither could, nor wanted to forget. Ivor used many of the experiences he gained in St. Kitts, and as often as he could, to benefit Nevis. Yet, at times, he was seen as a traitor in his own political party, because he maintained a working relationship with St. Kitts. Ultimately, through persistence, that connection with St. Kitts worked very much in Nevis' favor.

That Ivor was born on St. Kitts, lived and grew up in Nevis, then spent an important part of his schooling and working life in St. Kitts, made him the ideal mediator between the two islands. Historically, any Nevisian attempting to serve in that capacity had been overwhelmed in St. Kitts, and ostracized on Nevis; that was not the case with Ivor. Through his varied experiences on St. Kitts, Ivor was able to empower Nevisians. Accordingly, Ivor must be credited for the work he did to improve social relations, political balance, and respect between the islands. Uhral Swanston concluded, "Ivor Stevens was often more the man than the politician. He used politics to achieve goals for Nevis. He often acted to benefit others. It did not matter how he did it."

Final Days

When he sensed that death was approaching, Ivor did not sit around, pine, and wait to die. He was never a man to sit in fear and wait in awe—even for death. His life would have become too monotonous and too filled with moments of melancholy. Instead of waiting to die, Ivor continued to live life as actively as his aches, his pains, and his breathing would allow. As it was, he challenged the level of existence that time and fate allowed him. Being the soldier that he was, Ivor had no intention of just dying. He wanted to live, then, fade away to the nothingness brought on by death. Meanwhile, his intent was to live a full and vibrant life. Ivor wanted to see more done for Nevis. By 1997, he could be satisfied that his life had touched and brought change to the lives of many Nevisians. Prior to that political journey, they walked together, the common citizens of Nevis were often destined to be victims of the drudgery that pervaded life on the island.

I had an unexpected encounter with Ivor in December, 1996, 7 months before his demise. It was shocking to see his very frail body and to note how he struggled to breathe, and to speak audibly.

During that meeting with Ivor, this book was conceived. He had been transformed into a feeble man, who depended on others to get around. His voice was not resonant or distinct anymore. His hair did not blow in the wind as before, because Ivor could no longer walk alone, or in the wind. However, his mind was still very alert and lucid as he spent time reflecting on the ongoing politics on the island. That was also the period when Ivor would meet at the waterfront of Nevis on Saturday afternoons with special friends, Norman Jones, Elmo Liburd, Al Thompson, and anyone else who cared to join them. Despite his deteriorating condition, Ivor kept his sense of humor and would often joke with his wife that such meetings were, "To solve all the problems of the world."

I remember that afternoon well, and cherish the fact that I met and spoke with Ivor before he passed on. Our memorable encounters before, on the *Sakara* as it sailed to St. Kitts, included vibrant arguments about race, politics, cricket, and apartheid in South Africa. Back then, there was another encounter with Ivor Stevens and Sim Daniel aboard the *Caribe Queen*. That experience was humiliating for me. After Myrna Walwyn and I had a secret political meeting with Vance Amory, he related to Mr. Daniel what the Nevis Independent Party was planning for the upcoming Nevis local election, 1983. The Nevis Independent Party was the first political party to challenge the Nevis Reformation Party for political control of Nevis. I was one of the NIP's candidates; Myrna Walwyn was the other. We invited Amory to run with the NIP, in the St. George's constituency against Mr. Levi Morton, whom we were confident could be beaten. However, that morning on the *Caribe Queen* Daniel and Stevens spoke knowingly about the plans of the Nevis Independent Party, since Amory was on their side. That meeting ended my zeal for politics on Nevis. I realized that we had been betrayed. After the election, which the Nevis Reformation Party won outright, Mr. Amory left the St. Kitts, Nevis, and Anguilla National Bank to serve as Permanent Secretary of Finance for the Nevis Reformation Party, and the local government in Nevis. Seemingly, that move also set the stage for the introduction of Rawlinson Isaac to work as a banker on Nevis.

In that third and final encounter with Mr. Stevens, I seized the opportunity to speak with him. His physical being, his manner, and his forthright reflections made me realize our meeting that time would be our last. Ivor and I talked of things in general, and about the impending secession vote. He also took time to reflect and comment on some of the experiences he regretted in his politics. Finally, rather than talking about death, I suggested we could look at the possibility of writing a book about his life. I thought then, without malice, that the life and times of Ivor Stevens, and his contributions to the development and politics of Nevis, were worth documenting. Obviously, I still feel that way.

Our unexpected meeting ended with certainty about the following things: (a) Ivor was still concerned with Nevis and its politics, (b) he was not happy about that ongoing drive (1995-1998) toward secession from St. Kitts, (c) Ivor had enough time to reflect on his life and his legacy to Nevis, and (d) he was about to die. The mere act of living had become a burden and a daunting struggle for Ivor. That vibrant, aggressive man of yesteryear could only cherish memories of the giant of a human being he once was.

Mrs. Alvea Sergeant remembered many encounters with Ivor during the good times. "He was always robust and pleasant," she noted. She also recalled when Mr. Stevens became seriously ill and had to be hospitalized. She reflected, "He was always alert and thought about things constantly, even on his sick bed."

One commonly heard criticism of Caribbean politicians, who tend to hold on to political power, is their tendency to act as if they will live forever. There is hardly any engagement in the formalization of a strategy for succession beyond themselves, or beyond their time. Even as they face death, Caribbean political leaders usually refuse to move off the stage of action and allow someone else, perhaps a younger person, to assume leadership: to whit, Eric Williams from Trinidad and Tobago, Robert Bradshaw from St. Kitts, Nevis, and Anguilla, also the Birds from Antigua and Barbuda. That updated list of dreamers about a forever leadership in the Caribbean will include names such as, John Compton of St. Lucia, Joaquin Beleaguer of the Dominican Republic, and certainly, Dr. Denzil Douglas of

St. Kitts-Nevis. Even today, Caribbean politicians seem to hate the idea of term limits and moving on. Rather, for them, being a political leader is forever. Such leaders never see time as moving beyond them—their ideas and experiences. The same cannot be said of Ivor Stevens. He retired from Nevis politics while he was still vibrant, active, and very much alive. Further, while Ivor was actively involved in politics, he was careful and deliberate, as he gathered a group of younger Nevisians around him. He was intent on sharing his political experience, leaving a legacy, and a model from which future generations can learn.

Ivor lived for another good 10 years after he left politics. Reportedly, during the early '90s, he also suggested that then Prime Minister Simmonds should step back from politics and the leadership of the islands, allowing some younger person to take over. Against such advice, Simmonds stayed on in politics until he brought the wrath of society onto himself. It was sad and must have been a humiliating experience for him, when Dr. Kennedy Simmonds, St. Kitts-Nevis' first Prime Minister, was virtually forced out of office—an unflattering end to his political career. Dr. Simmonds' final humiliation came in the form of an election defeat by a virtual political unknown, Dwyer Astaphan, on July 3, 1995.

From time to time, Nevisians reflect, and admit there was a time when their society fell in love with the gray-haired, tall, fast-talking, wily, straight-shooting Kittitian. Ironically, Ivor was always keenly aware of his need to keep winning the admiration of Nevisians, and he took that challenge very seriously. Care was taken to demonstrate his interest in the island and its people, again and again. Ivor did it his way. He ensured that he left a great legacy to his time on Nevis.

CHAPTER 2

The Times

Education

Many children who attended public schools on the islands during the early 1900s and up until the 1950s did not go beyond grades 3, 5, or 7. Success at school was not seen as very rewarding then for working-class boys and girls. At that time those children had no hope of becoming lawyers, priests, doctors, or businessmen. As was the case with Ivor and his siblings, the middle-class sent their children to special private schools. The grammar school on St. Kitts was a bastion of class and privilege, for boys from elite families. Few children of poor and powerless plantation workers were allowed in its classrooms. In cases where children of working-class parents did well at school on Nevis, it was not unusual that such bright, young, boys and girls sat in seventh grade for up to 3 years, repeating the same seventh-grade examination over and over, at the end of every school year. Some of the children who were educated then can still count the number of seventh-grade certificates they attained. The secondary education available, at the time, was not offered readily to poor working-class children, particularly if they lived far away from the town, in places such as Butler's Village, where I was born. In retrospect, there was only a dead-end approach to working-class education in British Caribbean colonies.

A good, sound education, that included secondary school attendance, back then, was a luxury in St. Kitts, Nevis, and Anguilla. The idea was endemic that higher education was something for wealthy, fair-skinned people, and was designed to benefit, and be appreciated only by those living in the towns. Quite often, children living in the countryside were limited or doomed by location and class circumstances. Further, it was not until 1915, 4 years after Ivor was born, that the British government passed legislation indicating that it would pay for compulsory primary education in St. Kitts, Nevis, and Anguilla, up to age 14. Before then, that burden of educating the mass of children in the colony was undertaken by the churches. Up to that time on Nevis, school buildings were owned largely by the Anglican and Methodist Churches. In the White Paper that Ivor dictated just before he died, he was still convinced that Nevisians suffered from "lack of education" along with what he called "three other social ills: Love of freeness, too little attention to the youth and elderly, and not enough attention being paid to the economy and the island's infrastructure."

For a number of years after 1915, the least costly facilities available to school children were church buildings that had already been used for that purpose. Even the best schools were conducted in crude buildings. Besides being crude and outdated, by the 1960s, schools were overcrowded and barely conducive to learning.[10] Nevertheless, working-class society grew to revere them. Probably, their association with churches helped to make school buildings sacred places then. There was also a special respect and appreciation directed at the few educated people in the villages. Teachers were generally revered in their villages. Many years passed before the government of St. Kitts, Nevis, and Anguilla found sufficient money and interest in education to invest in the building of quality structures to house and school their children. In turn, the local government has, at times, imitated the lack of commitment by the British to academic development and social transformation in its Caribbean colonies. The story about elementary, secondary, and higher education in the U.S. Virgin islands has been very different. During both Danish and U.S. colonization, education in the islands received keen attention.

---

[10] Browne, W. T. (1992). *From Commoner to King*. Lanham, MD: University of America Press.

However, when masses of migrants from other Caribbean islands started to arrive in the U.S. Virgin Islands, from the late 1950s on, that privilege to have a good and free education was not readily shared. The children of immigrants were treated as second-class human beings (aliens), and refused at the public schools. It took a court challenge to the government in the famous case *Hosier vs. Evans*, 1970, which the immigrants won, to change public schools' discrimination against children from other Caribbean islands.

Meanwhile, for the British government, education in the colonies never appeared to have been important. Rather, there was always fear that it would encourage critical thinking and social discontent among the lower classes. Because the British were very stingy when spending in the colonies, there must also have been concern about the cost of education in the colonies. Consequently, the British carefully controlled who and how many people in the islands were exposed to higher education. One interesting criticism of such people was that they returned to the Caribbean even more British than the British. The author, V. S. Naipaul was probably envisioning such people when he wrote his book, *The Mimic Men.*[11] Meanwhile, the democratization of higher education was another of the subtle but profound differences between the British colonies and the U.S. Virgin Islands by the 1950s. Up until the 1960s, when the British Caribbean islands moved to become independent nations, there was still a list of banned books considered too radical to be read in the colonies. Topping that list were books written by Karl Marx.

Ironically, even after education became a popular liberating force in the colonies, there were those among the emerging leadership who still wanted to control the access of certain villages and social classes to education and enlightenment. They kept those "dreaded books," the works of Karl Marx, C. L. R. James, Malcolm X, and other revolutionary thinkers, hidden from the restless masses. Recently a friend from Nevis, who went to St. Kitts for advanced secondary education, recalled that he and some other students located a stash of revolutionary writings hidden in the attic of the public library at

---

11 Naipaul, V. S. (1969). *The Mimic Men.* Harmondsworth, UK: Penguin.

Basseterre. They enjoyed sneaking into the attic on a regular basis to read the forbidden books.

Although the phenomenon was more common in the countryside, many urban boys and girls on St. Kitts and Nevis also left school having never mastered the art of reading or writing. Despite the efforts of demanding teachers and the diligence of truant officers, many young people did not see the fruition of their dreams in the school system. Further, the high level of poverty forced many families to put their children to work early. Often that choice was a deliberate matter. It was a useful strategy to boost the small earnings of the parents. Many parents also kept their children home from school to help reap the family's sugarcane and cotton crops. I still have vivid memories of those awful hot, sweaty, and tiring days I spent in my father's cotton and sugarcane fields, or reaping yams up in Maddens' Mountain, instead of being at school.

Many adults who received an inadequate education gave a thumb print or signed an "X" in place of their signature, having never learned to read or write. In time, as literacy became a more common achievement, some of those people, along with their children, became ashamed of that limited literacy. However, such low levels of literacy were a direct product of the times in which they lived. That experience still remains a haunting legacy of capitalism-driven agriculture in the British Caribbean colonies.

Just as it was with slavery in the plantation economy, the end result that mattered was status and profit, not how many human beings were uneducated or how many labored and died in silence on plantations. Mills, Jones-Hendrickson, and Eugene, who highlighted certain aspects of working-class performance culture in St. Kitts-Nevis societies during the early to mid 1900s, wrote, "The long passages from the Bible, or other narrative or verse they memorized, are a credit to these artists, many of whom, perhaps never had a chance to attend school."[12]

---

[12] Mills, F. L., Jones-Hendrickson, S. B. & Eugene, B. (1984). *Christmas Sports in St. Kitts-Nevis: Our Neglected Cultural Tradition*. U.S. Virgin Islands: Authors.

From 1915 on, public education was provided by government, but free secondary education was not possible even for those who lived in Charlestown or in nearby villages, then. Later, families who could afford the cost of secondary education often had their children walk the 2-6 miles to and from high school. However, young people in Butler's, Zion, Barnaby, and other villages further from town, did not have the same access to higher education on the island. They were 8-10 miles away. During the late 1950s some of the best students from Whitehall (St. James) School were invited to write the high school entrance examination. They are still awaiting the results. None received even a report about the exam. That's the way things were then. You did not get answers, and you dared not ask questions if you were of the working-class, or lived in forgotten places such as Butler's or Brick Kiln Village. I lived at Butler's Village, attended Whitehall School, and was one of the students who took that high school entrance exam. My classmate and good friend Roosevelt Daniel took that exam too. However, thanks are due to the late headmaster, Stanford Boncamper, who got me into the pupil-teacher system at age 14, and later the innovative thinking of Education Officer Willie Dore, who introduced the College of Preceptors (CP) and other experimental exams to St. Kitts, Nevis, and Anguilla schools, during the early 1960s. Although I had a stint of the apprenticeship program, with my father doing carpentry, and later with Jollife Hendrickson in Brick Kiln doing tailoring, I did manage to find my way in academia, to become an educator.

Sports and Recreation

The two different systems of agricultural production, large sugar estates on St. Kitts, and small-scale peasant holdings in Nevis and Anguilla, affected every aspect of social life, economics, and politics on all three islands. That included attitude toward leisure and how these shaped the evolution of contemporary political systems. Labor unionism, for example, was more popular in St. Kitts than in Nevis or Anguilla, where there was a strong preference for peasant farming and fishing, and a greater attraction to independence. There was also a high level of fascination with migration.

Mills et al. provided a useful and interesting review of Christmas Sports on St. Kitts-Nevis.[13] They highlighted the fact that Christmas was one of the few periods of the year when the working-class on the islands had leisure time and could take social liberties, poking fun at the upper-class without being forced to spend time in jail. The authors highlighted the persistence of African culture residuals. They highlighted the performers' skills and capacity to memorize long intricate passages for dramatic presentations: *Giant Despair*, the *Red Cross, the Pilgrim's Progress,* and some others.

The history of the Christmas festival also provides a useful illustration of the role politics plays in shaping and reshaping various aspects of society on St. Kitts-Nevis. Over the years, politicians have attempted to shape and remake every facet of the islands' society, including long-held popular ideas. Some of these have been designed and redesigned by the islands' political leadership or by their personal interpretation of how certain ideas can impact politics. Mills et al. also commented on the influence politics came to have on Christmas sports and carnival in St. Kitts:

> Perhaps the first incident dates back to Christmas 1947, when the leaders of the huge labor union of sugar workers was deadlocked in negotiations with the planters. Foreseeing the longest strike in the island's history, Comrade Llewellyn Bradshaw admonished those who play sports—mostly sugarcane workers—that they should not entertain bukra any longer, because they were the same villains who were intractably refusing to agree to decent wages and working conditions for the laborers. The early 1960s saw another low point in Christmas

---

13 Mills, F. L., Jones-Hendrickson, S. B. & Eugene, B. (1984). *Christmas Sports in St. Kitts-Nevis: Our Neglected Cultural Tradition.* U.S. Virgin Islands: Authors.

> sports following the advent of carnival. Politics reared its ugly side to the detriment of sports, when, in 1965, there were two opposing carnival groups: the Christmas Festivities Committee promoted by the upper-middle class, and a Soul Carnival Committee supported by the Labor government. This ludicrous situation was resolved in 1971 with the establishment by government action of a National Carnival Committee.[14]

On Nevis, politics also entered the Christmas festivities. It also affected athletic sports and influenced the evolution of Culturama. After the *Christena* mishap (see Chapter 5) there emerged an aggressive pro-independent Nevis politics, led by The Nevis Reformation Party (NRP), born in 1970. Nevisians openly indicated they wanted little participation in the National Carnival on St. Kitts. In their search for separation from, and parity with St. Kitts, Nevisians also reengineered their cricket and became determined to excel at the sport. From about the mid 1970s to the present, Nevisians have been the dominant performer in St. Kitts vs. Nevis cricket. The humiliating defeats at the hands of Kittitians, during the 1950s, and on through the 1960s, are no longer haunting memories for Nevisians. Nevis cricketers, Elquamido Willett, Keith Arthurton, Deryck Parry, Stuart Williams, and the late Runako Morton, also went on to represent the West Indies in world-class cricket.

As that search for independence from St. Kitts progressed into the 1980s, Nevisians received ready support from their politicians. The people co-opted the politicians and instigated a movement to create a Nevis alternative celebration to the St. Kitts carnival. By 1974-1975, the Nevis Drama Group, started during the 1960s by John Williamson, Sam Sweeney, and Sonny Walwyn, evolved into the Nevis Dramatic and Cultural Society (NEDACS). It

---

[14] Mills, F. L., Jones-Hendrickson, S. B. & Eugene, B. (1984). *Christmas Sports in St. Kitts-Nevis: Our Neglected Cultural Tradition.* U.S. Virgin Islands: Authors.

prospered through the creative efforts of young, confident, and aspiring Nevisians, including Irma Johnson, Lyra Richards, Tyrone O'Flaherty, and Victor Martin. Calvin Howell, who returned to Nevis from Canada some time in 1971-1972, was also an inspiration to that effort. Other leading lights in NEDACS included Melford Henville, Clifford "Boots" Griffin, Sylvester Griffin, Eustace Hunkins, and others. As with the Harlem Renaissance, some 50 years before, here was another occasion in human history when, by harnessing new education opportunities and focusing on the humanities, Nevisians were inspired toward self-actualization, thereby inspiring a social and political revolution on their island. The experience also contributed to the radical awakening of a people, too long neglected and forgotten. Like the Anguillans during the 1960s, the people of Nevis suddenly awoke to their objective interests and moved to restructure their association with St. Kitts. Eventually, that awakening became one of the instigators of both political and social change on the island. While he served as a member of the Nevis Reformation Party, Stevens became very much a part of the radical political thinking that developed then.

During that same period on the island, the organizational activities spearheaded by NEDACS, appeared to have gone a long way toward fostering the revolutionary mood that emerged on Nevis. Later, NEDACS also led the way in creating Nevis' own celebration: Culturama. Within a few years, Culturama on Nevis, late July to early August, became the Nevisians' answer to carnival on St. Kitts in late December, early January. It remains the premier cultural celebration on Nevis since 1974. Today, Nevisians everywhere know about Culturama. At Culturama time, every year, thousands of Nevisians who emigrated to other places around the world "go home again." Because of its message of independence from St. Kitts, Culturama was hailed and supported by both Daniel and Stevens. The celebration became another useful rung on the ladder that Nevisians constructed in their move away from a system of historical domination from St. Kitts.

Through the years, the economic and social factors associated with the sugar industry on St. Kitts encouraged the population there to be more spendthrift and more cosmopolitan than that of Anguilla or Nevis. As Barbadians did at an earlier time, Kittitians experienced a closer social proximity to the English planters and businessmen than was the case on Nevis and Anguilla. Seemingly, Kittitians were better imitators of the English in many aspects of their social life, particularly in their class system, leisure activities, and sports. For example, political and social life on St. Kitts were profoundly shaped by the ups and downs of British plantation economics on the island.

Leisure time in St. Kitts, for the wealthy, was more formally organized than in Nevis and Anguilla. There was at least one exclusive, now infamous, tennis club on St. Kitts; its members had to be from among the social elites, White or near White. For most of its existence, Afro-Caribbean citizens were not admitted. Formal, organized leisure activities were largely for the St. Kitts upper and middle classes. These included football, tennis, concerts, dramatic presentations, picnics, and cricket.[15] Leonard Harris became one of St. Kitts' outstanding cricketers, a product of the early two-tiered class of cricket that evolved in Barbados, and also on St. Kitts. In Nevis, like many things there, it was country vs. town, and town always got the privileges. Hundreds of young Nevisians had their formal education dwarfed on Nevis because they lived in far out villages, Butler's, Fountain, Zion, and Brick-kiln. Many of those children were barred from the opportunity to attend the high school in Charlestown. Later innovations, with the College of Preceptors Exam, were instituted in the St. Kitts, Nevis, and Anguilla education system by Education Officer William F. Dore, a Nevisian educator who migrated to St. Kitts. In time, Mr. Dore joined up with the Labor Party and Bradshaw. He talked of initiating other overseas exams including the General Certificate of Education Exam for nonsecondary students. In time, this new academic development started to revolutionize and equalize education opportunities in St.

---

[15] Mills, F. L., Jones-Hendrickson, S. B. & Eugene, B. (1984). *Christmas Sports in St. Kitts-Nevis: Our Neglected Cultural Tradition*. U.S. Virgin Islands: Authors.

Kitts, Nevis, and Anguilla. Eventually, a secondary education became commonplace and available to children of the working-class also. Further, with the decline of colonial control in the islands and a rise of working-class leadership, all the leaders from Robert Bradshaw and Lee Moore, to Dr. Kennedy Simmonds, and now Dr. Denzil Douglas instituted policies that liberalized access to secondary and postsecondary education. Today, education is undoubtedly a powerful transformational force in the social, economic, and political history of Nevis and St. Kitts.

During the 1700s, Nevis lost its economic and political place as "Queen of the Caribees." The island kept spinning downward economically. Estate owners shunned it as they rushed to the sugar booms on St. Kitts and elsewhere in the Caribbean.[16] Thousands of Nevisians also migrated to other places, in the Caribbean and around the world.[17] In both Nevis and Anguilla, by the 1940s and beyond, there was a predominance of poor infrastructure that limited development on the islands. Citizens on these two islands grappled with the psychological burden of being seen as the less important islands in the three-island colony. That was one of the realities that suggested emigration as a viable option to Anguillans and Nevisians, in their search for a more successful future. As early as the 1840s, many citizens of Nevis and St. Kitts fled in large numbers to other islands and countries whenever the opportunity presented itself. That migration trend persisted into the 1990s. By the 1990s there were even Nevisians who chose to live in Anguilla, instead of remaining on Nevis.

---

16 Frucht, R. (1967). *Community and Context in a Colonial Society: Social and Economic Change in Nevis British West Indies*. Ann Arbor, MI: Ann Arbor University Microfilm.

17 Richardson, B. C. (1983). *Caribbean Migrants: Environment and Human Survival on St. Kitts and Nevis*. Knoxville: University of Tennessee Press.

Superstition

In 1997, Stevens commented on the phenomenon of obeah, a residual of African culture in the Caribbean, and one of the social responses Afro-Caribbean people used to deal with the conditions of their time. By the late 1950s, music and obeah were among the vibrant African culture residuals on St. Kitts-Nevis.[18] Despite a claim to be very God-fearing people, experimenting with the supernatural continued on Nevis, and at one time seemed to have been very common there. Meanwhile, Pentecostal teachings from the U.S. were being presented in villages, challenging the teachings of the Anglicans, Methodists, and Roman Catholics. In time, the new teaching started to attract young and old Nevisians. However, there were enclaves on the island that depended on obeah as a way of life. Anything that could not be readily explained—strange occurrences, drownings, illnesses, or other misfortunes—were readily attributed to obeah. Usually, the best practitioners of the art were well known throughout the island, and appeared to have had quite a following. The clientele needed to have money to pay for the special service. There was always a cost. Seemingly, the practitioners would promise the world to those who perceived themselves as having problems, and came needing various forms of help. Usually, the clients came from every sector of society on the islands; even the upper echelons of society arranged for treatment. In time, the fame of certain practitioners of the art of obeah on Nevis even brought seekers after wealth, health, and love, from other Caribbean islands, including St. Kitts and elsewhere. Calypsonian, Lord Barkey, was on board and caught in the *Christena* sinking, because he was on his way to see an obeah practitioner on Nevis. Barkey wanted to check out his status in a recent love affair. Were it not for some foam on the ferry, that trip could have cost Lord Barkey his life.

---

[18] Mills, F. L., Jones-Hendrickson, S. B. & Eugene, B. (1984). *Christmas Sports in St. Kitts-Nevis: Our Neglected Cultural Tradition*. U.S. Virgin Islands: Authors.

Dick Stapleton of Zion, Sugar Goddy of Butler's, and Ezekiel Kelley of Simmonds' were reputedly famous obeah-men. Mum of Rice's was a well-known obeah woman. Kelley often walked around Nevis or traveled to St. Kitts, kettle-drum and all, to sell his skills. He often terrified school children when he walked around Nevis at selected times, playing his kettle-drum as he walked alone. Those men and women were all well known in Nevis for their expertise, operating on the island at different times. Nevis' last well-known and self-proclaimed obeah-man was Jerry Weeks of Zion. During his lifetime, he made repeated statements about his skill, competence, and exploits in the art of obeah. Mr. Weeks spent his final years in England.

Some Nevisians who professed Christianity often came into direct conflict with this legacy of African folk-life and the demands of Christianity on the island. There were strange stories of people walking into the sea and drowning mysteriously. Once, a man from Butler's turned up in a lady's yard suddenly, and confessed to the theft of her goat, pleading that his life be spared. In another well-known St. Kitts-Nevis incident, the boat *Crown* was supposedly sunk mysteriously because it offered the *Lady Nisbett* too much competition. These are only a few of the well-known obeah stories repeated throughout Nevis over the years. Since the 2000s, there are stories out of Nevis that suggest the obeah phenomenon is again raising its head on the island.

Claims have also been made that anyone who trespassed on another person's land to steal could be kept there, trapped, although there was no fence. At times humans changed into dogs. Some animals talked. And there were people who developed strange, life-long sores. There have also been new house owners, who could not live in the houses peacefully, because someone had set obeah in them (as supposedly occurred in the story about Malcolm, once a well-known immigration officer, on St. Thomas, U.S. Virgin Islands). At times frogs were placed in bottles, then clandestinely set in the foundation of houses. The owners could never live in such buildings peacefully.

Such stories still abound in the rural areas of St. Kitts and the villages of Nevis. As recently as August 2000, there was a strange Jumbie fire in Conaree, St. Kitts. The phenomenon was attributed to an obeah-practicing person from Nevis—a claim made in a song by calypsonian, Mick "Stokes" Heyliger of St. Kitts. There was also that murder case on Nevis in 2005, when allegedly a number of strange occurrences took place during the court trial for the young men held in the case.

When politicians and community leaders became clients, they tended to receive special treatment from obeah practitioners. Such leaders could arrange for protective baths prepared by the obeah-man or obeah-woman. Today, however, many of these stories have taken on the dimension of legends, having been handed down from generation to generation.

Today, with increased access to education, migration still in progress, and growing commitments to Evangelical Christianity, obeah may not have vanished from Nevis, but it is no longer as common an experience on the island. Ivor did not defend this feature of Nevis culture; he admitted that it existed. In reflections on culture and religion in Nevis, Ivor observed: "From the Christian standpoint the community has always been accepting to Christianity. However, it must not be overlooked that a small percentage of the community has at one time or another been receptive to necromancy (Devil device)." The phenomenon was a very real part of the cultural mix in Nevis during the time Stevens referenced.

Herbalists, at one time called bush-doctors, were numerous and in great demand on Nevis. Some mixed their bush art with obeah. The persistence of that African tradition was useful at a time when modern medicine, and doctors, were alien to the masses. Until recently, as was the case when the *Christena* sank in 1970, Nevis was frequently without a resident physician. Many Nevisians grew up with the herbal tradition, tending to trust it more than they trusted modern medicine. During the 1960s, for example, it was still common to hear older Nevisians claim they had not been to a doctor in all their life. Interestingly, contemporary research in alternative medicine is suggesting positive, holistic cures from the use of selected bush medicines Nevisians and other Caribbean people once used for healing.

Evangelical Christianity also impacted the emerging and developing societies on Nevis. One peculiar aspect of Christianity on Nevis at that time centered on the travelling Pentecostal preachers. They went from village to village, faithfully, with gas lamps, and conducted open-air evangelical services. However, despite their diligence and commitment, many of those people were illiterate, semiliterate, or simply responding to emotions. Often, such people were the subject of many jokes in the villages. "Darrel da Goose," for example, only repeated what he heard others say. He always ended his presentations with the line, "Ah do me best, ah do me best." Brother Smith traveled alone. He always made it to our house in time for the next meal. As children, we had so much fun imitating his mannerisms and prayers before he ate. Then, there was Brother Charles Freeman, a serious and deeply spiritual man. It was always a moving experience to see and hear him pray. Brother Freeman also conveyed the idea that the religious life is a serious matter.

In an unprecedented situation at Brick Kiln Village, many people left the Anglican Church when Mother Anderson came from the U.S. with clothing and food, and started an independent Baptist Church. At Christmastime, however, even the very religious were absorbed in the cultural traditions that were depicted in Christmas Sports. Such traditions included dancing and reveling to nonreligious music, the serving of special drinks and food, and of course, celebrating one another. One report circulated on St. Kitts stated that a Baptist preacher, Pastor Connor, was seen in a j'ouvert band the morning after Christmas. When asked what he was doing in the center of the parading steel band, Brother Connor reportedly answered, while moving to the steel-pan rhythm, "I'm looking for my members. I'm looking for my members."

Economic History

By 1911, sugar production was failing, but still dominated the agriculture-based economy of the British colonies. It was some 73 years after the abolition of slavery in British colonies such as St. Kitts, Nevis, and Anguilla, but Afro-Caribbean workers were still on plantations, trapped in capitalist-driven cheap labor production, and systematically alienated from the political process in their native islands. Plans were afoot to add technological innovations to revitalize sugar production on St. Kitts. It was a time when the drudgery of sugar production, particularly on St. Kitts, persisted, dominating the lives of plantation workers. Politically and economically, the plantocracy ensured a dictatorship of the wealthy classes. The poor and powerless sugar workers hardly mattered in that sugar-dominated society; only their labor on the plantations mattered.

Generally, the role of one's family in the sugar-production process determined its condition of existence. During the early 1900s, sugar production on the islands dominated and determined the structure and culture of society, based on the worst aspects of vulgar capitalism. The sugar economy determined the very being of those who lived in the colony, and, in time, came to temper the mettle of the workers on Nevis. Should they remain on their island or migrate to some other place? In contrast to what was happening on St. Kitts to boost sugar production in 1911, on Nevis, the sugar industry was experiencing a long slow death, starting as early as the 1700s. During 1911, there was also a problem with water on Nevis.[19] Providing water for all the people on the island was a difficult challenge. Usually, there was not enough of the commodity to share with the farmers. There were questions raised as to whether there was any British representative living on the island during the year, and whether anything would be done to help resolve the water problem on the island.

Interestingly, the failure of sugar on both Anguilla and Nevis contributed to the early development of a peasantry and to the evolution of personal independence, but a less aggressive politics

---

[19] Robinson, A. (2008). *The Shaping of an Abolitionist: James Stephen 1758-1832 Exploring the Scottish and Caribbean Influences on Abolition's Chief Strategist.* Liverpool, UK: The Society for Caribbean Studies.

than that which pitted the planter class against sugar workers on St. Kitts. By 1912, sugar production received new life on St. Kitts. The processing became centralized there, with the establishment of a modern factory, linked by rail to estates around the island. While the factory was ready for operation in 1912, the rail connection to all the estates was completed in 1926. Despite the increased attention to sugar production by the planter-class on the island, the new technology and economic thrust became a limiting force to the lives of all working-class Kittitians. Ultimately, the threats to their survival forced a radical response by the workers. They organized and marshaled themselves in the labor union movement.

Meanwhile, the empire created by the British government was in clear decline, even though it still fostered and oversaw the poverty and squalor its system had created in the West Indies. When Ivor was born, poverty was still a glaring reality in the colony of St. Kitts, Nevis, and Anguilla. The shackles set in place by capitalistic exploitation caused the islands to experience gross underdevelopment, which forced thousands of Anguillans and Nevisians to migrate to Cuba, the Dominican Republic, the U.S., and elsewhere, hoping to achieve social and economic success. The poverty situation coupled with the British government's stingy approach to spending in its Caribbean colonies also made Nevis and Anguilla a burden to the more prosperous St. Kitts.[20] The two less prosperous islands were dependent on the central government on St. Kitts. Notwithstanding, each of the islands in the colony of St. Kitts, Nevis, and Anguilla was concerned about its individual identity. St. Kitts struggled with its dependence on Britain. Meanwhile, Anguillans and Nevisians felt humbled by their dependent relationship to St. Kitts.

During the early years of the 1900s, the descendants of African slaves living in the Caribbean should have been free citizens. However, they enjoyed few freedoms. Education for independence was not a priority for colonies dominated by the British government. Its real interest seemed more about economic exploitation and psychological control of the people in the colonies. Further, the

---

20 Innis, P. (1983). *Whither Bound St. Kitts-Nevis.* Basseterre, St. Kitts.

British insistence on a Eurocentric focus in its Afro-Caribbean societies blurred the vision of the emerging future in all segments of the population. Descendants of African slaves, indentured servants from Asia, European plantocrats, and representatives of the European governments at the control, were all forced to look toward Europe, instead of at their own objective interests. Alternate views of the world were discouraged.

Consequently, until the early 1920s and 1930s, few people took what was then an emerging Afro-Caribbean identity seriously. At that time in the Caribbean, matters such as shades of skin color, family status and history, marriage, and the exposure to education, determined at what level each group participated in the affairs of the community. Generally, members of the working-class, because of their color, history, education, or other ascribed factors, found themselves in the middle of such matters, but at the fringe of society. Notwithstanding, many of the working poor found enough survival inspiration to live for the future. And, they committed themselves to changing that future for their children. Even then, as they examined their migration history, many Caribbean people were beginning to reconnect with Africa, and forcing a critical review of their false consciousness engendered by Eurocentrism. Despite the arrogance and airs associated with Eurocentrism in the Caribbean, many Caribbean people of African ancestry started searching for their culture and identity shortly after Europeans came and brought their ancestors from Africa to the West Indies. Despite the control strategies of the Europeans, African people on the harsh plantations started to look back to Africa—the place from which they were stolen. Unlike the Europeans, the new Caribbean people were willing to accept the idea of a common humanity—one shared by all human beings. They saw themselves as important, and equal to all the other people of the world. Their experience of oppressive exploitation had to end. A determined undaunted African people yearned for a time to create and accept opportunities for changed and less limiting experiences.

One former governor of the Leeward Islands, Governor Blackburne, wrote in 1976 that St. Kitts society was surprisingly more limiting and racist than that of Barbados, then called "little England." Everywhere in the Caribbean, judgments were made about the possibilities for Afro-Caribbean people to perform at high intellectual and social levels. This was held to be evidence of the creative thinking necessary to lead the islands. To Europeans, it was not evident in African societies. Thus, Eurocentricity came to be held as an "eternal verity," in the Caribbean. Accordingly, the local population was criticized and mistreated by the dominant, White, planter society. At a time when the sugar industry was tired and declining, the poor and powerless Black working-class was harassed for underproduction. Consequently, the working-class was blamed continuously and pushed to the limit, to save an exhausted and slowly dying sugar industry. In time, with the aim of empowering themselves and creating an inclusive Caribbean society, the workers did push back against their oppressors. During the 1930s, and into the 1940s, for example, St. Kitts and Nevis were embroiled in unprecedented social, political, and economic unrest. Every citizen had to decide whether he was with the planter-class or with the working-class. There was no middle ground.

At the forefront of that conflict were the planters, lined up behind their organization, the Sugar Growers Association, committed to keeping the working-class poor, ignorant, and dependent. On the other side was the working-class. By the 1940s, they had their organized movements too, and lined up behind them. First, they had the quasi-labor organization, the Universal Benevolent Society as early as 1917. However, until 1940, the planters prevented laborers from uniting in a formal labor union. Later their quasi-labor organization, at that time called the Workers' League, was formally renamed the St. Kitts, Nevis, and Anguilla Trades and Labor Union. By the late 1940s, Ivor Stevens had been to war, had returned to live in St. Kitts, and worked at the sugar factory where the ongoing struggle was centered. He could not avoid being caught-up in the struggle around him, even if he did not openly choose a side.

Soon, the changed circumstances, on St. Kitts in particular, led to a number of economic, labor, social, and political eruptions on both St. Kitts and Nevis. The despised working-class had organized itself and was taking a stand—it fought back in defense of its rights and dignity, a fight its ancestors started against planter authority on St. Kitts as far back as 1639. During the late 1800s and on into early 1900s, the struggle was re-energized, in that effort to change the leadership and ideology of the society. Men such as Fredrick Solomon, Joseph Nathan, James Halbert, Edgar Challenger, Thomas Manchester, and Joseph Sebastian, were among the pioneering leaders of the labor-union struggle. They gave the labor union structure, vision, and meaning to the working class. That band of men preceded Robert Bradshaw by many years. They are among the original leaders of the workers' struggle for justice on St. Kitts. It was that early group of leaders, who organized the resistance and gave form to the leadership of the working-class organization. They also galvanized the masses, then ignited their desire to fight back and vanquish the then fading plantocracy—a situation Joseph Nathan understood and exploited repeatedly.

When Bradshaw came along later, he served in the movement as a contemporary of Stevens. In time however, Bradshaw was named among the indomitable champions of the workers' cause on St. Kitts. Today, he is still remembered as a flamboyant, fiery, political crusader in the islands. Over time, he became intricately involved with the conflict as a defender of the masses' cause. He led numerous battles against those in the sugar industry who reaped most of the profits. It seemed that at some point, Stevens became influenced by Bradshaw's skill and aggression as a politician and leader of the people. He remained unopposed for many years at the head of the powerful working-class union, and leader of the Labor Party on St. Kitts. As the transformation in the islands developed, both Bradshaw and Stevens were exposed to the ideological influence of the Fabian Socialist, Bishop Hand, from the Anglican Church.

Bishop Hand was a preacher, activist, and crusader for social change in the Caribbean. Bradshaw and Hand met in Antigua while Bradshaw attended a labor-union conference there. Shortly after, Hand moved to St. Kitts to work as a regular Anglican minister. He became a close friend and adviser to Bradshaw, and a well-known person in the community, because of his preaching and interest in drama. Since Hand held a practical ideology about Christianity and socialism in the Caribbean, he was always ready to exchange ideas about politics and society with Afro-Caribbean listeners. Apparently, Bishop Hand was also intrigued by the emerging labor and political unrest in St. Kitts-Nevis. Finally, there was a challenging of the absolute right to domination by capitalism in the islands. It was quite possible that because of his commitment to socialism, Bishop Hand had become a subtle but powerful influence on the lives and politics of Bradshaw and of Stevens—two future leaders in the islands' politics. The Fabian Socialists' goal was to encourage change in the class and race politics they saw in Caribbean societies, where they found themselves. Accordingly, the emergence of labor unionism in the islands, at that time, inspired hope among the Fabians for change in the colonies.

However, the very populist path that Ivor eventually took appears to beg the question, "Why didn't he declare his position and take an open stand against the planters while he worked at the factory?" Seemingly, during those times, jobs such as the one Ivor held at the factory were few. Had Ivor challenged the plantocracy, he might not have received the support of his parents, whom he held in very high regard. Further, social mobility and his family's social status were important to them. At the time, these were determined and awarded by the planter class only. During those times too, when the wealthy planters discovered that people, including Mr. Stevens, were sympathetic to the workers, the planters could be merciless in their reaction. That was evidenced in the stories of Laughton McKinnon and Thomas Manchester. They were both hounded to death for supporting the masses' cause.

Nevis under British colonialism experienced neglect for many years. Later that was coupled with a dictatorial politics from St. Kitts, fostering further injustice, ignorance, poverty, and a great sense of powerlessness on the island. Such was the situation that kept Nevisians in a state of backwardness, almost into the 1980s. There was very limited electricity, poor schools, unpaved roads, an inadequate water supply, no telephones, and more. Quite often, the people on the island dealt with their sad plight through disorganized or individual emotional outbursts, short-term organization, and self-deprecation. By the 1970s, Nevisians were searching for a radical political experience along with social and infrastructural change for their island. However, they were not as politically organized as the Kittitians. Nevisians needed to learn and understand the nature of political power, the culture and limitations of dominance, and how they could use the political forces available to them, to organize themselves, and to alter their condition of existence.

When Ivor was born in 1911, the colony of St. Kitts, Nevis, and Anguilla was barely three generations from chattel slavery. Labor issues were in dire need of attention. The plantation workers were crying out for change, some individually and openly, clamoring against the oppressive plantation economy. Often, the conflict erupted in serial skirmishes pitting sugar workers against the planters. This was seen more frequently on St. Kitts, where sugar production was still successful. The problem heightened there after sugar production was centralized, associated with the demand for greater productivity from workers. Those emerging conflicts were repeatedly played out in dramatic class rivalry on St. Kitts and elsewhere in the Caribbean, during the early 1900s, and on into the 1950s. On Anguilla and Nevis, where sugar production had lost its agricultural dominance, independent men turned to the sea in Anguilla, while a peasantry developed in Nevis. On both Nevis and Anguilla, the labor vs. planter battles on St. Kitts were generally misunderstood. The political and social realities on St. Kitts, Nevis, and Anguilla, at the time, mirrored those in the wider British Caribbean. There was the privileged planter elite, usually White, and there was the underprivileged, powerless, working-class, generally Black. The time had come. Each side competed for political dominance on the islands.

Reflecting on the social reality in the islands at that time, Mills et al. wrote:

> Plantation society throughout St. Kitts and Nevis was characterized by, among other features, two struggling cultures. During the long period of

> slavery, the super-ordinate Europeans considered the culture of the Africans to be not only inimical to theirs but a threat to their safety, and thus spared little effort in eradicating the major elements of the slaves' cultural equipage . . . . Consequently, this conflict of identity has been a social prison in which the majority of Kittitians and Nevisians are still inmates.[21]

In other words, the colonial powers of the day attempted to instill feelings of inferiority in the Black population. They used the strategies of false consciousness to reinforce the notion that African culture was inferior to European culture. Over time, that domination strategy had great success. Accordingly, for the mass of people on St. Kitts-Nevis, all 86 years that Ivor Stevens lived (1911 through to 1997) were challenging times for the people of St. Kitts and Nevis. They were always years when Nevisians and Kittitians, as a people, searched for escape, through individual or group action, using politics or migration. Some traveled to Costa Rica, Panama, Cuba, the Dominican Republic, Curacao, and Trinidad and Tobago. There were some adventurers beyond the region to the U.S., England, and Canada. Kittitians and Nevisians also migrated to the U.S. Virgin Islands and to the British Virgin Islands. Other people became engaged and caught-up in organized labor, and eventually in politics. They chose these as their strategies with which to challenge and change the system on the islands.

At home, most Nevisians tilled land with shallow, rocky soil, in plots they did not always own. They often had to give designated portions of the harvest to the landowners. However, some sharecroppers learned to outmaneuver their landlords as they fought to survive a harsh economic climate. At Butler's Village, for example, my father, the late William Browne, told his children

---

21 Mills, F. L., Jones-Hendrickson, S. B. & Eugene, B. (1984). *Christmas Sports in St. Kitts-Nevis: Our Neglected Cultural Tradition*. U.S. Virgin Islands: Authors, p. 14.

about the many times he reaped cotton by moonlight, so that he could avoid giving the prescribed share to the landowner.

By the early 1930s, large portions of land on Nevis had declined in productivity. Much of it was abandoned or put up for sale by fleeing estate owners facing bankruptcy, because of poor sugar crops on the island. Some planters left for St. Kitts, the U.S., Canada, or other Caribbean islands. Others returned to England. Despite the generous land-sale deals instigated by government, the poverty faced by many Nevisians prevented them from becoming landowners. Some tradesmen, hucksters, and a few professionals did understand the power of land ownership plus its eventual economic and social worth. Those who had access to money, some through relatives abroad, did sacrifice and somehow found the money to buy small plots of land across the island. However, most Nevisians had to pass on the offer, because they simply could not afford the money.

Further, many of the villagers who made land deals were uneducated and could not read or write well. After they made land-purchase agreements, some were duped by estate owners or their children. A number of the verbal and written agreements were not honored later by the landowners. A number of the sale documents had not been prepared legally during such exchanges, since most of the workers were illiterate. However, they trusted the planters and their family members to deal with the exchanges ethically. Often, such contracts were made between desperate planters and trusting workers. There were promises that if work was done by the laborers, eventually that land would pass from the planters to the laborers' families. However, in many cases on Nevis, the land was never exchanged, as had been agreed. In Butler's Village, for example, by the late 1900s, many families that trusted such agreements lost their land. A number of those agreements were declared to be unreliable contracts. In a number of cases, no documents had been preserved to verify agreements between the contracting parties. Many agreements were verbal. Consequently, the surviving children of the planter simply argued there was no legal proof of ownership, even when the family had been reassured for years that they owned the land on which they lived. Such situations were repeatedly exploited by the relatives of estate owners. In all 5 parishes of Nevis, there were cases where families had to purchase the same land twice, or give up land they had been told for many years they owned.

However, whether they worked the land as owners or as sharecroppers (metayage), there was a fairly vibrant peasantry on Nevis, by the 1950s. In contrast, St. Kitts, with its central sugar factory, had fostered an elite planter class that owned most of the land until Robert Bradshaw moved to nationalize estate lands and the sugar factory, during the early 1970s. Meanwhile, despite that opportunity for land ownership on Nevis, as far back as the 1930s, hundreds of Nevisians continued to migrate to St. Kitts and elsewhere. Some preferred the relatively secure seasonal work on the sugar estates. Many found that in spite of the hard, blistering work in the cane fields, the pay was more than they could earn on Nevis, on St. Kitts there was a "pay day." To some of those migrants from Nevis, the wage earned on plantations in St. Kitts provided for them, once struggling Nevisians, a feeling of being better off than their family and friends back on Nevis. There was a certain monetary stability achieved from the regular weekly wages and a bonus secured when the labor union and sugar producers came to amicable wage agreements. Over time, that promise of better wages from plantation work on St. Kitts did entice hundreds of Nevisians to choose living on that island rather than on Nevis. There was also an attraction of many Nevis educators to St. Kitts during those years. The group included men such as Obadiah Williams, William "Willie" Dore, Edward Griffin, Stanley Amory, and some others. These men made invaluable contributions to education in both St. Kitts and Nevis. For example, Dr. Edward Griffin who now lives on St. Croix, was my fifth grade teacher. He was transferred to Sandy Point where he inspired hundreds of young Kittitians such as Dr. Simon Jones-Hendrickson, the late Asyll Warner, and many others. Meanwhile, Dr. Frank Mills continues to laud another Nevis educator on St. Kitts, Analdo Richards. To many of his students, Dr. Griffin is still remembered as one of their most inspiring teachers. He stood out as a major guide through that challenging path to an early education; then later secondary education.

Major crops grown on estates in Nevis included sugarcane, cotton, and ground provisions. Sugar was refined locally in Nevis until the late 1950s. After the cessation of sugar production at New River, all sugar cane produced on Nevis was sold to the government and shipped to St. Kitts to be refined at the central factory. Sailboats such as the *Oceana, Lady Nisbett, Gotham, Princess Royal,* and of course *Crown,* were household names on Nevis then.[22]

Just as with sugar production, preparing cotton for market was labor intensive. Whole families, the larger the better, at times worked together or alongside hired hands to complete the tasks. Children on Nevis, particularly those in the countryside, often had to choose between attending school and working in fields of sugarcane or cotton. Because of the limited academic and professional opportunities available to them then, the choice was often to work on the crop that was in season, or to withdraw from school early to become apprentices and learn trades. Carpentry, masonry, and tailoring were available for boys. Girls could learn dressmaking, work as maids with well-to-do families, or assist their mothers at home. As education became increasingly available, teaching, nursing, and the police force started to be more attractive to young people.

Notwithstanding, farming remained a dominant approach to economic development on Nevis. During 1961, commensurate with the growing animosity between St. Kitts and Nevis, an argument developed over the export tax charged on cotton from Nevis. This was the incident that served to reopen the secession issue in Nevis.[23] Meanwhile, because cotton had become the important export cash crop on the island, particularly after the 1950s, that move by Bradshaw and the Labor members of the legislature to raise the tax on cotton export, was unacceptable to Nevisians. The decision was to raise the export tax on cotton 500% (from 1 cent per pound

---

22 *The Crown* became legendary when it sank mysteriously off Basseterre in 1948. Three men who could not swim, including Captain Buller Hicks, drowned. That story was later immortalized in a song, "Crown Went Down," by Johnny Walters and George "Too-too" Webb.

23 In 1882 the British forced Nevis to join the government of St. Kitts and Anguilla.

to 6 cents per pound). Because Nevis' major agricultural product was cotton, both representatives for Nevis, in the St. Kitts-based Parliament, Wilmoth Nicholls and Eugene Walwyn, protested vehemently. They took the issue back to the farmers on Nevis and thus the idea of secession from St. Kitts was reignited in 1961. In a protest rally on Nevis, one placard read, "St. Kitts married to Nevis in 1882. Divorced in 1961!"

Along with cotton, Nevisians grew a variety of fruits, vegetables, and other cash crops. These were consumed locally or sold on St. Kitts. Selling one's produce on St. Kitts was more profitable than doing so on Nevis. The intense level of sugar production on St. Kitts prevented the cultivation of enough food crops on St. Kitts to feed the population. In time, some Nevisians came to depend so much on trade with St. Kitts that they never attempted to produce sugarcane or cotton. Many people on Nevis traded directly with St. Kitts, while others sold to middle-men who traded as "hucksters." Eventually, a stable thriving trade in fruits, vegetables, ground provisions, and animals for slaughter developed between the two islands. Scores of hucksters made a comfortable living and became engrossed in the St. Kitts and Nevis trade, until the *Christena* accident in 1970.[24]

Social Conditions

Because of Nevis' economic situation and its historical and political circumstances, relations with St. Kitts deteriorated during the 1960s and on into the 1970s. Compared with St. Kitts, the infrastructure of Nevis and Anguilla was in a deplorable state at that time.

Telephone service on Nevis was severely limited; telephones were cumbersome, intimidating, and a luxury to have. They were

---

24 Browne, W. T (1985). *The Christena Disaster in Retrospect.* Charlotte Amalie, St. Thomas: BL&E; Browne, W. T. (2001). *The Christena Disaster Revisited.* Charlotte Amalie, St. Thomas, VI: BL&E Enterprise.

available to the police, a few government offices, and persons from the upper class. During the 1950s, there was one telephone at Butler's Village. The roads were poorly maintained dirt roads, so the telephone was a definite asset in cases of emergencies. However, everyone else knew about it when a telephone call came for a person in the village. Peter Griffin, the telephone-exchange operator, lived at the bottom of Mannings' Road. He developed the remarkable skill of using his very loud voice to call for a person anywhere in the larger Mannings' area and Butler's Village area. At times too, other persons who heard the call joined in the message relay.

Throughout the island, many poor and unfortunate families were often locked in a continuous struggle for survival against scathing poverty. For a number of years, the village of Rawlins, above Market Shop, supplied Nevis, and to a lesser extent St. Kitts with breadfruit, which was part of the Nevis staple diet during bad times. People from throughout Nevis went to Rawlins by donkey or on foot to buy precious breadfruit for their own use or for resale. At times, the owners of breadfruit groves also made trips on their donkeys to the villages around the island to sell their produce.

During those times, shoes were such a luxury in some families that they were frequently worn in the hands, or over the shoulders. A popular joke from that era poked fun at a person who wore his shoes over his shoulder and eventually struck his foot against a stone, bursting one toe open. He quickly consoled himself with the comment: "Suppose I was wearing my shoes. What would have happened to them?" Until the early 1960s, few Nevisians had more than one pair of "going out" shoes. They might also have been handed down and too tight, but, they were a pair of shoes.

Even in St. Kitts the use of shoes as an everyday part of one's dress came relatively late. The poor working class was often heard boasting, even during the 1960s and beyond, "It's Papa Bradshaw give us shoes"; a reference to the health and social improvements that came through working-class politics led by Robert Bradshaw after 1952. Bradshaw's leadership also greatly influenced the development of public education, set the stage for new levels of public health, and in particular brought a new politics to the islands for the masses.

Bradshaw achieved the inclusion of the masses, and development of political awareness among the masses on St. Kitts, by challenging the plantocracy. Such political arousal and consciousness came to Nevis much later, when political leaders such as Sim Daniel, Ivor Stevens, Uhral Swanston, and others, mirrored Bradshaw's opposition to the planter-class, against Bradshaw and his Labor Party. They challenged Bradshaw to change from what was seen as blatant neglect, along with very unfair treatment of Nevis and Nevisians.

BOOK II

Ethics and Politics

CHAPTER 3

ETHICS

When Ivor worked at the sugar factory on St. Kitts, Ivor's wife, Dora, in whom he confided, recalled times when he disagreed with the attitude and actions of management toward the workers. She confided that Ivor disagreed with the claim that the sugar workers were lazy. On many occasions, Ivor had rallied his group of workers to perform beyond their normal limits. He also disagreed with the criticisms and accusations of poor performance frequently leveled against the sugar workers. Usually though, the poor working masses had limited recourse against such snobbery, false accusations and disrespect by the planters, who considered them social inferiors. Ironically, those very workers provided and secured the profits and privileges the planters enjoyed. On more than one occasion, Ivor's team won the prize given at the factory for good performance and outstanding production. Again, and again, he saw irony, injustice, and arrogance in a society dominated by an elite planter-class. He disagreed with the planters' position on labor matters.

However, although Ivor was a mover, shaker, and independent thinker, he was not one to openly and suddenly turn on a friend or an employer, even when they disagreed on a matter. He went on to depict that stance during his political life. For example, few people knew about Ivor's long-term conflict with Mr. Daniel, until after Mr. Stevens left politics. During that earlier situation at the factory, Stevens said an amicable good-bye to the sugar industry on St. Kitts, then made his way over to Nevis quietly, when his father became ill in 1953.

Unlike some of his political colleagues, Stevens hated the idea of being offered bribes by individuals or businesses. He never accepted such exploitative favors. When he made up his mind to become a politician, Ivor saw so much that needed change on the islands, that he simply did not have the time or the will to be bribed by anyone—he was an ethical man and wanted to do what he did honestly. Mr. Stevens considered bribery to be beneath his dignity. The fact that certain people tried to bribe him made Stevens angry. He refused to accept the lavish Christmas presents sent by the management of The Four Seasons Hotel and certain other businesses on Nevis and St. Kitts. Donors were politely thanked, but their gifts were *always* returned.

From start to finish, throughout his political career, Stevens had one set mission and one specific goal for his politics, and he kept at them with determination and tenacity. He wanted to better Nevis through improved infrastructure. He wanted Nevisians to achieve success and prosperity through better education and the creation of a vibrant, versatile economy. They also needed to experience a caring leadership and a responsive government. Stevens believed that certain aspects of the functioning of government on Nevis should be independent of those on St. Kitts.

Despite the difficult challenges he saw during the early years, Ivor committed himself and promised Nevisians that before he died, fundamental changes would come to the island, for all to see and appreciate. The condition of infrastructural backwardness and social squalor, which Stevens saw everywhere in 1953, had to end. At the same time, he wanted to preserve as treasures for generations to come, those things on the island that were considered worthy of such preservation. To him it was important that Nevisians, particularly those children yet unborn, should come to know and appreciate them too—the sandy beaches, the coconut groves, shoal-pot fishing, Annancy stories, and the simplicity of village culture.

Today, astute politicians take time to observe and carry out surveys. They evaluate their constituents carefully, then make judgments about them. That is one strategy by which politicians determine whether they will win or lose political races, or what position they should take on important matters. At the same time, politicians, too, are observed, evaluated, and judged on a constant basis, by people inside and outside their constituencies. Such patterning of evaluation is particularly true in so-called democracies, where citizens vote for political candidates based on their political ideology, people friendliness, administrative ability, perceptions of their leadership ability, other experiences, and certainly for money too—a growing phenomenon in Caribbean politics.

Beginning in the early 1950s, and up until his death in the 1990s, Ivor was in the public eye on St. Kitts-Nevis. He was talked to, talked at, and talked about, during all those years. Even now that Ivor is dead, he is remembered and still being talked about as people on Nevis, in particular, evaluate and reevaluate how and in what ways Ivor Stevens contributed to the designing and structuring of contemporary society on St. Kitts-Nevis. Quite often, politicians can perform unique acts and make special contributions to their societies. In time too, such leaders can take on a special aura, catching the attention and admiration of the citizenry.

Many years ago Shakespeare commented about the human inherent capacity to be actors through life, noting that each human being also plays different parts over time. Meanwhile, a number of persons observing the lives and actions of the same individuals can see different things. They may even arrive at opposing conclusions. However, there is general agreement in both St. Kitts and Nevis that Ivor Stevens, particularly in his later role as a leader in the NRP-PAM coalition government, was more than an ordinary actor—he was a convincing actor. The roles thrust upon him, Ivor performed them well. Notwithstanding, the question is still relevant today, "How did Kittitians and Nevisians see Ivor Stevens?" Following are some the stories, anecdotes, and reflections that speak to how Kittitians and Nevisians saw and remember Mr. Stevens.

St. John Payne

The late, St. John Payne was a politician in St. Kitts and a member of the Labor government for a number of years. Both Payne and

Stevens were elected to the St. Kitts-Nevis House of Assembly for the first time in the general election of 1971. Fond and vivid memories of their interactions remained with Mr. Payne through the years. He spoke of remembering Ivor with good feelings. Our conversation flowed quite easily and freely as Mr. Payne talked about observing Ivor the politician closely, and admitted to admiring him:

> Ivor was very capable of seizing the moment and twisting things in the direction he wanted. He spoke always on behalf of Nevis. Ivor was humorous, a good speaker, and often frank without being obnoxious. He had a penchant for detail, too. For example, if Ivor wanted to speak about how bad the roads in Nevis were, he would give details of incidents on the roads, then stress that an unfeeling government on St. Kitts just did not care about such things. Despite his criticisms of the Labor government, Bradshaw and Ivor were always good friends; so too were his brothers, Hope and Cecil. Ivor's attacks on Bradshaw were usually in a very general sense. On one occasion, probably when Ivor's mother died, Bradshaw made an announcement in the House of Assembly, then paid glowing tribute to Ivor's mother giving details of his friendship with the Stevens' family. Before Bradshaw finished speaking, Ivor cried like a child. There was Bradshaw in public saying those good things about his family.
>
> Ivor was a good advocate for the people of Nevis. He kept very close to his constituents. Often Ivor would claim to be just an ordinary fisherman and simply reporting what the people said under the Iron Shed, often making his points graciously and well. At times, Ivor taunted the Speaker of the House. He used the leniency of the House to

bring to light public issues that he cared about. Ivor always found some way to bring attention to the issues that concerned him.

Everything Ivor did in the House of Assembly, was for Nevis. I remembered teasing Ivor about how he could justify his acceptance of a Ministry in the People's Action Movement-Nevis Reformation Party (PAM-NRP), coalition government when he had always been negative in his comments on government. Stevens' response was, "Johnny boy, I have to do the work of the people of Nevis. Remember, I am only a fisherman."

During his early tenure as a Minister of Government, Ivor was surprised when someone wrote him from Bermuda decrying his inconsistency as a politician. How could Ivor, a sworn secessionist then, accept a ministerial position in a coalition government of St. Kitts-Nevis and move away from secession? Apparently the individual followed St. Kitts-Nevis politics via ZIZ Radio, heard in Bermuda. Ivor read the letter in the House of Assembly. His response to the letter's query was: "I am doing the work of the people of Nevis. There is no contradiction."

We found Ivor to be much warmer than Sim [the other representative from Nevis], who did not relate well to the other members of the House. Although Ivor attacked Bradshaw from time to time, their two families had an amicable friendship outside of politics. Once, during a storm the crane on the pier in Nevis fell into the sea. Since Ivor was then the Minister of Communications and Works, he readily took a crane from St. Kitts and sent it to Nevis. When a politician in St. Kitts complained,

Ivor's response was, "I have work up there for it to do." Ivor was a very good actor. He often reminded me he was from Sandy Point. But he made a very sound case for Nevis. I believe that a good politician should have some acting abilities. Ivor had both the ability and capacity. He also used them well. During the 1970s and the presentation of Nevis' Resolution for Secession, no one remembers if Sim talked. But everyone remembers that Ivor talked, and did so for 3 days in the Assembly, on one occasion, in 1974.

At that time, Ivor had one job, and that was to talk about the secession of Nevis from St. Kitts. When a time came that Ivor advocated the islands should work together, it was because he saw an opportunity there, to do something to help Nevis . . . Sim kept shifting his position. He never followed through and negotiated. Meanwhile, Ivor was bold enough to declare he would find a way to keep the PAM-NRP government in power. He was going to work for the people of Nevis, whether he was outside or inside the government.

The matter of single legislative membership for Kittitians and dual membership for Nevisians, as proposed in [a] White Paper, caused quite some debate on the two islands. The Labor politicians wanted to limit elected office to one body while the coalition government was allowing for two different bodies. There was also some concern over whether persons on Nevis elected at the local government level could, or should serve at the federal government level. Ivor gave a sharp and defiant retort to that query, "If Nevis people want to elect crooks, let them elect crooks."

Despite Ivor's initial acceptance of the White Paper, he later admitted it was inconsistent and flawed. However, the islands' constitution was an interesting political and social document . . . usually, the poor tends to elect those perceived as their betters. Thus, Ivor, from the top of the tree, appealed to those under the shed. Some even called him, "Massa Ivor." When the issue of whether Ivor fathered a child out of wedlock came to the fore it tempered Ivor's style, and he acted somewhat more reserved. The fact that he fathered the child was an embarrassment to Ivor. There was also the story that at one point he did not acknowledge or support her.

That attack against Ivor by Fitzroy Bryant came again and again during Ivor's second term in office, after he had launched an attack on Bryant about his commonly known boast about promiscuity. The result of Fitzroy's revelation to everyone about Ivor's illegitimate daughter was a surprise to many. That revelation by Fitzroy did serve to back up and frazzle Ivor, at least for a time. The two men had ethical failures. One was open and cavalier about his. The other was initially unwilling to own-up to his human failings and unethical behavior.

Notwithstanding, it was difficult not to like Ivor. Usually, he made his points with finesse and grace. There were times in the House of Assembly when he would tease Lee Moore, who served as Attorney General, 1971-1979. When Ivor made his presentations, he would make statements such as, "Yes Mr. Attorney General, when I am going out of line you tell me." However, Ivor's real intention was to get out of line. There were also times when Lee became very irritated by Ivor. He understood

> what Ivor was doing, and Moore was not humored by such tactics. Quite often, what Ivor said had nothing to do with truth or absolute truth. It had more to do with presenting his case for Nevis. If I had to choose one politician to represent Nevis I would have chosen Ivor again and again. He had a flamboyant personality. He also had the uncanny ability to present Nevis' case so well, that even the fishermen—those under the iron-shed, they understood and appreciated his commitment to their island.

Ralph Harris

Ralph Harris had migrated from Nevis and lived on St. Croix at the time I interviewed him. He was quick to remind me that he was 79 years old then, but that he continued to work at boat building. During a much earlier time, Mr. Harris was one of the political pioneers who labored with Ivor and the other activists to defy Bradshaw and the Labor Party, in their effort to change the dreams and the destiny of Nevisians. The saga of Nevis politics engaged Harris in more than 50 years of personal struggle, hope, disappointment, and then disillusionment. Throughout that time he remained a pure secessionist and a staunch crusader for the independence of Nevis from St. Kitts. Harris remembered being in the political trenches with Ivor and others. However, Harris always saw Mr. Stevens as a St. Kitts-man and never thought he should be trusted with the affairs of Nevis. Little wonder, Harris was not very complimentary of Ivor in his comments. Some of the things he said in reference to Ivor follow.

> When Ivor ran his first campaign in 1957, I was able to work out that he had the support of the Labor Party. Its leader, Robert Bradshaw, came to Nevis and gave a speech in the street across from the courthouse. He told Nevisians, "I have a man

for Nevis." Later on, Attorney Wigley of the planter affiliated, Democratic Party, of St. Kitts, came to Nevis and warned us, Nevisians should vote for a son of the soil. Ivor responded by calling Eugene Walwyn, his opposition, a Democrat. However, since Walwyn was a Nevisian by birth and there was no other person who had declared for that seat, the only person Bradshaw could have been speaking of was Ivor Stevens. Further, if the Stevens' were not close to Bradshaw, Ivor's sister, May would not have received the appointment to head the hospital on St. Kitts during the 1950s. Also, during the campaign of 1957, Ivor did refer to Eugene as "that Black bastard." For me, it was more than an insult to Eugene. Since elite families at that time despised persons of illegitimate birth, that comment was also an attack directed at all Black people on Nevis, the very people whom Ivor was canvassing for their votes.

There is no doubt that Ivor helped Nevisians at Brown Hill, Brown Pasture, Church Ground, and the Burden Pasture area, during the sugar era. He provided them transportation for their sugar cane. I am not convinced that Ivor or Sim did enough to help Nevis. There were many times, too, when it was very difficult for Sim to get the support of the others on certain St. Kitts vs. Nevis related matters. I knew those things because I used to be a member of the party's executive body. I was not there then, but Ivor never campaigned with, or did anything to show support for the NRP, after he retired from politics. Seemingly, he had accomplished what he wanted for himself. That to me showed that he was committed to the success of Ivor, not Nevis.

Ivor did support the People's Action Movement. He was fired, from the Trades and Development Corporation, after he won for the NRP in 1971. His winning for the NRP, a Nevis party, was not acceptable to the People's Action Movement supporters, behind the corporate operations.

At one time Ivor wanted to lead Nevis. When De Grasse was asked to step down by Bradshaw, the Nevis politicians invited De Grasse to Nevis and asked him to lead the opposition. The aim was to get Uhral Swanston in the House as a nominated member. He was needed to second the motions moved in the House on behalf of Nevis. They usually died for the lack of a supporting vote. However, Ivor protested and said he would resign from the party if De Grasse was appointed over him. The NRP executive then told Ivor to resign from the House, too . . . . In the end, Ivor backed down.

The secession clause is there in the constitution, not because of Ivor [only] but because Sim, Ivor, and particularly the people of Nevis wanted it there. No one was certain how future Labor Party regimes would behave toward Nevis.

Very few Kittitians, even when they live on Nevis, and that included Ivor, really care about Nevisians. They think we are fools. Consequently, Ivor could not have been a Labor man and fully support secession in Nevis. However, he did encourage Nevisians to have more affection for the People's Action Movement than for Labor. Nevis thrived under the People's Action Movement because Nevis politicians were given more internal control.

> Through Ivor, the two islands came closer together. One of Ivor's successes was the purchase of *Caribe Queen*. It was to ensure that Nevisians in particular, can travel to and from St. Kitts in safety. Stevens always relived the specter of the *Christena*, in 1970.
>
> However, it was noticeable that during the night of the 1998 referendum vote, the ferry-boat slept in St. Kitts, not in Nevis.

Phineas Griffin

Phineas Griffin worked closely with Ivor in the Department of Public Works. Seemingly, Phineas cherished that relationship with Ivor because he found it very rewarding and he felt respected. Phineas continues to speak about the man quite glowingly. Following are some of the things Phineas said about how he knew Ivor, and related to him.

> Mr. Stevens was an honest, admirable man who was usually fair in his dealings with other people. While I worked with him, Ivor took me on my only trip abroad for government. He had a way of calling me Nevius. He said to me, Nevius, get a receipt for all your expenses. Make sure you account for every cent that you spend . . . Ivor did things up front. I never found him to be crooked. When Ivor liked you, he stuck with you, even if you let him down. Once when I referred the misbehavior of one of his friends to Ivor, his response was, "I understand, but when I like you, I like you." However, it appeared that Ivor did scold the person afterwards.
>
> Although Ivor thought the Social Security building was too small, he attended its opening. The building

was named in his honor. Before the ceremony began Ivor was introduced to Premier Amory's wife. He complimented her on her beauty, in his usual chivalrous way. Then, without skipping a beat, Ivor discredited her for "marrying that man Vance." I remember that Ivor was not mild in his criticisms of Vance. I was also quite shocked that Mr. Stevens was so straightforward, criticizing Premier Amory, in the presence of his wife.

At one time Ivor had assisted successfully in negotiating a loan for Nevis from the Social Security fund. When Ivor came to Nevis with the check he said to me, "Man I am loaded." The money was secured in late 1991 or 1992. During the period when Ivor was out of political office. There were those times when Sim had to depend on Ivor, even though he would have preferred that Ivor was not involved in Nevis affairs. That was one of the times.

Sim did not consult with Ivor or anyone else about his secession idea in 1992. He simply presented the matter as an issue during the campaign. Generally, Sim knew Ivor had become more popular in Nevis than he was. Unfortunately, Sim did not know how to deal with his low popularity situation. Ivor went out of his way to assist me at times while I was in politics. Sim on the other hand did not favor me. He did nothing to help me. When I won the St. James' seat, Sim met me and in a facetious manner said, "You lucky . . ." There was little doubt that Ivor was a major player in the NRP. It was very much his party.

Dr. Keith Archibald

Dr. Archibald's family and Ivor's family, on Nevis, were close. Keith knew all the Stevens siblings well, except Ivor. He got to know Ivor on his return to St. Kitts-Nevis from the war, during the early part of the 1950s. Keith was there as Nevis politics emerged and came into its own. He had the opportunity to observe Ivor the politician, as he developed, grew, and matured. At times, Dr. Archibald's observations and comments about Ivor went beyond politics:

> When Ivor returned from the war he worked at the sugar factory. The reports were that Ivor and the people he supervised worked well together. He respected them and they respected him. Ivor and Eugene Walwyn generally disagreed over politics. However, I often saw the two men talking under the Iron Shed. At one time, even Ivor was persuaded to join the United National Movement. He was willing to give up on his differences with Eugene. There was one time when Ivor even spoke on the same platform with Walwyn. They marched together after a big meeting next to the courthouse. Then, they collected signatures of Nevisians together, to send to the then Administrator, H. A. C. Howard. Later on, Ivor was among the leaders of the 100 or so persons who went from Nevis and walked to Government House to protest against how St. Kitts was treating Nevis. Walwyn, Stevens, Nicholls, and Parris, all promised then, that they would take their protest to England. In the ensuing election of 1961, Ivor chose not to run against Eugene.
>
> Stevens shifted his politics from time to time. At first, maybe up until 1966, Ivor might have been supported by the Labor Party. During 1966-1971,

he was with the People's Action Movement, or probably independent. Ivor won his first election in 1971, as an NRP candidate. . . . Eugene Walwyn, having shifted loyalty to the Labor Party, accepted the position of Attorney General, with the coming of Statehood in 1967. However, Ivor refused to become involved with the Labor government. At that time, he opted against making any compromise with the Labor government.

Ivor seemed to have always been suspicious of Walwyn. Later, when Sim joined with Ivor and the other political activists on Nevis, it was because Sim knew about Ivor's stance on self-determination for Nevis. Generally, Ivor was positive and determined when it came to arguing matters related to Nevis. In every way Stevens attempted to show he was totally committed to Nevis; his dream for Nevis was that water, electricity, and the other infrastructure on the island could be improved. He once said to me, "I am going to revolutionize the telephone system. We will get that high tech thing." Ivor was also keen on promoting agriculture production, to include Sea Island cotton, and the livestock industry. Those had to be strengthened to help the small man.

At times, I thought Ivor was not too much in favor of the party system in Nevis. He felt that a few people could run the island. I also felt that Ivor was somewhat ill at ease around intellectuals, but he was a totally honest man. During the time that Ivor was involved in politics, he was always good at speaking with those whom he needed to communicate. That was probably a carry-over influence from his military experience.

Eustace John

Deputy Governor General, Eustace John, still remembers Ivor Stevens very fondly. They shared a long, interesting, and unique friendship. Following is some of what Mr. John shared about how he knew Ivor.

> My first contacts with Ivor came during 1957-1959, and it was not about politics. When I was assigned by government to work as a customs officer, I had absolutely no idea what I was supposed to be doing. Ivor recognized my problem and decided to help me. He, along with Lindy Parris and Arthur Evelyn, worked out a plan to assist me. Their aim was to help me learn customs work since it was a process that required new learning. Following that experience, all of these people became my very good friends for life.
>
> I remembered when Ivor went into the House of Assembly, as an opposition member in 1971. I also remembered when he talked for 3 days and gave the longest speech on record in the Assembly. Ivor and I hardly ever discussed politics. He understood and accepted the fact that my family supported the Labor Party. At times, Ivor was very adept at rising above politics, divorcing it from everyday life and from his relationship with friends. For me, Ivor also joined the rank with Bradshaw, as one of the honest politicians of St. Kitts-Nevis.
>
> Mr. Stevens could not be bribed. He refused to accept gifts. I do not recall he was ever involved in a political scandal. Ivor also had a high standard of personal integrity and he listened well. He was careful to hear and digest well what was being said

> to him, and he was always approachable. During his last days at the hospital, Ivor often asked about my family. Even as he neared the end of his life, Ivor was still concerned about others.
>
> As far as I can remember, Ivor was the greatest non-fisherman's fisherman, that I ever knew At one time, Ivor was a member of the labor union and supported some of Bradshaw's policies. He also became very much a friend of Lee Moore. However, in dealing with Nevis politics, Ivor did not argue as a Kittitian. Further, there was never a time when I thought Ivor worried about his personal safety in Nevis. Usually he could be approached and spoken to by anyone, on any matter.

Bertram "Tramming" Mc Mahorn

Bertram "Tramming" Mc Mahorn worked with the ferry service during the time that Ivor served as the Minister, responsible for Communications and Works. Over time, he and Ivor became good friends. This was how Tramming remembered Ivor:

> I knew Mr. Stevens and was associated with him from 1981 to 1987. In many ways, he was like a father to me. Mr. Stevens often encouraged and helped me. I remember one time at the pier, he took up some board and put them on the boat to Nevis. His comments were, "I take things for Nevis; they cannot lock me up."
>
> One time, Ivor also sent over an old crane from the factory. He was honest and straightforward. With Mr. Stevens you got what was due you. On one occasion, Mr. Haynes, the Permanent Secretary, refused to pay Mrs. Knight her increment. When

the matter was brought to Stevens' attention, he insisted that Mrs. Knight's increment be paid.

Wilmoth Nicholls

On June 21,1997, a column by Wilmoth B Nicholls, one of the early Nevis politicians, was published as a letter to the editor in the *Democrat,* after Nicholls became aware of Mr. Stevens' death. Back in 1961, after his election loss to Brookes, and the subsequent disillusionment he experienced, Nicholls migrated to St. Thomas, Virgin Islands. However, Nicholls made the effort to keep abreast of developments back home in Nevis. In that letter to the *Democrat* newspaper, Nicholls commended Ivor for his wit, good sense of politics, and the consistency he exhibited in his fight for Nevis. That letter is reproduced here:

> Dear Editor,
>
> *Ivor Is Gone But The Dream Lives On.*
>
> It was just Tuesday, June 10, that I telephoned Ivor's home to have a chat with him after I had written a letter to the *Democrat* in which I had used his name concerning his efforts in the "FREEDOM FIGHT" that he had put up for Nevisians.
>
> His wife took the call and informed me that he was admitted to the hospital. She also informed me how Ivor had read my "letters to the Press," and was happy that I was carrying on the fight. I told her that I was doing my best on his behalf and on the behalf of all true Nevisians.
>
> Nevisians cannot imagine the shock I felt when my wife, who had typed my letter, told me that she had heard on VON Radio, Thursday, that he had

died. It was to me the kind of news that could have caused one to faint.

I remember Ivor for his famous "Three days speech in Parliament" as he carried the fight for Nevisians. I do not believe any other Parliamentarian had performed such a devoted effort for his people. I also remember Ivor for his stirring address to the members of the St. Kitts-Nevis Mutual Improvement Society as a Guest Speaker during one of our Annual Celebrations.

I recall that as Master of Ceremonies and Vice President at the time, I promised Ivor that I will always support the cause which he had volunteered to carry on, on our behalf. Governor Juan Luis of the Virgin Islands was also flabbergasted to know that our parliamentary system allowed for a hero to talk for three days, and praised Ivor for his devotion to his country.

In his usually captivating style, Ivor's speech brought laughter and cheers to the over three hundred members and friends who attended the function. It was one annual ceremony where the caterer had to request a fresh supply of food to satisfy the three hundred plus guests.

I am certain that all members of St. Kitts and Nevis join with me in expressing their heartfelt loss of one of the best representatives that Nevis ever had. May his family take solace in knowing that Ivor will go down in history as one of the great patriots of his country, and the true Nevisians would continue to fight for Ivor's dreams to be realized. I know that former Premier Daniel has lost a great friend and a

> loyal supporter of the cause which most Nevisians hope to achieve.
>
> Wilmoth B. Nicholls, Former Legislator, St. Kitts-Nevis & Anguilla.

Tom Joseph

Tom Joseph (a pseudonym, since the interviewee did not want his real name used) was a close friend of Ivor. He said the following about the man:

> Ivor was a good person to deal with. He got things done, but he bluffed when he wanted to. The fishermen did receive valuable assistance from him. At one time, I knew that Ivor paid the fees for certain children at the secondary school. In politics Ivor was very forceful and aggressive. He spoke up and stood up. He did not get the support from Sim. Sim did not assist or accept some the things Ivor did. But, Ivor never wanted to smash the party. . . . Ivor's motto was, "Do things first. Argue about them later." There were times when Sim felt he could not trust Ivor and Swanston. He thought they were sympathetic to St. Kitts. Based on that thinking, Sim once commented, "I cannot say anything in Nevis before Kennedy knows it in St. Kitts." Ivor resigned from politics before he wanted to, because of the mistrust he felt and because of Sim's feeling that Ivor wanted to take over the party. Sim hated opposition; he was cunning and cut throat. He did not like when he could not control.
>
> Ivor had more freedom in St. Kitts. If Sim had worked with Ivor, more would have been done for Nevis. Once when Sim was asked to meet with Ivor

> and some others from the NRP's leadership, he refused. Sim's response to them was, "Oh, you all are politicians; go ahead without me." Ivor was very disappointed with that response. Ivor always met with the party-faithful, and he listened to them. Then he would talk to Sim later. Sim did not spend time, as Ivor did with the common people.
>
> Bryant and Ivor were once engaged in an argument, when he accused Ivor of fathering a child he did not take. In anger, Ivor said to Bryant, "You are not from here." Bryant's response was, "You are a Kittitian but you speak as a Nevisian."
>
> Yea man, Ivor did try his best. Three weeks before he died he called someone to take him to town so that he could buy a coil of rope for a fisherman friend. Unfortunately, he did not get the rope.

Rhoan Liburd

Rhoan Liburd was one of the founders of the Nevis Reformation Party. He knew Ivor well and was part of that force in the 1970s, for secession from St. Kitts. Following are some of his thoughts about Ivor.

> The name NRP was given to the party by Ivor. Later, Ivor and Sim were responsible for the downfall of Nevis. Both talked secession but did not mean it. Ivor was never for secession. That is reflected in what he did, and in what he said.
>
> In 1979, on one of the independence trips to London, Lee Moore came to speak with Ivor and Sim. They refused to see Moore, but Ivor coughed where he was hiding. Lee Moore left after he had a

> drink with me and Swanston. At another meeting in 1983, Stevens said to Ted Hobson, "Labor Dog, follow your master, hoots!" Ivor was always a Bradshaw man, up until he died. Neither Sim nor Ivor was fair to Swanston. They did not look after Swanston or give him a fair deal. Once they got power, they forgot the people around them. Stevens once said, "Not over my dead body will you see Nevis secede from St. Kitts."

Vance Amory

Vance Amory served as the Permanent Secretary of Finance to the Nevis Reformation Party government during the early 1980s. He had a close relationship with Daniel, not Stevens. However, the two men could not have avoided each other. They were required to work together in the said government. From 1992 until 2006, Vance Amory served as Premier of Nevis. Even as I write in February 2013, he has recently been returned to that position on the island. Following are some of his thoughts about Mr. Stevens.

> Ivor was a people's politician. He had a unique way of communicating and appealing to the people. He knew how to get maximum mileage from those he chose to represent. As an administrator, he was persistent. He even bulldozed his way at times. Ivor always got what he wanted. During the late 1980s, the NRP started to show a general move away from the people. That was why I became involved with the opposition movement. There were times when I felt Ivor was moving to undermine Sim.
>
> At times Sim showed himself to be a deep thinker. He was also very forward looking. But he left the planning and organizing to others. One weakness of Ivor was his sensitivity. At times, that weakness led

> him to become involved in personal attacks against others. One could always count on Ivor to rally and fire-up Nevisians, whenever that was necessary.

Wendell Huggins

Wendell Huggins worked as a Permanent Secretary in the Nevis Reformation Party government toward the end of its first tenure in Nevis Island Government. Mr. Huggins worked more closely with Daniel, but he had contact with Stevens, too. Following are some perspectives he offered about Ivor:

> Ivor was a patriotic Nevisian. He was always willing to help, and he had a good sense of timing. There were those times when he exaggerated, but he might not have understood economics well. Early on Nevisians had no one in the corridors of power during the period of the Unitary State. We got minimal services. Ivor recognized the situation and acted to help Nevisians overcome the neglect. Ivor saw himself as a Joshua, or a Moses to bring Nevisians out of bondage. He brought healing, too. He was the consummate populist politician. He read widely and was always a serious and intense combatant.

Levi Morton

Levi Morton was also a founding member of the Nevis Reformation Party, and for many years served in its administration. Morton noted that he was much better acquainted with Ivor's brother Garnet, until he and Ivor were brought together in the NRP. During those years, Levi had enough time and a good opportunity to develop an opinion of Ivor. Following are some of his thoughts about Nevis politics and Mr. Stevens:

It was I, who named the party the NRP. We knew early on that Ivor was associated with the People's Action Movement. However, the NRP was to bring a new politics, and to encourage change on the island. There was no intention to continue things as they were. Ivor wanted to get Eugene Walwyn off the Legislative Council. Since he was part of the high society in Charlestown, Ivor felt he would have made a better representative than Eugene. Besides, he appeared as if he wanted to get at Walwyn. Probably some rancor existed between them.

There was also the need for a new approach to dealing with Nevis politics. We helped Stevens to remove Eugene and we also wanted to get Bradshaw out of the Premiership. It was the NRP, not the People's Action Movement that really provided Bradshaw the tougher challenge right up to Bradshaw's death. Billy and Co. were lame. The People's Action Movement is still lame.

Ivor's association with the People's Action Movement did not really help Nevis. At times Billy seemed to be Ivor's child. He had a special regard for Billy's ideas. But Billy used the government to cushion and hide certain illegal things he was doing.

Ivor genuinely wanted to get rid of Bradshaw. That probably came from his association with the People's Action Movement. With me, Stevens and I often agreed to disagree. On the matter of the 1980 coalition, I wanted the sun to be shining and people to be awake when the discussions were taking place. Stevens appeared to be in a hurry. Sim just tagged along with him.

> Ivor pretended to be a commoner. He set up a chicken farm and sold his eggs. But he did make important contributions to Nevis. Ivor was in a position in St. Kitts to help improve water and electricity on Nevis and he did so. He was also very friendly with the fishermen at Cotton Ground and Jessups.

Arthur Anslyn

Arthur Anslyn was captain of the government's ferry, *Caribe Queen*, for most of the period that Ivor served as Minister of Communications and Works. The two men became close friends because of Ivor's interest in the sea—fishing, and sailing. At one time Anslyn also owned and ran a fishing business on Nevis. Some of Anslyn's thoughts about Ivor follow.

> Ivor always showed a keen interest in the fishing industry. He was a member of the Nevis Fishermen's Cooperative and he did attend the meetings. Ivor also kept in close contact with the fishermen, showing interest in their concerns, and sometimes gave them advice. At one time or other, Ivor owned boats which he sometimes used for fishing. It was Ivor or probably his brother Garnett, who introduced the first outboard motor in Nevis. However, Ivor always preferred the use of more primitive fishing equipment such as hand-held lines.
>
> He was a man for the people and could be approached anytime, anywhere, about anything. Ivor always took the time to listen. He had a genuine interest in the people of Nevis. Although he was born on St. Kitts, Stevens considered himself a Nevisian and did all he could to help Nevis. He was a strong

secessionist and was involved in most the secession battles since 1961.

On the political front, Ivor wanted to have no personal obligations to special interests. He always sent back gifts given to him by the various firms at Christmas or other times. Meanwhile, Ivor went out of his way to build good relations with those he supervised. Usually Mr. Stevens was not offended when his instructions were not carried out, particularly those times when something he ordered someone to do was illegal or contrary to regulations. Further, he was always willing to hear other views. Stevens expected civil servants to do the logical and wise thing, even when his instructions were otherwise. Ivor reasoned that often his actions were to win votes. On the other hand, civil servants had their jobs to protect. He was a very generous person. There were also times when he was probably used by others.

Ivor made snap decisions sometimes; afterwards, if he reflected and disagreed with it, he was always big enough to apologize. In those situations where Ivor was frustrated and stretched to the limit, he would display a nasty, almost uncontrolled temper.

Mr. Stevens often used his authority and position with the federal government to help push special projects on Nevis. Many Sunday mornings he held court and met with interested friends for general discussions. At times, the office he used was the Iron Shed, or the back of the treasury building. Overall, Ivor was a very unorthodox, but successful politician.

Conclusion

The foregoing comments represent the varied ways in which different people saw, knew, and understood Ivor the man, along with Ivor the politician. Although they looked at him through a wide range of lenses and experiences, there were certain things some people seemed to have noted in common: (a) Ivor was dedicated to making Nevis a better place for Nevisians; (b) he played very hard politics; (c) everything that Ivor presented was not real; sometimes he was acting the role his politics dictated at that moment; (d) he did manage to affect and influence the recent development of Nevis; (e) Ivor was an aggressive, but reflective and competent human being; (f) Ivor was not perfect; in time, he too, had to confront his human weaknesses and deal with character flaws; and (g) the relationship between Sim and Ivor benefitted Nevis, but each man used the other in his personal politics. Often, there was more mistrust and suspicion than love between the two men. Ivor Stevens, was everything reported here and more. He came back to Nevis in 1953, and by 1957 Ivor had joined the island's political process. The island needed change that would come only through politics. Despite the great challenges, Stevens worked overtime and the rest of his life, to bring "better," for Nevisians. When he passed in 1997, the common people knew, and all who eulogized him said, "Ivor was a politician who kept his promise to Nevis."

CHAPTER 4

POLITICS

During the time that Ivor aspired to politics in Nevis, and after he was elected to serve as a member of government in St. Kitts-Nevis, his brothers and sisters who were alive at the time gave their support and rallied behind him. Ivor was always certain of their full support. Sister May, who outlived Ivor, remained a best friend and ardent supporter of her brother. She made unique contributions to this documentation until just before the manuscript was first compiled in 2001.

When he entered Nevis politics, Ivor Stevens committed himself to becoming an important catalyst to fashion fundamental changes on the island. They would be critical infrastructural, educational, social, and psychological changes that Nevisians wanted to have implemented, as part of the process of transforming their island. Ivor grew up on Nevis, but he had travelled abroad and was exposed to other cultural experiences. He had also developed a different vision of what life on the island could become. As with the migrants who returned to St. Kitts during the early 1900s and gave new direction to the labor movement on that island, Stevens assisted in bringing a new vision to the politics of Nevis. He saw the problems on Nevis differently from the average Nevisian, but Ivor was ready to work with all Nevisians in charting a path to the change they dreamed about. It was a time when Nevisians were searching for local heroes in their cricket, politics, and other areas of their social life. The people wanted their champions to be persons they knew personally, and with whom they could identify. As fate dictated, Ivor Stevens was one such person. He was agitating in the islands' politics, in anticipation of his moment in the arena.

Stevens was Kittitian, a product of the emerging middle class, and veteran of the Second World War. His varied experiences had taught him commitment and self-confidence. There were infrastructural limitations on Nevis at the time, and Ivor's life had been touched by all the challenges in the societies. Like Frederick Solomon, James Nathan, and that now famous band of earlier pioneers on St. Kitts who came together during the early 1900s, there was need for organization on Nevis. It was that organized mass movement on St. Kitts that laid the foundation for social and political transformation on the island. Ivor saw and understood that a similar need existed on Nevis; consequently, he accepted the challenge to be a champion for Nevis. Undoubtedly, Ivor had his own ego dreams, but he was determined to fill the role as leader and instigator of change on the island.

One positive development for Nevisians during that period was the booming and reliable trade with St. Kitts. Another was their Christmas sports that captured and engaged the entire island from year to year. The dramatic sports presentations were events that brought much fun and laughter to Nevis during Christmastime. A third but subtle factor was that although the labor union was viewed negatively in Nevis, it was actively working for social and political changes, which, in time, both Kittitians and Nevisians would appreciate and embrace. Because of labor unionism, benchmarks were set for the later development of St. Kitts and Nevis, in their society and politics.

When Ivor Stevens came back to Nevis in 1953, he brought a fair measure of formal and practical education. He served in, and survived, the Second World War. He also witnessed the results of mass revolt and mass political mobilization on St. Kitts. Through his manipulation of those experiences, Ivor intended to help build and affect people's mobilization and organization in Nevis. He was determined to bring change along with a measure of success, in that move toward social progress on his adopted island. Yet, Stevens was no magician. He understood that real political power in St.

Kitts and Nevis, at that time, came from acceptance by the masses. Ivor grasped and was determined to live by that truth. Early in his planning for a new politics, Stevens also understood that to make a difference in Nevis society, he could not lead alone—leadership is never one-man-ship!

According to Uhral Swanston, he and Stevens were teaming up and planning to impact Nevis politics shortly after 1961. They both understood that they needed organization and unity, since no one person could have single-handedly transformed the misery and backwardness seen on the island during the 1950s, and on into the 1970s. Thus, at first, as then seemed necessary, Ivor worked cooperatively with Eugene Walwyn, Wilmoth Nicholls, and Uhral Swanston. Later he also worked with Premier Sim Daniel and other members of the Nevis Reformation Party, to enter the arena of political power. When Stevens thought it beneficial for progress on Nevis, he would work closely with Prime Minister Simmonds, along with other members of the People's Action Movement political party, particularly during the time of the PAM-NRP coalition (the government that served St. Kitts-Nevis from February 1980, until November 1993). Stevens was willing to reach out and build all forms of cooperation that would work at bringing about real change on Nevis. He always gave the best he could to make his adopted island a better, more welcoming place. Stevens also understood how the struggles of labor politics on St. Kitts won the right to universal suffrage, mass education, improved health care, and eventually political independence.

It did not matter what social, economic, or political problems he saw in Nevis; Ivor felt he could work on them, preferably with others of like mind. Together, they could find solutions. In spite of his middle-class background, Ivor took the position that even the poorest person on the island had ideas and perspectives that should be heard, if real changes were to be brought to the island.

When Ivor Stevens decided to enter the islands' politics in 1957, both Nevis and Anguilla were underdeveloped. The islands lacked many of the amenities for the good life. They offered young people very little of anything to which they could attach themselves as they built commitments, and hope for the future. Nevisian, Victor Martin, recalled that time in these colorful sentences:

> Cast your mind if you will to the Nevis that was, 40 years ago. Walk with me over the lay of the land and see the struggles of the people. Our forefathers have told us that life in those times was a difficult existence. Cotton was king. But cotton was a brutish king. Water was scarce and electricity came only to a few households in the year 1956. Young men were seeking to emigrate to England, to the Virgin Islands, to Aruba, to Santo Domingo, and to elsewhere in the world beyond Nevis.

During that period, the view ahead for Nevis was blurred and dreary from every angle—few jobs, hard labor, much poverty, and limited social mobility. The average working-class Nevisian could only dream of drudgery and stagnation. That was fate and destiny for most Nevisians who remained on the island. There was no grander vision for the island, no end of the rainbow; no pot of gold, neither was there the sight of any silver lining. During the 1950s, 1960s, and 1970s, the powerful enticements were always somewhere beyond Nevis. Consequently, thousands of Nevisians said tearful goodbyes, then left the island of their birth, many of them never to return.

Ivor was attuned to many of the social and political realities on Nevis when he chose to enter politics. That decision was made despite the complex and depressing social situations he observed on the island. There were those times when Ivor acted the part of an idealist, but he always had confidence in his ability to make a difference anywhere he was needed—even on Nevis. Besides, Ivor had surmised by then that he was needed in Nevis. He was confident he could make a difference in the island's politics. During one of his political speeches in 1957, for example, Stevens asserted, "If good men do not dip their oars into the sea of politics, then not so good men will tell the truly good men how to live." He obviously had dreams for Ivor Stevens and thought he could realize them in Nevis, not on St. Kitts. The ruthless, pro-working-class leader, Robert Bradshaw, was there, and Stevens did not think he could win that challenge.

As the French Revolution of 1789 did to Haiti, the labor union movement in Europe of the later 1800s also came to inspire the African Diaspora in other areas of the Caribbean. It came at a time when exiled Africans in the area were beginning to reconnect with Africa. They were also demanding inclusion and empowerment in their new homeland. The labor movement, which eventually transformed societies on the Caribbean islands, was legalized first on St. Croix and the other Danish West Indies, 1915-1916. Labor unionism was not granted legal status in the British West Indies until after the Moyne Commission Report on labor unrest in the British colonies (1934-1939). The first legal labor union in St. Kitts, Nevis, and Anguilla, started in St. Kitts, May 15, 1940. During the first election in 1952, after universal adult suffrage came to St. Kitts, Nevis, and Anguilla, solid political support was given to labor-union candidates, who represented the interests of the sugar workers. Planter control and its related politics was in no mood for the impending change. But the labor leaders were adamant. Their time had come. They were in a revolutionary mood and they had the numbers! After attaining universal suffrage for the election of 1952, the next move was a formal political party, the St. Kitts, Nevis, Anguilla Labor Party, by 1957[25]

Over on Nevis, the earliest named home-based political parties, the Nevis Progressive Party, and the United National Movement, were launched at a later time, between 1957 and 1961. Robert Gordon, an early Nevis politician, claimed he launched the Nevis Progressive Party on Nevis as early as about 1957; the United National Movement was launched by Eugene Walwyn along with his supporters about 1961. Ivor Stevens also claimed that the seeds

---

25 Browne, W. T. (1992). *From Commoner to King*. Lanham, MD: University of America Press; Borg-O'Flaherty, V. M. (2004). *20th Century Election Results: St. Kitts-Nevis*. Basseterre, St. Kitts: Author.

for the Nevis Reformation Party started to be sown in an early political coming together by Uhral Swanston and himself, in 1967, 3 years before the political party was officially launched.

Once the labor movement was legalized, it blossomed and became very vibrant on St. Kitts, bringing an early political consciousness to the masses on the island, which was not seen on Anguilla or Nevis. It took the later efforts of Eugene Walwyn, Wilmoth Nicholls, Ivor Stevens, and others in the late 1950s, and early 1960s, to start encouraging some sense of political independence and political consciousness among working-class Nevisians. The initial result was the United National Movement, and probably the party Gordon claimed to have started, the Nevis Progressive Party. Recently, I had a conversation with my fifth grade teacher, now Dr. Edward Griffin. He claimed that Mr. Gordon and he were associated back in the 1950s. Dr. Griffin suggested that Gordon had some kind of political organization—even if it was rudimentary. At that time, leaders and supporters of the working-class Labor Party, and the planter-class Democratic Party, kept insisting that the political parties on St. Kitts become the dominant political parties on both Nevis and Anguilla. Accordingly, the working-class vs. planter-class politics that fostered so much tension on St. Kitts, also crossed to Nevis and Anguilla. All three islands became very much a part of an intense class politics during the 1950s-1980s. The Labor Party spoke for the masses. The Democratic Party, which evolved later—to become the People's Action Movement, spoke for the planter-class. That "pepper in your rice and bones in your soup" comment attributed to Bradshaw, was a product of that class politics which had been brought to Nevis and Anguilla—a part of the then battle for control of the masses' minds.

The United National Movement had some early success on Nevis. But the Labor Party kept skillful lieutenants working on the island also, chief among them, Edread Walwyn. There was soon some thinking that the UNM and its leader, Eugene Walwyn, had also become agents for the Labor Party on the island. The People's Action Movement had some following on Nevis, too, with Fred Parris winning the St. James seat in 1966. However, the first Nevis political party that really stirred broad mass interest in politics on the island was the political movement started by Ivor Stevens and Uhral Swanston. It broadened later to include others. The list of pioneers includes the names, Rhoan Liburd, Ralph Harris, Sonny Parris, Levi Morton, and Edgar "Popie" Hicks, a preacher and returnee from the Dominican Republic, who lived at Brick Kiln Village. The party was officially launched in October 1970 and named the Nevis Reformation Party. Sim Daniel, who became the first leader, was not an original founding member of the NRP. He came to the party after it had been founded and was about to be launched. The organizers wanted to have a lawyer as part of their organization, because they feared the response of Bradshaw to an independent political party on Nevis, opposing the dictates of the Labor Party.

During 1951, the property clause, a vehicle used by the planter-class to block universal adult suffrage for the working-class in St. Kitts, Nevis, and Anguilla, was removed from the laws of the Leeward Islands. Following that event, and coupled with the activities of labor unionism, political awareness among the working-class continued to heighten in these islands and throughout the Caribbean area. Over time, as the working-class grasp of politics and political power increased, workers became empowered politically, economically, and socially. Later, that political awareness was combined with their numbers and growing education, to transform the economic, political, and social realities on the colony of St. Kitts, Nevis, Anguilla—forever. There is now very little doubt that the political enfranchisement achieved in 1951-1952, played a pivotal role in remaking the world for all the people of St. Kitts, Nevis, and Anguilla. The dominant thrust and ideology of the islands' politics finally swung away from the elite planter-class, as it finally included and started to empower the despised working masses.

Shortly after returning to Nevis in 1953, and only months after the 1952 election there, Ivor started to work at becoming an important figure in the islands' society and politics. However, his move toward a life in politics was viewed quite quizzically by his family. To them, the then shifting class-dominated politics was strange and unpredictable territory for Ivor. At that time too, politics was seen as being taken over and moving towards control by the less educated working-class under the keen, committed, and formidable leadership of Robert Bradshaw. Another factor the Stevens' family must have contemplated was that their family was not from Nevis. They were migrants there, and the family was not on social common ground with the mass of voters on the island. Notwithstanding that reality, members of the Stevens' family were always very supportive of one another. So, when Ivor declared his intention to enter the islands' politics, his family too accepted the challenge and tossed their lot in beside him. Soon, his interest in St. Kitts-Nevis politics became a powerful obsession for Ivor Stevens. Once he had offered himself to the politics, Ivor never stopped campaigning—he kept on even when it was not election time. However, despite his commitment and interest in politics, Ivor's move into Nevis politics did not always go well for him or his family.

Early in his effort, Ivor virtually set up shop under the Iron Shed, an old colonial building at the entrance to the Charlestown pier. It was there that a large number of people hustled to St. Kitts in the morning and returned in the afternoon, particularly on Fridays and Saturdays. Quite often, morning and afternoon, Ivor could be found at the pier, tall, straight, and wiry, usually well dressed, flaunting a bow-tie. At times he would seem to be preoccupied with a few strands of unruly hair, out of place and blowing in the wind. However, Ivor never lost focus as he campaigned relentlessly among the porters, fishermen, hucksters, and anyone else on the crowded pier who stopped to shake his hand or to hear his views. Mr. Stevens was never afraid of approaching the common people of Nevis, to do verbal wrestling over ideology or politics. Stevens was not only relentless, he was also very calculating. Every action taken, every friendship made, was a seed sown toward his future politics.

Interestingly, the politics in Nevis had an inheritance of viciousness even then. Nevisians never forgave the British government for forcing a union of St. Kitts-Nevis-Anguilla, into a tri-island colony in 1882. Meanwhile, growing economic prosperity on St. Kitts, and the birth of the labor union there, further pitted the islands against each other. Nevisians who supported the political views held on St. Kitts were ostracized and marked as traitors. Notwithstanding, it was a time when some Nevisians were observing and learning from St. Kitts politics. Many negative aspects of class and party politics had also crossed the channel and infected society on Nevis. During the 1950s, politics on Nevis was in its infancy and open to all who dared to enter. Despite the many factors that appeared to limit his chance for political success on Nevis, Ivor Stevens dreamed about it, then chose to enter the political fray on the island.

Limited political franchise was allowed in St. Kitts-Nevis-Anguilla from 1937 until the coming of universal franchise in 1952. The three persons elected to represent Nevis up to that time were Hubert B. Henville (1937), F. Henville (1940), and Robert J. Gordon (1943, 1946). Two electoral districts were created in Nevis in 1948. R. J. Gordon and James W. Liburd won the popular votes in 1952. Later, the said James Liburd, accompanied R. L. Bradshaw to Trinidad and Tobago, where they served at the West Indies Federation on behalf of St. Kitts-Nevis-Anguilla. Unfortunately, the move toward Caribbean federation was too contentious. It lasted from 1958 to 1962. When that attempt at uniting most of the British West Indian colonies under one federated government fell apart in 1962, Bradshaw equated the effort and its failure to, "A cow giving a bucket of milk, then kicking it and toppling it over." He was very pained by the immaturity and other weaknesses seen in Caribbean politics at that time. However, Bradshaw returned to St. Kitts after the federation effort ended, and wanted to continue a politics as usual stance with Nevisians. Paul Southwell led the islands while Bradshaw served the Caribbean Federal Government, in Trinidad and Tobago.

There were two political constituencies on Nevis, during the 1960s. One combined St. James' and St. George's parishes. That was once dominated by J. R. Gordon, who lived at Fenton Hill. The other combined St. Paul's, St. Thomas', and St. John's parishes. In 1952, that constituency was represented by James (Jimzey) W. Liburd, who had worked on St. Kitts, and was closely associated with the Labor Party. However, Jimzey was from Rawlins Village, in the Gingerland area of Nevis. On his return to Nevis he was set up and encouraged to run in the St. Thomas', St. Paul's, and St. John's area, as a Labor Party candidate on Nevis.

This story, probably apocryphal, illustrates the naïveté among Nevisian voters at that time. It is a story about what supposedly happened during an early election on Nevis, when few Nevisians in St. James' and St. George's parishes could read and write. Apparently, the voters in Gordon's constituency were not happy with his leadership. There was some concern about the lack of material results from his representation in St. Kitts. At that time, because of concerns about literacy among the working class, and in order to ensure enfranchisement for all eligible voters, the voting was done then, and is still done, using specified symbols—a hat, hammer, hand, bottle etc.—on paper ballots. The symbols represented individuals or parties participating in the election. To vote, the letter "X" was placed in a box next to the symbol representing the candidate of one's choice. Since some people were not very adept with the voting process, Gordon reputedly capitalized on their ignorance. Supporters of Gordon were asked to spread the word. "Since the voters are angry with Mr. Gordon, they should "X" him out of office." So, they did. It was later, after the fact, that voters realized they had voted Mr. Gordon back into office, not out of office.

Not long after Stevens returned to Nevis in 1953, both Gordon and Liburd lost their places of dominance in Nevis politics. Gordon was ousted by a 23-year-old teacher from Camps Village, Wilmoth B. Nicholls; Liburd was replaced by the young lawyer from Charlestown, Eugene Walwyn. Ivor Stevens also ran in that election, but he lost to Walwyn. Meanwhile, since labor unionism never took deep roots in Nevis, that reality left the masses on the island less politically astute than their neighbors in St. Kitts. Thus, the earliest politicians on Nevis were largely independent and not party men. Back then, none of the politicians, Gordon, Walwyn, Stevens, or Nicholls, had mass party following and support, as was the case on St. Kitts by the mid-1950s.

However, by the end of the 1950s the time was ripe for a new birth and a new vision of politics on Nevis. Eugene and Wilmoth were young, energetic, driven by dreams of change and new beginnings. With relative ease, they pushed aside the senior politicians from that earlier era. While Ivor was not successful in his first try, he too was there in Nevis dreaming of change through politics. He was looking on and beginning to dream his own dreams for Nevis. Ivor, too, had ideas and wanted to be a decision maker for the island. However, he was destined to be an observer for the next few years, and looked on from outside the Assembly, instead of being at its center. All that time, however, Ivor kept thinking politics and was very careful to keep himself in society's limelight. He remained in campaign mode, meeting people, doing them favors, and he repeatedly introduced himself to voters all around the island. That was a strategy to keep feeling the political pulse of Nevisians, while getting himself well known to everyone.

Based on what he saw and heard while moving around the island, Stevens became even more determined to enter the political arena. There were concerns about water supply, roads in disrepair, lack of electricity, and the ongoing domination of Nevis from St. Kitts. However, the more Stevens saw, the more he became determined and steadfast about becoming a champion for Nevis. He intended to wage a relentless war against underdevelopment, political control from St. Kitts, and the need for a more liberal and inclusive system of education.

To become a player in Nevis politics, however, Ivor had to challenge and get past Eugene Walwyn. It would be a daring challenge, but one that Mr. Stevens accepted with dogged determination. The personal and intellectual demands of that task did prove to be difficult. Walwyn was also an ambitious young man. He was smart, college educated, a lawyer, and as charismatic as Ivor. At first, he was a darling to Nevisians. Eugene was full of confidence about his future as a leader on the island. He was a man propelled by a desire for success. However, Eugene was of darker complexion than Ivor, and in St. Kitts-Nevis, during the 1950s, complexion mattered in social status and perception of self. Like

Ivor, Eugene's father was descended from a well-known emerging, middle class, and an upwardly mobile family. However, Eugene was born to unmarried parents, and reportedly his mother had worked as a maid to Ivor's family. Despite such detracting factors, unlike Ivor, Eugene was born on Nevis, and had a well-connected father, by then an emerging banker on the island.

At that stage during the 1950s, Eugene Walwyn saw himself as being well positioned on Nevis to be the legendary "'one-eyed-man' in a land of the blind." He saw the opportunity and, like Stevens, kept dreaming. He too had vowed to make an important mark on Nevis's history. In time, however, Nevisians came to realize that all of Eugene's motives were not selfless or as lofty as they first appeared. Later, he joined openly with the Labor Party, and at times worked against the wishes of Nevisians. Up until he died in 1995, Mr. Walwyn was still viewed with disdain by many people on Nevis. Archibald (2010, p. 37) noted, "Walwyn was in a hurry, driven by his personal ambition for wealth and political influence in Nevis and St. Kitts."

There was one other towering political hurdle Ivor had to circumvent or overcome. It was labor-union politics in St. Kitts-Nevis, led by Robert L. Bradshaw. Bradshaw's approach to politics and use of labor unionism, allowed him to become self-confident, uncompromising, and a very powerful force in the everyday life of Kittitians, Anguillans, and Nevisians. Most children growing up on the three islands learned about Robert Bradshaw early in their lives. They were taught to love him, or to hate him—at times for the rest of their lives. Nevisians also learned early that their poor roads, lack of water, and everything else that was wrong on the island happened because of Bradshaw's leadership. No one bothered to teach that the colonial system from Britain, superseded and supervised even Bradshaw, in setting the tone and managing the affairs of the islands, at that time. Rather, everything was attributed to Bradshaw and his political style. And, he did little to deflect the criticisms about him being dogmatic, doctrinaire, and divisive. Seemingly, just as the colonialists did before, Bradshaw was focused on understanding how to manipulate the masses and their ideals to win favor for himself and to ensure his political survival. In time, as the British did throughout the Caribbean islands, Bradshaw's politics and policies created two tiered societies in St. Kitts, Nevis, and Anguilla. While Bradshaw came to be accepted as a charismatic leader, he was also playing out the role of a benevolent dictator. Probably, Nevis and Anguilla, more than St. Kitts, bore the brunt of his authoritarian politics.

With Bradshaw as leader, it was held on St. Kitts that politics in Anguilla and Nevis should be derived only from that espoused on St. Kitts by the Labor Party. Even the politicians who emerged on Nevis were expected to pay homage and subject themselves to St. Kitts and its political leaders. But, it was the British who initiated subjugation of Nevis to St. Kitts, back in 1882, to limit the colonial administrative costs to Britain. However, when the administration of the colony shifted to the emerging working-class leadership on St. Kitts, in 1967, Bradshaw accepted the colonial pattern of relationship with Nevis and Anguilla as given. He hesitated about acting to change it. Accordingly, there was a continuous relationship of domination over the other two islands, on the part of St. Kitts. There was also an active attempt to encourage the citizens of Anguilla and Nevis to accept St. Kitts-based politics as the ideal for their islands. However, although the islands were together as three islands in one colony, each island had a distinct system of production, resulting in each island having its peculiar history and a distinct cultural formation. Each group of human beings sees the world differently and hold very distinct ideals for their lives. Anguillans and Nevisians always protested against that union of the three islands, as far back as the 1850s and 1880s. They disagreed that because St. Kitts is the largest of the three islands, and has held economic dominance since the late 1700s, due to its successful sugar industry, that Kittitians should see their island as the only one that mattered among the three that formed the colony.

Thus, for many years, St. Kitts possessed the best infrastructural development of the three islands. It was kept more advanced than Anguilla and Nevis in every way. Demographically, St. Kitts always has the largest population. It also shares a mixture of people from all three islands. Further, because of the prominent role St. Kitts played in the Caribbean labor struggle, Kittitians have historically been much more politically advanced and involved than Nevisians or Anguillans. Meanwhile, there has been an attitude on St. Kitts that sought to stifle any move toward independent leadership development on Nevis or Anguilla. St. Kitts-based politicians acted with intolerance and moved to outmaneuver or kill innovations toward autonomy in Nevis and Anguilla, particularly if such moves were not initiated on St. Kitts or sanctioned by Labor Party politicians. It became increasingly clear to Nevisians and Anguillans that Kittitians felt they were destined to dominate Nevis and Anguilla forever. Ironically, the protest movement on St. Kitts that culminated in labor unionism there, was shaped by similar human dynamics, when the privileged planter-class worked to hinder empowerment and leadership development for the working masses on St. Kitts.

Another critical factor in the St. Kitts-Nevis-Anguilla conflict and dynamics was the marked differences among the three islands in land-ownership patterns, their systems of production, working-class experiences, and other peculiarities brought on by each island's history of production. Not surprisingly, by the 1960s, Nevisians and Anguillans were consistently rejecting the idea of political domination from St. Kitts as naive and unworkable. The new generation of Nevisians and Anguillans wanted more participation in the existing colonial structure. Each island also wanted its indigenous political leadership—not one designed by, or coming from St. Kitts.

Stevens was one of the early politicians on Nevis who increasingly took advantage of the existing and growing anti-St. Kitts thinking on the island. He was among the political activists at the time, who took the lead in opposing the popular thinking on St. Kitts. Stevens also committed himself to organizing, establishing, and institutionalizing a Nevis brand of politics, different from, and independent of that on St. Kitts. Ultimately, Stevens wanted to work with Nevisians to find an alternative path to politics, and a changed future for their island. For him, it had to be a politics with deep roots in Nevis' social and cultural history, and a politics that demonstrated realistic changes from the stifling past. The new politics on Nevis must meet the real and present needs of the island. It must also be prepared to move the island beyond where it was standing—behind time.

In reference to that early, difficult, and intensely antagonistic era between St. Kitts and Nevis, Stevens wrote in 1997,

> The situation in St. Kitts was so maneuvered as to bring further hardship in Nevis, so that emigration became the order of the day for Nevisians, who in some cases nearly gave away their property so as to get enough money to pay their passages to England, which is affecting the country up to now.

By the early 1960s, it had become evident that the endemic animosity between Kittitians and Nevisians was becoming worse, and that loud crescendo of conflict moved on into the 1970s and 1980s. As could be expected, the politicians noticed the trend on the islands and manipulated every event to their benefit. Soon, the different socioeconomic and cultural groups on the islands, separated across a 2-mile channel, engrossed themselves in an intense, unhealthy politics that pervaded every sector of the islands' life. Citizens saw and labeled one another as ugly, greedy, untrustworthy, dangerous, arrogant, superior, and inferior; these perceptions were based on whether one worked on the plantations, owned them, or according to the island on which a person lived.

During that period people said thoughtless, painful things about one another. Politicians on each side of the channel and from the varied political parties tried to secure political dominance, as they worked for the trust of the electorate. For many years in St. Kitts and Nevis, personal political power, more than economic power for the group, empowerment, and inclusion through politics, became the passion of a people struggling to build native Afro-Caribbean leadership. Ivor Stevens was there amid it all, battling for change, new thinking, and new ways of dealing with the future relationship between St. Kitts and Nevis. When voting rights on the islands became more democratized, after 1952, the privilege to vote became a prized possession, attracting people from every class and educational experience. It empowered the working-class, in particular, and gave them confidence they could reshape the islands' future.

Since the colonization of the islands in the 1600s, for the first time, men from the working-class, the planter-class, and the emerging middle-class, 21 years and older, all had the opportunity and wanted to control the islands. Back then, women were either not allowed, or did not find the courage to apply for leadership on the islands. However, on every island women were actively involved and were a part of the great coming-out revolution in the colonies. Notwithstanding their equal passion for change, women were encouraged to lay their effort at the altar of a labor union movement dominated by men. The men were also quite adept at controlling the mobility and influence of women in the organization's leadership. Today, St. Kitts and Nevis still have a poor record of supporting women in politics. Somehow, there seems to be a mythical notion that political leadership on St. Kitts-Nevis is a men's thing.

Probably, one of the most widely heard and best remembered political statements from the 1950s and 1960s, during those battles for minds on the islands, was one supposedly made by Robert Bradshaw. In the statement Bradshaw was said to have vowed to give Nevisians and Anguillans, "Bones in their rice and pepper in their soup," if they refused to accept his leadership and the politics dictated by the Labor Party on St. Kitts. However, everyone forgot that Bradshaw was in a battle for the islands' soul against the planters, who said in 1937 that the Afro-Caribbean people in St. Kitts, Nevis, and Anguilla could not, and did not deserve to govern themselves—hundreds of years after they had been humiliated and dehumanized by a vicious plantation system.[26] If Bradshaw did make that statement, one wonders about the deceptive statements the planter-class was making to Nevisians, Anguillans, and Kittitians,

---

[26] Browne, W. T. (1992). *From Commoner to King*. Lanham, MD: University of America Press.

as they attempted to outmaneuver the emerging working-class leadership, and maintain the status quo. The situation must have made Bradshaw quite desperate, as he challenged the planter-elite status quo, in order to set-up his working-class transformation toward the acceptance of a new and emerging labor union inspired leadership on the islands. Bradshaw must have reasoned that if the masses on the islands persisted with planter-class leadership, they would continue to experience an arrogant, alienating leadership equivalent to having "bones in their rice and pepper in their soup." Seemingly too, Bradshaw was angry that after all the planters had done to humiliate and limit the workers, there were still some people willing to admire and imitate their former "massas." Did people from the working-class, in St. Kitts, Nevis, Anguilla, expect the planters-class to suddenly provide a better life for them because they got the vote? That was what Bradshaw's bone and rice comment seemed to be alluding to. Further, St. Kitts, Nevis and Anguilla were very much one British colony at that time. Britain and the planter-elite, not Bradshaw, had the last say about how the islands were managed.

However, that angry, divisive statement was reported widely in St. Kitts, Anguilla, and Nevis. No one ever queried to what extent it was embellished and used by the planter-class. Neither is it known whether the statement was ever corroborated by Bradshaw. The intensity of class politics on St. Kitts at that time could easily have allowed such a statement to be taken out of context, and manipulated to ensure maximum political mileage for the planters.[27] As far as his wife and others close to him remembered, Bradshaw never took time to confirm or deny the statement. Notwithstanding, it remains one of the buzz statements through which many Nevisians and Anguillans still see and remember Robert Bradshaw.

Whatever the truth or the circumstances surrounding the statement, it found ready acceptance on Nevis, Anguilla, and also on St. Kitts. The planter class and their political party, the

---

27 Browne, W. T. (1992). *From Commoner to King*. Lanham, MD: University of America Press.

Democratic Party, could have easily framed the statement to be used for every bit of political mileage it would bring them among the working-class. At the same time, Bradshaw and his St. Kitts-Nevis Labor Party were being dubbed villains and hated intensely in Nevis and Anguilla. The use of that statement as an example of Bradshaw's disdain for Nevisians and Anguillans contributed to the anger and venom that kept the three people angry and divided over the years. Meanwhile, the recent history of all three islands does seem to suggest it was largely those from the planter, elite leadership, who consistently thwarted the success of workers on the islands. Today, many Kittitians, Nevisians, and Anguillans who have taken the time to reflect and understand where the islands are at this time, see Bradshaw in a different light. They now understand that the workers' struggle on St. Kitts was a deliberate, conscious decision to change the politics of planter domination and control on the islands. In most instances, the new politics has been more humane and a source of unprecedented empowerment for the working-class in the islands. Little wonder, the planter-class responded with such rancor, and sought to control the process, when the right to vote was first offered to workers, in 1937.

Testing the Waters

That was the political melee into which Ivor agreed to thrust and engage himself when he entered Nevis politics in 1957. His early politicking did not matter much to anyone but himself, when he worked quietly in his brother Garnet's garage. During 1956, he accepted a managerial position with H. F. Wildy, one of the earliest firms from St. Kitts to set up a branch of its operation on Nevis. H. F. Wildy sold cooking gas, oil, and soft drinks on Nevis. The enterprise was started long before the St. Kitts, Nevis, and Anguilla Trading and Development Company (TDC) was formed and moved part of its operation to Nevis.

Despite their early relationship, some people felt that after a time, Wildy became concerned about Ivor's politicking, since he spent so much time away from his job talking politics and introducing himself to the people. Accordingly, Stevens' job performance suffered. It was also reported that Wildy feared criticism from the Labor government on St. Kitts. If Ivor Stevens, one of the branch managers for Wildy, on Nevis, became involved in an independent politics on the island, that would be a challenge to the Labor Party. A possible second line of thinking at Wildy was suggested by Mrs. Stevens. "Supposedly, Ivor was to have no political ambitions, particularly if they were not acceptable to the firm, and controlled from St. Kitts."

It was not much of a surprise then, that independent-thinking Stevens left Wildy and went to work for H. F. Henville Co, a Nevis-based firm. By then Ivor had become well known in Nevis as one with political leanings and interest in the welfare of the common man. Stevens had also been dubbed on the island, "the man in the bow-tie," as he campaigned among the workers on the island. There was also the thinking in certain circles on Nevis that Ivor's early politics was shaped by and related to Labor Party politics. At that time, labor union politics was the politics that continued to emerge, to permeate, and to dominate all other political thinking on St. Kitts, Nevis, and Anguilla.

Since the firm H. F. Henville, Co., was run from Nevis; with Stevens working there, he was less concerned about being attacked by St. Kitts politicians. Further, since Nevis was surging into a new political era, with a number of confident young men reaching for change and glory on Nevis, H. F. Henville provided Ivor nurturing and security, as he contemplated and formulated his political vision for the island.

Stevens grabbed all the opportunities to campaign, as they came his way. He also took the time to speak out on critical matters related to Nevis and its domination by St. Kitts. Ivor was very concerned about the general wellness of the island and its people. Accordingly, he immersed himself in understanding all the existing and emerging matters that impacted life on Nevis. Over time, Stevens also secured the friendship of fishermen, the turn-hands, hucksters, and farmers on the island. Mrs. Stevens reflected on her husband's political interests and his altruism at that time. She recalled,

> He was motivated by the fact that people were disadvantaged and he could have spoken for them. He was a member of the Cotton Growers Association. They needed to be able to speak with someone interested in them. During the 1950s, Nevis-based initiatives received very little recognition or support from St. Kitts.

Mrs. Stevens also observed,

> Nevis was neglected by the colonizing British government in England. There was no water, no electricity and very poor roads. When dry periods came, people from Barns Ghaut, Jessups, and Fig Tree had to walk for miles to Charlestown Police Station in order to obtain water.

Those from Butler's and Brickkiln often walked 4, 6, or more miles to and from Madden's Mountain for the precious liquid. During that time in Nevis, life for the ordinary person had become intolerable. There was a dire need for someone to challenge the government on St. Kitts and the British government in England, in order to force changes on the islands.

It was ironic, but Ivor, a Kittitian, was expressing great concern about the struggles of Nevisians, as they attempted to survive and live successful lives on their island. He made a commitment to their cause and began his challenge for change. Admittedly, the interest in Nevis affairs was not all altruism on Ivor's part. This view is borne out when one looks at Ivor's life and political history in its totality. From time to time, Ivor was careful to make subtle references to his superior family background. A number of people on Nevis still believe that color and class were persistent factors impacting the political relationship between Sim Daniel and Ivor Stevens. They were journeying together as leaders in the island's politics, but, there were class and culture factors that separated the two men, and over which each man struggled quietly. Ivor also made occasional references to his roots in Sandy Point on St. Kitts; and, despite Ivor's open shenanigans, it has been established by many people that Bradshaw and Ivor's family always maintained a special friendship. That relationship existed even during the worst political times between St. Kitts and Nevis. Also, while serving as part of the PAM-NRP government leadership, Ivor was the leading person in Nevis to organize, plan, then go the extra mile to bring the two islands closer together.

Mr. Stevens made his first plunge into Nevis politics when he opposed Eugene Walwyn in a contest for the St. Thomas, St. Paul's, and St. John's constituency in 1957. It was the second general election in the islands after universal franchise was legalized by Britain in 1951-52. The voting took place on November 6, 1952. Mr. Stevens' goal was to beat Walwyn and win one of the two Nevis seats in the St. Kitts, Nevis, and Anguilla Legislative Council. Both Walwyn and Stevens were locked in a fight to the finish for that St. John's, St. Paul's, and St. Thomas' seat. Back then, there were just two constituencies on the island and no Nevis Island Administration or local elections.

Elmo Liburd, a former educator from Brown Hill, became a friend, admirer, and confidant of Ivor, after being associated with him in the Nevis Island Administration for a number of years. Elmo did not know Mr. Stevens well, back in 1957, but he recalled some highlights of that election contest. Elmo noted that both Stevens and Walwyn were young and ambitious. They had recently returned to Nevis having experienced life beyond the Caribbean. Both were excited, fired-up, and yearning to move Nevis in a different direction from the one it had taken for most of the 1900s. To them, not much had changed during the years they were away from the islands, so, on their return to Nevis, both men were infected with a sense of altruism, inspired by a growing idealism and hope, mirrored in the future. In quick time, they both stepped forward and offered themselves as change agents to Nevisians—for the island and its politics.

To the best of Elmo's recollection, Ivor ran an unorthodox but skillful campaign. He had his own views, and at times a peculiar perception of things. However, throughout the campaign, Ivor showed genuine understanding of, and commitment to, the poor and powerless on the island. Fishermen, porters, farmers, and other poor workers were among those who became his friends and well-wishers. He met with them regularly, under the sheltered area at the entrance to Nevis pier, called the Iron Shed. Stevens also met with his friends and supporters elsewhere. He was always on the campaign trail. Stevens found where his constituents were, here, there, and everywhere. And he went to meet them.

At times, he even thought it appropriate to condescend and wore a necktie or a piece of rope, rather than a belt, around his waist—just as his fisherman and porter friends did. The vehicles he owned were hardly ever new; they were always old and beaten-up. That was part of Steven's presentation of self: he wanted to appear "like the common man" and to fit in with the Nevis working-class. Those were among Ivor's carefully considered strategies to identify with the masses—to win their trust, their confidence, and in time their votes. Stevens did not have the large, ready-made, and captive labor force in Nevis that Bradshaw had on St. Kitts, so he had to create a reliable group from which to get the numbers he needed. Such secure numbers are what win elections; he had observed this about the labor union on St. Kitts. The strategy meant that Ivor had to devise varied techniques and improvised approaches, to remain in a continuous campaign mode, bringing more and more voters into his friendship and trust.

According to Liburd, "At that time the less educated followed Ivor, while the better educated followed Eugene." When Attorney Eugene Walwyn came back to Nevis, many Nevisians thought "a star is born." Thus, support for Stevens in that 1957 election was not as broad as for Walwyn. The result was that Stevens lost his first contest at the polls. Walwyn went on to join Nicholls as the Nevis representatives to the House of Assembly on St. Kitts. Stevens was disappointed about his loss, but he remained undaunted. Soon he was on the streets and at his usual campaign spots again, preparing for the next election. Later on, Ivor was heard commenting quite frequently, "Win or lose: Once I entered politics I campaigned continuously." Thus, Elmo Liburd's observation was corroborated by Stevens himself. He declared it a normal strategy for his politics.

Secession Talk

During his losing years, Ivor did more than strategize: he persevered. He did not give up after that loss to Walwyn in 1957. Soon, he was back in the trenches campaigning for votes. However, as new talk about Nevis seceding from St. Kitts gathered momentum in 1961, led by Walwyn and Nicholls, Stevens joined in to become part of the demonstrations and marches for secession on Nevis. Since Walwyn and Stevens marched and campaigned together for secession, in a continued show of solidarity in 1961, Stevens decided to forego his own political ambitions, at least for that one time. Accordingly, Stevens put his personal politics on hold and lined up his support behind Walwyn. He did not compete against Walwyn for the election of November 16, 1961. The thinking was growing on Nevis that if Nevisians spoke to St. Kitts and Bradshaw with one voice, someone would probably listen and pay attention. At the time, like most other Nevisians, Stevens thought Walwyn could be trusted to carry a common message from Nevis. Nevisians asked Walwyn to indicate that a new era was emerging on the island and that there was growing need for a changed relationship between the two islands.

It was during that time in the political history of St. Kitts-Nevis when, according to Dr. Keith Archibald, "Nicholls and Walwyn walked out of the Assembly after declaring, Massa day done." Subsequent to that event, the political party, the United National Movement, was formed by Eugene Walwyn, Fred Parris, Wilmoth Nicholls, and James Brooks. The creation of the UNM was one of the strategies designed to bring all the political ideas and forces on Nevis together. At that time a growing body of young, educated, Nevisians was yearning to see change in the existing colonial relationship between St. Kitts and Nevis. There was a demand to win greater self-determination for Nevisians, and a move was also afoot to bring the growing intelligentsia into the center of the emerging movement to transform the island and its politics. Early in the period, although Ivor and Eugene had political and other differences, they were seen together, from time to time, having discussions—an indicator that at one time both men reached beyond themselves and mended some bridges for Nevis.

Even Ivor seemed to have been persuaded to join the United National Movement, after he managed to mute some of his differences with Eugene. They appeared on the same political platform and spoke with one voice, as the new secession movement evolved. There was a time, too, when Stevens and Walwyn marched together for Nevis, demonstrating for secession and against continued domination from St. Kitts. They also participated in collecting signatures of pro-secession Nevisians, and took them to the residence of Administrator H. A. C. Howard on St. Kitts, where they were delivered. In that unprecedented secession demonstration of 1961, on both Nevis and St. Kitts, some 50 to 100 Nevisians went over to demonstrate on St. Kitts, after a much larger demonstration at Grove Park, in Nevis. It was reported that Administrator Howard met the leaders—Walwyn, Nicholls, Parris, and Stevens. He promised to pass on their concern to the British government. Bradshaw was serving at that time with the West Indies Federation Government in Trinidad and Tobago. Reputedly, when Bradshaw heard about the demonstrators from Nevis, his response was colored with disdain. Bradshaw reportedly said, "The masquerades came at Easter." Masqueraders from Nevis usually danced on St. Kitts during Christmastime. It was April 3, 1961, Easter Monday.

However, that coming together of Nevis' new politicians, Stevens, Walwyn, Parris, and Nicholls, was not to last long. Nicholls and Walwyn fell out and became sworn enemies before the election of November 16, 1961. The two men remained enemies until death. By the time of the general election in 1961, Walwyn was accusing Nicholls of plotting to accept favors from Bradshaw, so Walwyn threw his support behind businessman James Brookes, whom he helped and encouraged to oppose Nicholls in the St. George—St. James district. That was a very clandestine move by Walwyn. On his own, man to man, Brookes could not have beaten Nicholls in that election, but he pulled it off with the support of Walwyn. It was Walwyn who attacked Nicholls, stating that he made overtures to Bradshaw. Nicholls later argued that he did so, to win favors for Nevis.

Not long after that move by Walwyn against Nicholls, Walwyn became involved as a champion of pro-labor politics. That move positioned Walwyn for an all-out conflict with Nevisians, and his political downfall on Nevis. Businessman, James Brookes operated a soft drink plant. He might have had political ideas but he was unable to present himself well to the electorate. Brookes simply did as he was told by Walwyn. One election strategy by the Walwyn-Brookes team included the distribution of free sodas in the villages. It was a stunning surprise for Nicholls and for Nevisians, but Brookes won that election by 876 vs. 530 votes. Walwyn, meanwhile, ran unopposed, because Stevens kept his promise and did not oppose him in the election. For many young Nevisians then, that was a first real illustration of how elections can be bought. It was a vote the people of St. George's and St. James' regretted. Meanwhile, that political loss haunted Nicholls until he died on St. Thomas in 1999. He never found the will to forgive Walwyn for his betrayal. That election, however, was the beginning and the end of Brookes' hey-day in Nevis' politics. He was easily beaten by Fred Parris, a People's Action Movement candidate, on July 25, 1966, Parris received 751 votes. Brookes ran as a United National Movement candidate and received 489 votes. Another businessman, Ernest Warner, ran as an Independent. He received 108 votes. Few people took Warner's candidacy seriously.

Today, Nevisians do not remember Brookes for his political skills. They were very limited. During his tenure in the House of Assembly, Brookes' comments to his constituency were always preceded with the statement, "The lawyer [Walwyn] say . . ." It did not appear that Brookes thought or said very much for himself. He is better remembered for catchy one-liners such as "Flour or no flour, NRP; fish or no fish NRP." Not for his politics. These comments were made in 1975, during a critical point in the political development of St. Kitts and Nevis. The Labor Party was campaigning to take St. Kitts-Nevis into independence. It needed political support and approval by Nevisians, so the Labor Party had its own candidates on Nevis. They were Almond Nisbett and Fred Parris. Generally, Nevisians saw them as traitors to Nevis and the popular Nevis Reformation Party. The government in St. Kitts distributed free flour and tinned fish (from UNICEF) in both St. Kitts and Nevis just before the 1975, general election. It was another attempt to win votes on the island through bribery. Nevisians could not be persuaded to think twice about who to support with their votes. Stevens, the Nevis Reformation Party candidate in the St. Thomas, St. Paul, and St. John District received 1,039 votes against Nisbett, the Labor Party candidate's 307 votes. In the St. James and St. George District, Daniel, the NRP candidate received 948 votes, against Parris, the Labor Party candidate's 158 votes. Nevisians were single minded. They took Mr. Brookes' advice, "Fish or no fish it was the NRP; flour or no flour, it was the NRP!"

During 1961, Walwyn accused Nicholls of planning to betray Nevis, and of making overtures toward Bradshaw and his Labor Party. Nicholls responded by suggesting that any move he made toward the Labor Party was a subtle attempt on his part to get some benefits for Nevis, from a powerful controlling government centered on St. Kitts. Walwyn's accusation caught some attention on Nevis. His suggestion about Nicholls also started what became an unwritten political position on the island. Even today, when a Nevis politician is accused of being overly friendly with the Labor Party or its politics, that situation automatically makes his political future on the island questionable. In time, that was also Walwyn's experience. Just recently, for example, in the Nevis local election of July 11, 2011, the cozy relationship between Premier Parry of the Nevis Reformation Party, and Prime Minister Douglas of the Labor Party, was questioned. It mattered little that the relationship has been one of the most productive between Nevis and St. Kitts, up to the present time.

Ironically, a few years after Walwyn's accusatory attack on Nicholls, he made the same political maneuver for which he had accused and derided Nicholls. Walwyn made overtures toward the

Labor Party on St. Kitts and became a member by 1962. The people of Nevis, including Ivor Stevens, became very angry with Walwyn when he made the move to join with the Labor government. He took that direction instead of challenging the Labor Party on behalf of Nevisians, as he had promised to do. There is still agreement on Nevis that greed and personal profit were among Walwyn's chief motivators behind his political actions. Eventually, he did become a virtual outcast on Nevis. Notwithstanding, Walwyn's actions reinvigorated the challenge from Ivor Stevens. He reasoned that the promise Walwyn made to Nevisians had been betrayed. Stevens became very bitter about the betrayal, because he had laid his own politics aside, thinking Walwyn really intended to follow the political agenda Nevisians had come together and set for Nevis. Just as the situation was with Walwyn and Nicholls, Stevens and Walwyn became sworn enemies. They never saw Nevis politics from the same perspective again. As it were, the two men came to a fork in the road. Each one took a different path on his political journey. And they never met again.

It was eventually realized that the political move by Walwyn to oust Nicholls in 1961 was a selfish maneuver. It destroyed what could have been an early productive unity in Nevis politics, and a creative political relationship between two young, aggressive, forward-looking Nevisians, committed to changing the island's future. How did it happen that Walwyn later capitalized on the idea for which he criticized and ridiculed Nicholls—an idea he used to destroy the political career of a colleague, but to build his own? Was Nicholls the teacher more insightful and ethical than Walwyn the lawyer? The three men, Walwyn, Stevens, and Nicholls are all dead now. Walwyn died in 1995, Stevens in 1997, and Nicholls in 1999. Each has contributed to the struggle that transformed the island. They are all on the list of pioneers for Nevis' new politics. However, none of the others won the confidence of Nevisians, or impacted their lives as positively as Ivor Stevens did.

Back in the 1950s, these men brought youth, a different thinking, and initially, a common advocacy for more autonomy on Nevis. They all challenged the status quo situation of having the leadership for Nevis determined by Bradshaw from St. Kitts. In time, however, the conflicts and divisions over the best approach to transform Nevis became very deep and divisive. They were men who were friends, who once were committed and dreamed together about working for Nevis. Later they became sworn enemies—enemies for the rest of their lives. Shortly before he succumbed on St. Thomas, VI, Wilmoth B. Nicholls still spoke angrily and openly about a lack of respect, and his lasting resentment toward Walwyn, but he praised Stevens for his accomplishments in a task he, Nicholls, was forced to leave unfinished. Accordingly, Nicholls expressed little remorse when he received news that Walwyn had passed on. Some 34 years had gone by, however, time had not lessencd thc rancor Nicholls continued to feel toward Walwyn.

For Stevens, the relationship between Walwyn and him never returned to a point of civility and trust. As far as Nicholls was concerned, too much rancor developed between him and Walwyn and it simply festered through the years. For political and other reasons, the relationship between Stevens and Walwyn never returned to a point of mutual respect. Interestingly, as that drive for positive change came to the island, all those men were young emerging stars on the horizon of Nevis' social and political history. Each man had the dream and zest to be placed in the islands' political arena. However, in time, it was that same politics that corrupted the vigor and synergy of their relationships. Despite how far the island has come, one is still tempted to ask, "What would have happened if they had held together, all those years, from 1961; could they have attained that desire which drew them together initially—secession for Nevis?"

Difficult Years

From 1958, on through to the election of 1961 and beyond, times were difficult in Nevis. Initially, C. A. Paul Southwell was at the helm in St. Kitts, since Bradshaw had opted to serve as a West Indies Federation Executive at the federal capital in Trinidad and Tobago (1958-1962); a job for which Bradshaw was praised highly by Palmer (2006). Meanwhile, for Nevisians, there was little light at the end of the proverbial tunnel, in positive changes to their lives. However, Ivor Stevens kept helping Nevisians in whatever ways he could. Two areas of Nevis life where he made crucial contributions at that time were travel between the islands, and transportation of the sugarcane grown in Nevis, from the sugarcane fields to the wharfs for shipping to St. Kitts. During that period, Mr. Stevens owned trucks and boats. The trucks took the sugarcane to the pier at New Castle, or Charlestown. The boats then ferried it across the water to be processed in St. Kitts, at the Basseterre Sugar Factory.

Despite his business ventures, Stevens never lost sight of his desire to be a politician and represent the affairs of Nevis. In 1966, he was ready to oppose Walwyn again in the St. Thomas, St. John, and St. Paul district on Nevis. Like most other Nevisians, Stevens withdrew the trust and confidence he had placed in Walwyn during 1961. At the same time, it was widely known on Nevis that Stevens received the support of the People's Action Movement Party on St. Kitts when he ran against Walwyn in 1966. His wife refuted that thinking. She claimed that her husband never ran for a St. Kitts party, Labor, or PAM. However, a booklet that chronicles past elections, published on behalf of the St. Kitts National Archives by Victoria Borg-O'Flaherty, suggests otherwise. Stevens is listed as having run, officially, as a PAM candidate in the election of July 25, 1966.[28]

Uhral Swanston and Ralph Harris, two political activists in Nevis at that time, also stated emphatically and knowingly that during the early years of his politics, Ivor supported the Labor Party, then later the PAM on St. Kitts. Harris pointed out that during the election of 1957, Bradshaw made statements about "having a man on Nevis." He reasoned that every factor examined at that time pointed to Stevens as Bradshaw's man on Nevis—a position corroborated by others. However, for most of his early politics, Stevens claimed to

[28] Borg-O'Flaherty, V. M. (2004). *20th Century Election Results: St. Kitts-Nevis*. Basseterre, St. Kitts: Author.

be independent. Seemingly, by 1966 something caused a shift in Stevens' thinking, enticing him to move his support to the PAM.

Dr. Keith Archibald was observing the political developments on St. Kitts and Nevis back then. He reflected, "Ivor ran a very good campaign in 1966, but he lost to Walwyn." Archibald also noted that the two men still communicated, even though Ivor withdrew from the Walwyn-organized party, the United National Movement, choosing initially, a more independent posture. He noted, too, that eventually Ivor did shift toward the People's Action Movement. Throughout the 1970s, little changed in infrastructural and economic progress on Nevis. Further, there was the painful human and economic loss, from the sinking of the *Christena.* As time would show, one bright and meaningful light that came to Nevis during those difficult years was the formation of the Nevis Reformation Party (NRP).

Steering the Course

Stevens argued that his loss to Walwyn, by 42 votes, in 1966, was the result of a cheated election, orchestrated by Eugene Walwyn in collusion with his cousin Edread Walwyn. However, despite that second loss to Walwyn, Ivor stayed his course and did not give up. By then the evidence was all over Nevis. The Labor Party and Walwyn were dying forces on the island. Consequently, Ivor continued his organizing and politicking. He intended to capitalize on Walwyn's increased commitment to the Labor Party on St. Kitts and his growing rejection in Nevis. From 1966, through the 1970s, Stevens kept pushing a pro-Nevis agenda, and, in time, a politics he later labeled as *divisionist.* After 1970, Stevens entered one of the most important, decisive, and some persons add, glorious era in Nevis' emerging political history. Through his dogged persistence, Ivor seemed to have seen it all coming, and he was determined to be there, becoming in every way a part of the "Grander Vision" that eventually caught on in Nevis, by the 1980s.

Over time, four critical factors worked in Ivor's favor, so that by 1971, an election win for him became inevitable: First, after the 1966 election, Walwyn committed what for Nevisians became an unpardonable sin. He crossed the floor of the Assembly, to demonstrate his open support for the Labor Party government. Reflecting on that matter, Ivor wrote in 1997,

> NRP was born in 1967 in Low Street as a result of Eugene Walwyn having promised that he would carry the resolution for the Secession of Nevis from St. Kitts. However, the reverse took place in that he neither intended to push nor produce secession in the House of Assembly where constitutionally it should have been first debated; so that when he and his party arrived in England the question was posed, if he had taken it to the House. Having decided in the negative, he was told by the British government that nothing could be done. That was well known to Eugene from the start.

The crossover left the idea entrenched in the minds of Nevisians that Eugene accepted the post of Attorney General, rather than pursuing the Nevis secession issue in the House of Assembly. In other words, he became a supporter of the Labor Party, then cemented his position by stating in public that he would sink his ankles in blood to keep Basseterre the capital of both St. Kitts and Nevis. For Nevisians, such a statement was inexcusable. The statement was made in 1967, but up to his death in 1995, Nevisians never forgave Eugene for making it. He lost their trust as a politician, and as a fellow Nevisian.

A second factor was that in 1967, the Anguillans revolted against their political association with Nevis and St. Kitts, and the move to Statehood in Association with Britain. On February 27, 1967, while St. Kitts and Nevis held formal Statehood ceremonies, the Anguillans staged a mock funeral, signifying the end of their association with St. Kitts-Nevis. This became more formalized by the end of May, and on June 10, 1967, the Anguillans also made an attempt to invade St. Kitts, supposedly with the intent of kidnapping Bradshaw.

The activities staged by the Anguillans were unprecedented in the colony's recent history. They also had a destabilizing impact on the government of St. Kitts, Nevis, and Anguilla, and, to some extent, it impacted the rest of the Caribbean.

In time, Nevisians became very vocal about their situation. Mr. Stevens was at the center of that dissent. Nevisians also started to make threats, suggesting that they, too, would revolt and break from St. Kitts. Meanwhile, a very hurt and angry Bradshaw looked on almost helplessly as matters moved beyond his control. He moved to seek help from other Caribbean nations to invade Anguilla with the aim of restoring his sense of control over the islands. But other Caribbean leaders were uncertain that the government in St. Kitts was making a right decision to invade Anguilla. Bradshaw also stationed troops in Nevis, and on the passenger ferry when it travelled between the islands. Initially, the British seemed skeptical about the matter, but Britain eventually sent troops to Anguilla in March of 1969. Commenting on that incident, Westlake (1972) wrote about, "the British invasion of Anguilla on March 19, 1969, in which nobody was killed, but many people were embarrassed."

The moves by a frustrated Premier Bradshaw toward the Anguillans and Nevisians were very interesting. However, the situation favored Stevens and the other opposition politicians in St. Kitts-Nevis. Meanwhile, the Anguillans were lauded as heroes throughout the Caribbean and elsewhere. There was that infamous attempt from Anguilla to invade St. Kitts, on June 10, 1967, reputedly, to kidnap Premier Bradshaw. However, the opposition politicians assured Kittitians and Nevisians it was a big lie. Later, a number of Anguillans confirmed the invasion. Since he understood how to manipulate such political issues when he saw them, Ivor had a grand time shaping the popular politics on Nevis. He had also become very adept at winning Nevisians over to his viewpoint. At that time, Stevens was very supportive of the People's Action Movement, and the PAM was tied intricately to the anti-Bradshaw events on Anguilla. Later, Nevis Reformation Party politicians also attacked the Labor government about its military outpost on Nevis. However, through the years, the Labor government did not relent.

That outpost existed on Nevis until the Labor government lost the 1980 election. Only then were the soldiers removed from Nevis by the new PAM-NRP government. While Bradshaw did not win independence for St. Kitts, Nevis, and Anguilla, or become the first Prime Minister of St. Kitts-Nevis, he did achieve domination of the islands by labor politics, from the early 1950s until 1980.

The third factor was the sinking of the ferry *Christena* in 1970. After the tragedy, along with its resultant politics, there was further alienation between St. Kitts and Nevis, Their social relations and the islands' politics continued to take on ominous dimensions. Hate and vengeance became common denominators, as the two people interacted with each other. According to Lee Moore,

> The politics of that time exacerbated the tensions between St. Kitts and Nevis . . . . It concretized the hate for Bradshaw and the Labor Party on Nevis. I went to Nevis to hold political meetings with Bryant after *Christena*. Often we were close to being lynched. It did not weld us as a people. It intensified the hate.

Mr. Moore was right. On one of those occasions the crowd was very large and very angry. It refused to allow Mr. Moore and Mr. Bryant to hold their meeting. Many Nevisians still remember that evening by Stanley Henville's shop in Charlestown. There were loud and vibrant displays of anti-St. Kitts, post-*Christena* anger on Nevis. No one wanted to hear Labor Party politicians at that time. Their speeches could not sooth Nevisians, lessen their pain, or change their bewilderment. Even Premier Bradshaw came to fear speaking in Nevis. During that time, when he visited the island, it was always with attending bodyguards. Such protection was considered unnecessary, when he visited Nevis before. After the sinking of *Christena,* the tone of the welcome Bradshaw and the other Labor Party politicians received on Nevis, changed dramatically.

The fourth factor was the formal launching of the Nevis Reformation Party in October 1970. Despite Stevens' claim in his

White Paper that the NRP was formed in 1967, most Nevisians remember the party emerging and gaining momentum in 1970, after the *Christena* incident. Besides, during the 1960s Stevens was moving between the emerging People's Action Movement party on St. Kitts, and an independent politics developing in Nevis.

During the 1970s, the emergence of the Nevis Reformation Party, with Sim Daniel and Ivor Stevens among its leadership, served the death blow to the political success of any Nevisian who supported a political party on St. Kitts. It also ended popular acceptance of any St. Kitts-based political party in Nevis. Fred Parris, the then People's Action Movement representative on the island, soon found himself out in the cold. Nevisians, young and old, at home and abroad, started to demonstrate a high level of nationalism, solidarity, and a political consciousness never seen before. Almost every Nevisian rallied to support the NRP. Few Nevisians were brave enough to show support for any other party on the island. Even Nevisians who claimed to be independent thinkers suffered the wrath, rejection, and suspicion of those who supported the NRP. Not being an NRP supporter meant being labeled a Labor agent or "a wolf in sheep's clothing." Whether the claims were true or not, the strategy worked well for the NRP. Ironically, from 1992 to 2006, when the NRP was out of power on Nevis, it had to take doses of its own medicine, and it did not like how it tasted. None of the political parties likes being in second place, or out in the cold.

With the coming of the Nevis Reformation Party and an overwhelmingly pro-Nevis politics, Stevens beat Walwyn in the 1971 election by 122 votes, 769 vs. 647. Stevens was certain of victory even before the voting began. There was no doubt that the NRP was in a good position, poised to dominate and manipulate the politics of Nevis for the next 21 years. There was perseverance; and Stevens was also helped by a series of favorable political and other events in the history of the islands. In 1980, for example, Mr. Stevens was finally elected to St. Kitts-Nevis government, for the first time. After some 23 years he was legitimized as one of St. Kitts-Nevis's political leaders—a member of the PAM-NRP coalition government. At that time, Stevens was on his way to cement his place as a towering, indomitable political figure in the islands. Generally, he made thoughtful decisions that helped to reshape politics, society, and history on Nevis and St. Kitts, for the next 9 years and beyond. The horror of *Christena*'s sinking seemed to have haunted Mr. Stevens for many years. It appeared that the memory he held of the incident was always a factor, inspiring and propelling his life and politics. Whenever Stevens talked secession from St. Kitts, he also talked about how the *Christena* incident affected society on Nevis. He was there to see it all, and, Mr. Stevens understood how the event shaped his personal life and politics.

CHAPTER 5

THE CHRISTENA FALL OUT

The ferry *Christena* sank on its way from St. Kitts to Nevis some time after 3:30 pm., on Saturday, August 1, 1970. Prior to the incident, there were criticisms about the boat being overcrowded regularly, but no one in St. Kitts-Nevis really believed such an accident could happen, despite reports of strange dreams and premonitions. That afternoon, almost 250 Kittitians and Nevisians, male and female, young and old, were snatched to an untimely death in the ocean. To the people of any small island, such a horrific event can be overwhelming, painful, disorienting, and forever haunting. And, life has been that way for Nevisians and Kittitians, since the accident. To unsuspecting and unprepared Nevisians, in particular, the event was devastating. Its immediate and long-term effect on the social and economic life of the citizenry has been profound. Some people are still grieving and remain somewhat disoriented, as the islands move toward the forty-third anniversary of that sad event in August 2013.

Surveys conducted 15, 28, and 40 years after the accident (in 1985, 1998, and 2010) have suggested some people on the islands are still limited by the mishap. Some of the affected people are still reluctant to talk openly about the accident, the horror they experienced, and how it has impacted their lives. For them, the memories are still vivid and too painful to talk about, so they continue to live in a virtual daze. The *Christena* accident also caused sudden demographic shifts on Nevis. From about the 1950s till now, the population of Nevis has shifted from 14,000 to about 12,000, then to 8,500 people. In August 1970, the population of Nevis was barely more than 8,500, because of the mass deaths, a decline in the childbearing population, and migrations for various reasons, one being the ferry's sinking. There were also some changes in heads of some households. The number of people who died at child bearing age and younger also impacted the fertility rate on the island. It was at a virtual standstill for a number of years after the *Christena* incident.

Many children who lost parents were forced to join other family members elsewhere around the world. Others were taken in by foster parents, but there were those who gritted their teeth and opted to continue life's journey on their own. Over time, the resulting demographic and social realities did come to impact society, the politics, and the economy of the islands. Because of the profound nature of the *Christena* accident and its aftermath, certain political leaders were able to capture the moment. Within 3 months of the event there was the evolution of a new, unified, Nevis politics behind the Nevis Reformation Party. Politicians also used the political momentum they achieved after the disaster to heighten opposition politics on the islands. One of their themes was the uncaring nature of the government on St. Kitts; another, the continued promotion of the idea that Nevis must become independent of St. Kitts. However, at that time Nevisians had little organizational or administrative experience in politics. They were simply determined to build them. Later, as the political arguments shifted, even up to the referendum of 1998, Nevisians were unsure about their financial plan, or the organization that was in place to make secession a viable option for the island. Notwithstanding, the secession idea has remained an inspiration for Nevisians through the years. Meanwhile, there has been no consistent and organized plan in place to see it come true. During the 1980s, Nevis politicians and the people accepted a compromised shadow in place of their real dream. Today, the question is still being asked: Would complete secession from St. Kitts have been a better, more workable alternative for Nevis? However, since no one has a real answer, there are still moans and regrets from the secessionists, every now and then.

It is unfortunate that no one on Nevis has examined the dynamics or prospects of secession seriously and documented the findings. Throughout the 1970s, politicians simply held to the idea of secession because it united Nevisians, kept them emotionally charged, and in theory, seemed more attractive than continuing the link with St. Kitts. Further, the fact that so many Nevisians died on the *Christena,* the incident provided a ready reason to criticize the government on St. Kitts, labeling it as irresponsible, uncaring, and unconcerned about the welfare of Nevisians. Further, the impact of the *Christena* accident made the event an important catalyst for economic, social, and political changes on Nevis. It also led to important changes in the relationship between the people of the two islands.

Despite the horror and emotional despair displayed on Nevis, the *Christena* accident was an event that politicians on both Nevis and St. Kitts used opportunistically. Of course, no one applauded its timeliness, as an aid to the evolution of opposition politics on the islands, but they did examine it carefully to note how the event could detract from Labor politics, while enhancing their personal and party politics. Insightful observers were not surprised that the *Christena* accident served as a precursor to macrochanges, including new political developments on each, and between the two islands. More than ever before, leaders of the Nevis Reformation Party, on Nevis, and the People's Action Movement, on St. Kitts, saw their ability to challenge the Labor government successfully, grow, as anger about the *Christena*'s loss heightened on the islands.

In retrospect, that catastrophic event galvanized and cemented forces that were once disorganized protest groups. At an earlier time, they gathered, vented, then disbanded. Suddenly, thousands of Nevisians became united politically after the accident. They agreed with an unprecedented determination and will, that Nevis needed a politics different from the St. Kitts-derived Labor Party, or its alternative, the People's Action Movement. To Nevisians, although the PAM had begun to offer itself as a path to a new-look politics, it was a St. Kitts, not a Nevis party. Nevisians did support PAM politicians for about a decade, but it was a convenience. At one time, the PAM party offered Nevisians an alternative to Bradshaw and his Labor Party politics. In time, however, PAM came to share that anger Nevisians directed toward the Labor Party. Increasingly Nevisians began to see themselves as maturing, becoming better organized, and increasingly competent at politics. As time took them beyond the *Christena* incident, Nevisians moved to satisfy their yearning for a Nevis political party, and for their own brand of politics centered on Nevis.

Ivor Stevens commented,

> We worked to form a political party as early as 1967. Uhral Swanston and I started meeting at Low Street when we learned that Eugene Walwyn was more interested in betraying us and had no intent of leading a Nevis resolution to withdraw Nevis from St. Kitts, in order to set up our own House of Assembly on Nevis.

Nevisians kept dreaming of the time before 1882, when their politics was independent from that of Anguilla and St. Kitts. They also kept hoping that the evolving period would bring a vibrant politics to the islands, and also more economic development and prosperity for all.

Earlier, Robert Gordon, in the 1950s, and Eugene Walwyn, during the early 1960s, were inspired to make moves with the intent of organizing a Nevis-centered politics, but nothing appeared to provide that organizational glue until the *Christena* disaster occurred in 1970. It was a long, sometimes disappointing effort on the part of Nevisians, but eventually, the sad *Christena* incident became an inspirational and powerful political force on the island. After 1970, the People's Action Movement, the Labor Party, and its surrogate on Nevis, the United National Movement, all declined rapidly on Nevis. As he eulogized Mr. Stevens, Victor Martin, highlighted that in 1970, it was after the *Christena* matter, when Stevens, Uhral Swanston, Sim Daniel, along with some other political activists, came together and cemented the formation of the Nevis

Reformation Party—they were all committed to a better Nevis, no matter the time, the cost, or their backgrounds.

To their credit, Kittitians were forced into radical politics by the plantation system, much earlier than Nevisians. As a group, they started to become politically aware, and began to organize themselves to challenge and resist planter-class domination. The labor movement on St. Kitts and its associated politics, started to organize and became vibrant, during the late 1800s and early 1900s. Very early in the 1900s, men such as Frederick Solomon, James Nathan and others returned to St. Kitts from New York and elsewhere. They had been inspired by ideas such as, Marxism, socialism, and activities related to the Harlem Renaissance. Soon these men began to organize for change in the island's politics. Nevisians in contrast, started to develop a consistent politics much later, beginning in the 1960s. There were united, emotional outbursts against the central government on St. Kitts, but not much more. In time, there were rallies and uprisings in Nevis and Anguilla, during the 1960s. Eventually, the Anguillans revolted and organized an attack on St. Kitts in 1967. Undaunted, the St. Kitts government attempted to organize an invasion of Anguilla. During the same period, defense-force troops were sent to, and stationed on Nevis. The intention was to deal harshly with any open revolt against the central government on St. Kitts.

Meanwhile, on St. Kitts, there was a pattern of challenging every thrust on Nevis toward independent political development. At that time, Nevisians had not experienced a viable political growth or the development of a common political consciousness until after the sinking of *Christena*. Back in the late 1960s, in a survey on political consciousness in Nevis (1967-1968), it was concluded that because of the history of labor unionism on St. Kitts, the average Kittitian and Nevisian living on St. Kitts was more politically aware and had developed a greater understanding of political action than the average Nevisian living on Nevis. Of course, some of the political responses among the masses on St. Kitts, might well have been based more on survival consciousness, than on critical analysis of the emerging politics.

Further, in Nevis, despite Stevens' inside knowledge of the early political process, and his claim for a 1967 start of the Nevis Reformation Party, most Nevisians recall that the emergence of the mass-supported, vibrant Nevis political party happened after *Christena* sank. These two factors in Nevis's history, the sinking of the ferry *Christena*, and the formation of the NRP, should be remembered as being closely related and linked in time.

The anger, pain, and the frustration from the loss of loved ones, coupled with a general feeling of neglect from St. Kitts, drove Nevisians to search for a new and different relationship with the government. Consequently, Nevisians sought a less dependent relationship in what they saw as a controlling, insensitive colonial politics. They desired instead, a politics dictated by Nevisians, on Nevis, rather than the uncompromising politics driven by fear of, or subjugation to, the Labor government, and ideas vetted only by the political parties on St. Kitts.

A discussion with former St. Kitts-Nevis Attorney General, then later Premier, the late Lee L Moore, clarified how he understood the *Christena* incident as a factor shaping the islands' attitudes and politics.[29] According to Moore, "The new politics exacerbated the tensions between St. Kitts and Nevis, solidifying the hatred for Bradshaw and Labor on Nevis." Moore further noted, "When Bryant and I went to Nevis to hold political meetings, after the *Christena* incident, we came close to being lynched. The *Christena* disaster did not weld us as a people. It intensified the hate."

Thus, one major fallout from the *Christena* disaster was the further calcification of a Nevis politics, antagonistic to that on St. Kitts. It also provided Nevis politicians a focused mission, demonstrated by their anti-St. Kitts actions. Eventually it all became a driving force in the new, emerging Nevis vs. St. Kitts politics for almost the next three decades. The important mission that inspired Nevis politicians during the 1970s was the separation or secession of the Nevis government from that of St. Kitts. Nevis was too dependent and

---

29 Browne, W. T. (2001). *The Christena Disaster Revisited.* Charlotte Amalie, St. Thomas, VI: BL&E Enterprise.

in dire need of infrastructure development. Admittedly, the thrusts and arguments for more autonomy on Nevis started way before the *Christena* incident. However, the *Christena* matter did come to define and propel Nevis secession politics from the 1970s, through the 1980s, and beyond. During that time, Nevisians struggled with pain and great loss, agitated, then moved to revisit and reinvigorate their long and dormant political gripe—secession from St. Kitts.

Despite the aspirations of Nevisians, however, they had no recent experience in managing the affairs of their island. Since 1882, they had become a dependent people with their affairs increasingly managed from St. Kitts—one of the glaring reasons why so many Nevisians were caught on *Christena* that fateful afternoon. It was therefore some condescension for the Labor government, and a new beginning for Nevisians, when, just prior to the coming of Statehood, February 27, 1967, and following the advice of a British political expert, the Local Council Ordinance No. 2 was passed in the St. Kitts-Nevis House of Assembly. After that Bill, a fully *nominated* body of persons was sworn in as representatives on Nevis, February 27, 1967. That provided for a Local Council to be the chief facilitator, in a new and unprecedented Nevis Local Government: it was intended to be, one on Anguilla, and one on Nevis. However, the Anguillans never subjected themselves to the new arrangement supervised from St. Kitts. They resisted any further affiliation with the government there. A few months later, the new ordinance was superseded by the Local Council Act of November 4, 1967. However, for Nevisians, it was an evolutionary political process. Despite some structural change, Nevisians still felt colonized. They had limited autonomy in their island's politics. By November 23, 1971, with the *Christena* disaster on everyone's mind, the Nevis Reformation Party heightened its rhetoric in the argument that St. Kitts should be removed from dominating and controlling Nevis politics. Thus, the Local Council Act, was amended again, giving unprecedented power to the Nevis Local Council. Accordingly, the government in St. Kitts lost the authority to *nominate* members of the governing body in Nevis; they must all be elected in Nevis, by Nevisians!

The candidates for the Nevis Reformation Party won most of the seats in the local government election in Nevis in December 1971. The NRP controlled 6 of the 9 seats after the party campaigned relentlessly for secession, particularly because the two islands had achieved Statehood in 1967, and more authority was passed from the British government to the Labor Party government on St. Kitts. Only St. Kitts and Nevis participated in the general election held May 10, 1971, 4 years after Anguilla broke away from the three-island colony. An invasion by 315 British paratroopers in 1969 was "a witless attempt to put the rebellion down."[30] Up until 1980, the Anguillans were still defying any authority from the government on St. Kitts. Eventually, the British government allowed the Anguillans a special colonial arrangement. They were granted a political arrangement outside the control of St. Kitts. Nevisians were not as successful in their quest for complete separation from St. Kitts. In retrospect, the physical location of Nevis and Anguilla in relation to St. Kitts must have been a factor in the evolving political decisions. However, as time surges into the 21st century, Nevisians and Anguillans still ponder and question how British colonialism haunted and shaped their islands' political destiny.

The desire by Nevisians to achieve secession from St. Kitts was taken to another level by the NRP politicians. They moved quickly to consolidate their power in the Nevis Local Council and on the island. Nevis politicians were also confident that the citizenry supported their every action. There was a symbiotic relationship between NRP politicians and the electorate on the island. The better the politicians on Nevis became organized, the more they could argue the case for the development of a better Nevis, as they won increasing support from the people throughout the island. There was also an emerging and growing political consciousness on the island, even religious leaders became politicized. Meanwhile, an inspired and determined NRP political team, kept fighting the cause of Nevisians—in the process, becoming the island's tried and tested

---

30 Westlake, D. E. (1972), *Under an English Heaven.* New York, NY: Simon & Schuster, p. 11.

champions. Accordingly, politics on Nevis became aggressive, vocal, and demonstrative. On December 19, 1970, three Nevis politicians sent a petition to Joseph Godber, the British Secretary of State for Commonwealth Affairs seeking more autonomy for Nevisians. On learning about the petition, Mr. Bradshaw responded with disgust and contempt. He wrote a terse note to the Permanent Secretary of Home Affairs, to whom the letter and petition from the NRP had been forwarded by Mr. George Bradley, Government Secretary on Nevis, to the Secretary of State, and to the then Governor, Sir Fred Phillips. Bradshaw wrote,

> Mr. PS, Home (Mr. Permanent Secretary of Home Affairs)
>
> If, as it seems, Mr. Bradley, the Government Secretary in Nevis actually acquiesced to the wishes of Daniel and his jokers, to forward a copy of their so-called petition to the Chairman of the Nevis Local Council then I would be surprised. Surely the port is available to Daniel!
>
> Please simply circulate their nonsense to Hon. Members of the Cabinet, starting with the Hon. Dep. Premier.
>
> RB, Prim. 31/xii/70. (see Appendix B for original text).

Despite Bradshaw's attitude of disdain, the Nevis politicians came together in the Nevis Island Council and reiterated their argument for independence from St. Kitts. It came in the form of a resolution during a meeting March 8, 1974. Then, on April 17, 1974, the two elected opposition members in the House of Assembly, Simeon Daniel and Ivor Stevens of Nevis and the NRP, introduced the identical resolution in the House of Assembly on St. Kitts. Debate on the matter was never completed. On that occasion, Mr. Stevens outdid himself and spoke on the issue for about 25 hours. He started on April 17, 1974 and dominated the Assembly until April 19, 1974. Just over one year later, in August 1975, both sides agreed that further debate on the resolution should discontinue, and that Nevis' grievances should be addressed in a different forum. Accordingly, two meetings were arranged, one on each island. However, the secession matter was never resolved. Meanwhile, the government on St. Kitts had actively started to seek political independence for St. Kitts-Nevis.

On Nevis, however, there was intense opposition to any Bradshaw-led government in St. Kitts-Nevis. This thinking was passed on to the children from very early in their life. They learned that Bradshaw hated Nevisians and treated their island unfairly. That sudden drowning of numerous Nevisians on the *Christena* was used repeatedly as evidence. Consequently, for Nevisians, the *Christena* incident and its aftermath united and invigorated their opposition on the island. It also inspired an attitude of revolt from the Nevis Reformation Party on Nevis and the People's Action Movement party in St. Kitts. However, Ivor Stevens, more than anyone else, invigorated and carried the post-*Christena* attack on the Labor government in St. Kitts. It was Mr. Stevens, along with businessmen Levi Morton, Rhoan Liburd, Horace Liburd, Ralph Harris, and Uhral Swanston, who spearheaded the initial NRP opposition venture. Sim Daniel, a lawyer, was invited to join the group later, as the opposition evolved and solidified.

When the *Christena* tragedy occurred, there was political festering on all three islands. It would not have mattered who formed the government; such a dramatic and tragic event would have had a profound and overwhelming impact on the islands, affecting political relations and everything else. During the 1970s, neither the colonial government's machinery, nor the people's political, social, or philosophical consciousness, was prepared to manage and deal effectively with the impact of such a sudden tragedy. Generally, the responses were disorganized, at times self-serving, at other times inept. The ferry had a history of overcrowding; its system of communication was very poor; the security system aboard the ferry was ineffective; and the crew was barely trained to work on such a large passenger ship. Further, when the inevitable criticisms about *Christena's* operation were leveled by citizens, including members from the opposition political parties, the leaders in government chose to respond with political rhetoric for political rhetoric. Nothing was done to correct the problems—some of them glaring. The Labor Party government had been in power too long, had become too dominant, and was too distracted by the unprecedented and growing opposition from the nonplanter-class to see truth! Only feeble attempts were made to correct problems on the ferry. Meanwhile, attack as best defense did not help Premier Bradshaw, Deputy Premier Southwell, Minister of Education Bryant, or Attorney General Moore.

Nevisians and Kittitians were very angry. They brooded for a long time about their painful *Christena* losses. Despite the government's effort at diversion and push back, most citizens thought that government deserved blame for the mishap. On both St. Kitts and Nevis, the sudden loss of family and friends exacerbated the pain and psychological impact of the disaster on citizens, for many years. Few Nevisians and Kittitians are surprised that the aftermath of the disaster left indelible marks on the politics and society of St. Kitts-Nevis.

Shortly after the accident, Fred Parris, one of the then sitting representatives for Nevis in the House of Assembly (the other being Eugene Walwyn) commented on the disaster to the *San Juan Star* newspaper of Puerto Rico. His general theme was that the *Christena* incident gave a boost to the idea of Nevisians wanting to secede from St. Kitts. He said, "The loss of so many citizens from Nevis reopened serious historical grievances between the two islands." It was also noted that many of the statements the government made were false and could not be supported by available facts. Everyone knew that while the *Christena* was registered to take 155 passengers, it carried well over 200 on a regular basis. Later, it was admitted by the first-mate, Frank Tyson, that poor seamanship among the crew, not the overcrowding on the ferry, was the most critical factor leading to the ferry's sinking.

Despite the weak position of government in the matter, Bradshaw responded to Parris' criticisms about the sinking with anger, and with his usual disdain toward protests from Nevis. He even suggested Parris might have to answer in court for some of the statements he made about the event. Whenever there was criticism from Nevis, Bradshaw became angry: he was never compromising. At times too, Bradshaw made thoughtless statements about matters related to Nevis that he regretted later. Meanwhile, Stevens, Daniel, and the People's Action Movement politicians used the *Christena* matter and for a brief period, a growing political support on Nevis and St. Kitts, to taunt and challenge Bradshaw up until he died in 1978. It is still believed that the revolt on Anguilla and the fallout from the *Christena* accident were important factors that haunted Mr. Bradshaw's life. Together, they brought him debilitating stress which caused the return of a prior illness, and his eventual demise.

The next general election was legally due less than one year after the *Christena* disaster, and would be a test of strength for the government. In the inherited British electoral system on St. Kitts-Nevis, government controls the timing for elections. The people also needed some time to forget the incident. However, for the opposition parties, the People's Action Movement and Nevis Reformation Party, the loss of about 250 lives from the islands remained an unforgettable election issue. Meanwhile, there was also growing discontent with the government on St. Kitts. Scores of younger, better educated Kittitians were leaving the Labor Party to rally with the PAM party. However, that symbiotic relationship between sugar workers and the Labor Party politicians on St. Kitts remained a critical election matter. Further, by that time, Robert Bradshaw had undoubtedly become the grand master of St. Kitts-Nevis politics.

Notwithstanding the machinations of Bradshaw and others, fewer and fewer Nevisians supported the Labor government after the 1970s. Instead, the general population on Nevis kept suing for changes in their political relationship with St. Kitts. They were energized by the new politics espoused by Nevis Reformation Party politicians, and were determined to stay the new course. One night, shortly before the general election of May 10, 1971, a group of Labor Party politicians went to Nevis for a political meeting. When Bryant and Moore attempted to address the people, the meeting was disrupted immediately. Police could not hold back the angry Nevisians. They were in no mood to hear anything from Labor Party politicians. Lee Moore commented later that relations between the two islands deteriorated after the *Christena* sank.

In 1971, Eugene Walwyn and Ivor Stevens opposed each other again for the seat from the St. Thomas, St. Paul, and St. John constituency. It was not the same battle for a third time. The circumstances had changed. Stevens and other Nevisians understood that once Walwyn openly shifted his support to the Labor Party he could not win another election in Nevis. Walwyn's political bridges on the island had been burned forever. Most Nevisians felt betrayed when he took a pro-Labor position on three vital matters: Secession, the *Christena* incident, and the Anguillan revolt. Further, by 1966, Walwyn had done to Nevis exactly what he accused Nicholls of doing in 1961, when he caused Nicholls to lose his seat to Mr. James Brooks, in the St. James and St. George's constituency.

Ivor Stevens, meanwhile, made the *Christena* issue his political motto and focus. He kept its memory alive. Meanwhile, Stevens worked overtime to destroy the Labor government as sweet revenge for the *Christena* matter and for other reasons. Up to 15 years later, the disaster remained one of Stevens' most frequently used points for criticism of the Labor government. During the entire period, Stevens remained a major player in, and an important benefactor from *Christena* politics. He skillfully captured and caressed the new energy in Nevis politics, as the disaster brought back to life old, but powerful themes in the St. Kitts vs. Nevis saga. At one time, Stevens was among those who argued that because the government on St. Kitts neglected Nevis for so long, the future success of Nevisians lay in complete secession from St. Kitts. Further, because the leadership on St. Kitts failed in Nevis, only Nevisians can best understand and direct the affairs of Nevis. Stevens also noted that despite the deep blood relations and close proximity between the islands, Kittitians and Nevisians are two separate people, the product of different cultural formations, derived, more recently, from two different systems of economic production.

While Mr. Stevens was never the official leader of the Nevis Reformation Party from its launching in 1970 until he retired from active politics in 1989, Stevens was a leading activist, an astute strategist, and a leading spokesman for the party. Whenever he saw a political opportunity, Ivor sought to maximize it to his party's benefit. Also, because he openly tried to demonstrate a special empathy for the common people, Ivor Stevens often worked to project their hurt and helplessness. As he spoke, Mr. Stevens brought drama and new meaning to the Nevis experience.

Ultimately, for many Nevisians, the facts surrounding the ferry's sinking became the proverbial "last straw" in disrespect and unconcern for Nevisians. En masse, they criticized and rejected the uncaring government on St. Kitts. However, Nevisians still had need for a crutch and for a hero. Ironically, Ivor had observed Bradshaw at a similar stage in St. Kitts politics, as he struggled to secure political authority and credibility for the masses, through labor unionism. There was no powerful union on Nevis, but the *Christena* accident served a similar role. It brought Nevisians together. Mr. Stevens strategized and captured the moment. Within a short time, he became the most vocal, most charismatic, and most vibrant of the emerging Nevis politicians. He used the *Christena* incident continuously as he agitated against the Labor government on St. Kitts, while building a relatively secure political base for himself in Nevis.

At first, *Christena*-related politics did little to enhance the economic or social well-being of Nevisians. Nevis politicians were aggressive, not humble, and Bradshaw's government was too angry at the political upstarts to concede authority, or to help their political cause. Thus, throughout the 1970s, neither Daniel nor Stevens achieved much legislative success. It was reported that there were threats by Stevens that Nevisians could revolt, as the Anguillans did in May 1967. Accordingly, they would take over the inter-island ferry that replaced the *Christena,* and keep it in Nevis. Such talk did provoke Bradshaw into making a show of force. There were open displays of weapons, including large intimidating guns; and a deployment of well-armed soldiers to Nevis. Soldiers from St. Kitts made frequent and unprecedented visits to Nevis, and were known to have carried out special operations around the island. In the process, Nevisians came to see themselves as being under siege from the government on St. Kitts. However, Mr. Bradshaw was determined to have no repeat of that revolt he could not end in Anguilla.

Despite regular protests from Nevis, for a number of years, soldiers remained stationed on the ferry and on the island. That angered Nevisians, and left them increasingly dependent on the ideas and the leadership of Nevis Reformation Party politicians. One of their tactics was to walk out of the Assembly on a regular basis. Ivor spoke on the merits of secession for some 25 hours, and they refused to attend certain legislative meetings. However, while they managed to stage delays and interruptions in the Assembly, at that time, neither Daniel nor Stevens found an effective strategy to change St. Kitts' control of socioeconomic progress and infrastructural development on Nevis, through the existing legislative arrangement. The August 18, 1977 referendum on secession was a protest against the stationing of soldiers in Nevis, on the ferry, and against the deteriorating relationship between the islands. However, such matters remained unresolved until a change of government came in 1980.

Stevens understood quite well that those *Christena* years were not productive years for Nevisians. But, because he was a good actor, Stevens used every opportunity he found to dramatize, insult, frustrate, and show open resentment toward Bradshaw's government. Everyone knew about the hostility within the inter-island politics. There were also those occasions when the show of non-cooperation by Daniel and Stevens appeared overdone and out of time. But, there was a long, long history of political bantering and acrimony between the two islands. It would take unusual actions, including political risks, to bring about change.

Interestingly, a source once closely aligned to Stevens pointed out that despite Stevens' show on Nevis, Bradshaw and Stevens met occasionally on St. Kitts, and had tea at the home of dentist, Cecil Stevens, Ivor's brother. During such meetings, Bradshaw might have even discussed concerns in the Labor Party with the Stevens' brothers. For example, Ivor related to Hubert Brand that during one of those meetings at Cecil's place, Bradshaw leaked the story about Southwell's questionable investment of some $250,000 of government's money in a fool's gold scheme in Africa. Later, Ivor used that matter for political mileage; it provided variety, however briefly, from his obsession with the *Christena* and secession politics.

Dora Stevens remembers that period well. This is a part of what she recalls:

> The *Christena* period, 1971-1980, was the talking years. He was in opposition to Labor and not much was achieved. Secession became the big issue, and it was very frustrating. There was so much to be done on Nevis and so little being achieved at the time.

Joseph Parry, a Nevis Reformation Party stalwart, now its leader and one-time Premier of Nevis, worked with both Daniel and Stevens. In describing how the party managed to maintain itself during that time, Parry claims that it was Ivor who kept the party from capitulating to Bradshaw. Other knowing insiders indicated that Sim Daniel wanted to give up several times. There was also one point when Bradshaw tried to undermine the NRP, offering Daniel a position as magistrate in St. Lucia. The story is that Daniel relented only when an angry Uhral Swanston threatened to attack him with a truck's crank handle, if he dared to accept the position from Bradshaw.

As recently as August 1998, Nevisians were asked, again, to vote their preference on the secession matter. Earlier, even as Nevis and St. Kitts agreed on a constitution for a federal arrangement in 1983, secession for Nevis, on demand, was written into the constitution as Clause 113. There have been reports that it was Stevens who insisted on that clause being written into the constitution, at least temporarily. Meanwhile, despite Stevens' politicking, the period

1971-1980, as Mrs. Stevens noted, resulted in little legislative success for Nevis. However, Ivor's politics did cement in the minds of Nevisians that there was the possibility of secession and a totally independent Nevis. Further, Clause 113, of the St. Kitts-Nevis Constitution, makes secession for Nevis a vibrant, living idea, even though it has not always been feasible. It was that possibility for secession, embedded in Clause 113, that encouraged the referendum of 1998.

Robert Bradshaw died May 23, 1978. The dream that his Labor Party would lead St. Kitts-Nevis to independence fell apart then. A number of factors, including the revolt on Anguilla in 1967; the sinking of the *Christena* in 1970; the coming of the Nevis Reformation Party in 1970; the intransigence of Nevis leaders and their failure to cooperate with the Labor Party during the 1960s and 1970s; and the eventual death of Robert Bradshaw in 1978, should be seen as critical events that contributed to the Labor Party's failure in its attempt to lead St. Kitts-Nevis to political independence. There was also a sixth factor that undermined the process. It was the arrogant leadership and attitude of Lee L. Moore, 1979-1980. Almost singlehandedly, he caused the Labor Party to lose the election of February 1980. By 1980, the Labor Party had carried and dominated the politics of the colony for some 28 years. It had a long history of dictating the politics in the colony, even back to the time of early resistance politics on Nevis, during the 1950s, when Eugene Walwyn and Ivor Stevens returned to the island, dreaming of power, glory, and change through politics.

Eugene Walwyn, Ivor Stevens, and Robert Bradshaw

When Ivor appeared on the political scene in Nevis, he was somewhat of a stranger there. Many citizens on the island knew his parents—not Ivor. Some remembered seeing him growing up. But he had left the island and lived elsewhere for more than 20 years. Consequently, Ivor was not well known to most of the electorate, and had to reintroduce himself. Meanwhile, he was up against Eugene Walwyn, a bright young lawyer, newly out of college, and with strong family support on the island. Eugene had also been away from the island, but not as long as Ivor. Such positive factors for Eugene were not in Ivor's favor. Further, Stevens was born on St. Kitts, and neither of his parents was from Nevis.

Franklyn Brand noted that

> Eugene Walwyn brought a new dimension to politics and society on Nevis at that time. He was seen and eventually accepted as a very worthy contender to replace the old guard politics, and to enjoin the struggle against Bradshaw. His clashes with Stevens were something to note, and would evolve with time. Later it came to be assumed that more than just political animosity existed between Walwyn and Stevens.

Mrs. Stevens and sister May indicated that there might have been other reasons for, "bad blood," between the two men.

When both men declared themselves for Nevis and experienced their first joust at the polls in 1957, Walwyn won handsomely. In fact, sentiment during that period was so pro Walwyn, it appears that had he been patient, less mesmerized by materialism, and kept the faith with Nevisians; he could have been the kind of hero-politician in Nevis that Bradshaw became on St. Kitts. When Walwyn entered politics on Nevis, the people there saw light in the tunnel and anticipated a brighter future on Nevis for the first time in their generation. Nevisians saw a young man whom they thought could be their politician champion, and hopefully, a savior from Bradshaw and St. Kitts. Consequently, in that election of 1957, Stevens was no threat to Walwyn. He beat Stevens with a vote of almost 2 to 1. Nevisians believed in Walwyn and they showed it. They were suspicious and unsure about Stevens. He was a stranger and a Kittitian!

Despite the confidence the electorate placed in Walwyn's leadership, Stevens still wanted to be one of the political representatives on Nevis; and in the very constituency that was then dominated by Walwyn. For Stevens, "failure was not an option," in his desire for political office. He was convinced that if placed in an elected position, he could effect the type of change Nevisians were seeking in their struggle against St. Kitts, during the 1950s and 1960s. One aim was to achieve more autonomy for Nevis and less control from St. Kitts. Nevisians needed development of their basic infrastructure, including water, electricity, regular work, more efficient government, and opportunities for higher education. Stevens' divisionist ideal sprung from his observation of the differences between the islands, and how he came to understand these problems could be resolved. In time, his political and ideological commitment came together in one desire: Nevis above all else. As Norman Jones noted, "Ivor understood the psychology of politics. He did not wait until election-time to campaign. He campaigned daily. He interacted with his constituency constantly." Ivor really wanted to change what he saw on Nevis while the British and Bradshaw dominated the island.

Victor Martin remembers Ivor as a man of action who viewed electoral politics as serious business. He campaigned at the Iron Shed, at Chapman's, at the beach, and at the Base area. Ivor was always in campaign mode. He reached out and interacted with people in and outside his constituency. During 1961, Nevisians rose up in protest against the increase in the cotton tax. There was an appeal for political solidarity on the island against the Bradshaw-led government. In response, Walwyn promised to carry Nevis' cause to the House of Assembly, and Stevens trusted him to do so. An unfair percentage increase was added to the cotton export tax by the St. Kitts based and Bradshaw-led Assembly. Walwyn promised Nevisians he would fight against the cotton tax increase and argue the case of secession for Nevis. In lieu of that promise, Stevens made a magnanimous gesture. He chose not to oppose Mr. Walwyn in the 1961 election. Arthur Evelyn, businessman and at one time politician, referred to Ivor's remarkable and selfless gesture then as "A high level of political statesmanship."

However, Stevens was let down. Walwyn did not follow through with his promise to stand in the Assembly, to present a case for

Nevis' secession, then, or later. After that, the two men treated each other with civility, but Walwyn would never receive a high level of trust and confidence from Stevens again. Walwyn had also betrayed all other Nevisians who rallied behind his leadership and trusted him to lead Nevisians in the secession matter. Instead, Walwyn connived to aggrandize himself, then he moved to betray Nevis, by negotiating a close political relationship with Paul Southwell, the then leader of the St. Kitts, Nevis, and Anguilla Government, (1958-1966). The premise for that growing relationship between Southwell and Walwyn was that Bradshaw, who at that time served with the Caribbean Federal Government in Trinidad and Tobago, 1958-1962, was the real problem for Nevis, not the government on St. Kitts.

Stevens and other Nevisians, who were struggling to find a way to limit control of St. Kitts over Nevis, disagreed with Walwyn's reasoning. They suspected he was leaning full-time toward the Labor Party. He had no real interest in changing the fortunes of Nevis. That view was soon confirmed when Southwell created a tourist board in St. Kitts and appointed Walwyn as its chairperson. Thus, Nevis lost both Nicholls and Walwyn, two of its contemporary spokesmen for autonomy. Walwyn accused Nicholls of caving to the Labor Party. But even with that knowledge, he too was enticed by, and won over to, Labor Party politics on St. Kitts. Meanwhile, there was emerging new thinking on St. Kitts-Nevis, and growing unprecedented shifts in Caribbean politics. These developments brought other challenges to the Labor Party and its leadership, at a time when they sought to continue the traditional domination of St. Kitts, Nevis, and Anguilla.

The People's Action Movement party, a derivative of the previous planter-class-dominated, Democratic Party, emerged as a major political party on St. Kitts by 1965. It was ready to confront the Labor Party as the leading opposition political party in the 1966 election. The PAM organization also went to Anguilla, and to Nevis, in search of political support, and to counter the Labor Party's success on these islands. The PAM's intention was an attack on each island against Bradshaw and his Labor Party. Peter Adams joined the new party and became its candidate in Anguilla, whereas Fred Parris and Ivor Stevens became candidates for the PAM on Nevis.

According to Uhral Swanston, he and Stevens met frequently with executives of the PAM Party, and Stevens did run in the 1966 election under the banner of the PAM. That fact was also corroborated by Borg-O'Flaherty. She noted that Stevens ran as a candidate for the PAM party in 1966.[31] It appears that even if Stevens made a long-term commitment to PAM at that time, Swanston did not do so. Swanston noted, "We continued to struggle and kept toying with the idea of forming a political party for Nevis." When the NRP came along and pushed aside Fred Parris, the PAM candidate, he turned to the Labor Party for support, and he too lost the respect and goodwill he had built on Nevis.

Walwyn beat Stevens again in that 1966 election by 42 votes (834 to 792). Stevens remained undaunted by his second loss to Walwyn and continued campaigning. He made and lost a legal challenge against his 42-vote loss, since he surmised it was fraudulent politics. In time, however, Stevens became reconciled to that second loss and went back to the campaign trail. He also managed to remain actively involved in society, taking social responsibilities as if he were one of the elected politicians for Nevis. Mr. Stevens gave advice, expressed his views about events on the island, and kept himself in the limelight by doing whatever he could to bring positive benefits to Nevis and Nevisians. Stevens was in the center of the activity, along with persons such as, Arthur Evelyn and George Bradley, the afternoon when *Christena* sank. The people did notice. They appreciated his service and commitment.

During that early political period, Ivor made suggestions to the government as to how the agriculture program in Nevis could be enhanced. The plan was presented to St. John Payne, then a minister with the Labor government. He reputedly took the information to Bradshaw, thinking the suggestions were useful. Supposedly,

---

[31] Borg-O'Flaherty, V. M. (2004). *20th Century Election Results: St. Kitts-Nevis*. Basseterre, St. Kitts: Author.

Bradshaw responded, "Nevis shall be run as I want it to." He did not appreciate any suggestions from Nevisians about Nevis. It was the position Bradshaw took, again and again, about Nevis affairs.

With the failure of the British-contrived West Indies Federation (1958-1962), Bradshaw returned as leader of St. Kitts, Nevis, and a reluctant, protesting Anguilla. When Bradshaw opted for statehood in 1967, Nevisians and Anguillans both saw it as a wrong political move. That kind of relationship, without prearranged concessions, would increase Bradshaw's power over the islands. The Anguillans staged open protests, inspired and incited by their People's Action Movement connection on St. Kitts. On June 10, 1967, there was a daring but failed raid on St. Kitts from Anguilla. Supposedly, the intent was to kidnap Bradshaw and take him back to Anguilla as a hostage.[32] That tumultuous and unsettling event was an unprecedented act in the history of the then British affiliated Caribbean. Later, similar political disruptions were noted on Grenada, in 1979; there was an attempted overthrow of government in Dominica, 1981; and, an unprecedented attack on the government in Trinidad and Tobago, 1990. Undoubtedly, that St. Kitts incident had a profound impact on the history and politics of the three islands. Bradshaw, the astute politician that he was, could not bear to see himself pushed aside by the Anguillans. He was also virtually ignored by Britain and the Caribbean leadership. Bradshaw was not allowed to have his way in resolving the Anguillan revolt matter. Meanwhile, the Anguillans' position was almost openly supported by Britain, and by other Caribbean governments. Supposedly, the resultant stress did have a devastating impact on Bradshaw's future life and politics.[33]

By February 27, 1967, Britain awarded the islands a new constitution and moved them to a ministerial system of government. They were on their way to independence—Statehood in Association with Britain. However, the Anguillans, some 70 miles northeast of

---

32 Browne, W. T. (1992). *From Commoner to King*. Lanham, MD: University of America Press.

33 Browne, W. T. (1992). *From Commoner to King*. Lanham, MD: University of America Press.

St. Kitts, determined to go their own way, and moved to break from the three-island government. As noted in the Statehood anthem—a great trinity of islands. Actually, one that was hailed in song, but never existed! The Statehood concession for Nevisians, as close as 2 miles southeast of St. Kitts, was that Eugene Walwyn, a Nevisian, be appointed as the Attorney General for the new State, in Association with Britain. Bradshaw was named Premier, and continued to dream of leading St. Kitts, Nevis, and Anguilla as an independent nation. Meanwhile, the assignment of the political status, Statehood in Association with Britain, was another step in Britain's move to unburden itself of its Caribbean colonies, which, by then, had their resources depleted by Britain, and had become impoverished.

Following the deliberate move by Walwyn to the Labor Party government, Nevisians increasingly resented him. They turned from Walwyn's party, the United National Movement, in large numbers. Ralph Harris, Horace Liburd, Carlton Parris, and Rhoan Liburd, once staunch supporters of Walwyn, gave up their association with him, then approached Swanston and Stevens, asking that they work together to create a new Nevis political party. This seems to explain Mr. Stevens' assertion that the NRP was formed in 1967, 3 years before the party was officially registered. Swanston commented, "The UNM had served its purpose on Nevis. After Labor's big victory in 1966, the UNM affiliated itself with the Labor Party." For Nevisians, that blatant anti-Nevis move by Walwyn meant the UNM could no longer be the party for change on Nevis. However, when the UNM fell apart, pioneering political leaders became more determined to unite and form a real Nevis party. Ultimately, Walwyn's betrayal of Nevis' emerging politics inspired the formation of a more committed political party for the island and its people.

The Nevis Reformation Party

Regular meetings were held to discuss the growing demand from Nevisians that a new political party be organized. Quietly, Stevens and Swanston met with different political interest groups at Cotton Ground, Brick Kiln, Low Street, and Stoney Grove. When it was determined that the group should seek consultation with an attorney, they extended an invitation to Simeon Daniel. At that time, another Nevis lawyer, Theodore Hobson, was not consulted since he was viewed as being too closely allied with Walwyn, having once served as chairman of the UNM. Cecil Byron was another Nevis lawyer then; however, he did not appear to be interested in the emerging politics. The idea of including an attorney was initially viewed as a strategy to cut organizing costs. Asking the attorney to lead the group was a subtle enticement while deflecting the cost of the contract. Swanston pointed out that the group also received assistance from Ivor's brother, Hope Stevens, then a successful labor attorney and Caribbean activist in New York.[34]

In a discussion of his role in the formation of the Nevis Reformation Party, Stevens noted that the group struggled over a name for the party as the organization developed. Examples of names suggested for the party included The Nevis Liberation Army and The Nevis Revolutionary Army. Someone must have been thinking of organizing to deal with the soldiers then stationed on the island. Finally the name Nevis Reformation Party was deemed acceptable to all. No one really wanted to irritate further the sensibilities of Premier Bradshaw.

In an interview with the late Levi Morton, a stalwart and staunch supporter of the NRP, he took credit for proposing the name. Swanston remembers a series of meetings with Daniel, who eventually decided to accept the nomination as leader of the party. In time, Mr. Daniel resigned the position he held with the Labor government on St. Kitts. Daniel also had the opportunity to leave the experience of residing on St. Kitts, a situation that held some bad personal and family memories that he wanted to forget. On October 20, 1970, the NRP was launched officially on Nevis.

Despite his efforts and keen interest in the islands' politics, in 1970 Ivor was still on the outside of electoral politics looking

[34] Horne, G. (2007). *Cold War in a Hot Zone: The United States Confronts Labor and Independence Struggles in the British West Indies.* Philadelphia, PA: Temple University Press.

in. According to reliable reports, he had moved around from the Labor Party to being independent, to the PAM, and then to the NRP. When the NRP was launched, Ivor had already been actively involved in the islands' politics for about 13 years, but he had not won an election. Technically, one has to win an election to become a political insider and decision maker. Some political pundits still argue that the best test of one's political savvy is the ability to win elections. He tried hard, but, up to 1970, before the organization of the NRP, Ivor had failed that test.

The Barren Years

In 1971, Stevens finally won his first election, during a wave of support for the new Nevis political party. The vote count showed that this time Stevens beat Walwyn by over 122 votes. The next 9 years were punctuated by election successes on one hand, and legislative failures on the other. Ivor Stevens was elected to the Assembly in 1971, and in 1975. But, since he was in opposition to the Labor Party and not a member of the government, Mr. Stevens had little direct impact on legislation. He was out in the proverbial cold and in a sense barely heard in the Parliament.

Until February 1980, the Labor machine on St. Kitts did all it could to frustrate the NRP and the electoral success on Nevis for Daniel and Stevens. Neither of these men had a real opportunity to propose bills, and if they did, they were never heard or passed in the Assembly. Only bills presented by the majority, Labor politicians, could become laws. However, at that time, Labor and Ivor were very far apart, ideologically and politically: the two just did not meet. Meanwhile, Stevens worked to enhance his political fortunes on Nevis by constantly challenging the integrity of the Labor Party, its leaders, and their politics. He also made vicious and scathing attacks on other politicians in the Labor government. Later, Ivor would boast that those challenging years, when the Labor Party dominated the government and answered only to itself, were some of his most vibrant and aggressive years in politics.

Once the NRP secured political leadership of the Nevis Island government, the war of attrition continued with the Labor Party. Neither side yielded to the other. Stevens died believing that if a vote on the Nevis Secession Bill was allowed in 1974, he would have had some legislative success before 1980. However, Fitzroy Bryant blamed Stevens' excessive speech in 1974 as the factor that prevented a vote on his Secession Bill.

When Stevens won his first election in 1971, that placed him on the inside of the arena, close to political power. However, vicious party politicking kept him far from the real center of the political arena—legislative decision making. Neither his first phase of politicking, 1957-1971, nor the second phase, 1971-1980, was a pleasant experience for Ivor. Each of these periods had emotional costs and took a toll on his dignity. Further, neither one gave him the opportunity to fulfill his dreams. However, both experiences did challenge Stevens' commitment to Nevis politics. Despite the long period away from the center of the political arena, Ivor continued his style of politicking, opposing the Labor government, as one of the spokesmen for Nevis. It did not matter that those were wilderness years—harsh and barren in terms of productivity. During those wilderness years, Steven's wife Dora and the other members of his family provided invaluable strength and support. Nevisians from every level of society also offered Mr. Stevens much political loyalty.

Ultimately, those barren years worked in an ironic way to hurt the Labor Party and to favor Nevis' politics. While the Labor government endeavored to limit the Nevis representatives only to an opposition role in the islands' politics, Ivor used his moments on that opposition stage very creatively. He criticized Labor politics as myopic, anti-Nevis, and in dire need of change. Stevens usually said exactly what his Nevis constituency advocated and wanted to hear. He was also careful to repeat his pro-Nevis messages at every opportunity. Mr. Stevens knew Nevisians were listening!

When the time came, later in the 1970s, that the Labor government needed opposition support for its move to independence, the NRP paid back the Labor Party in kind. Although their 2-mile proximity to St. Kitts did not allow Nevisians the scope for independent action as was instigated on Anguilla, Stevens and Daniel took pleasure in frustrating the hopes of Labor Party politicians. They refused to endorse the necessary documents required by the British government before permitting St. Kitts-Nevis to move toward independence. In 1975, when Bradshaw declared that a vote for the Labor Party meant a vote to authorize his move to independence, both the PAM Party on St. Kitts, and the NRP on Nevis, begged the electorate to vote against any move to independence. On Nevis, the political cry that echoed was, "Secession from St. Kitts at all cost!"

During that period, each time he went into the House of Assembly, Ivor became orator and actor. It was a calculated delay strategy on his part, as he championed the cause of the poor, neglected, and powerless people of Nevis. The people also understood and appreciated the fact that Mr. Stevens spoke for them. Over time, Stevens had come to share the ethos of Nevisians. He also understood and empathized with their long difficult struggle for more autonomy from St. Kitts.

Meanwhile, a future political stage was being strategically fashioned in the islands. The ruling Labor Party sought a legitimate path to independence, whereas the opposition parties were bent on frustrating every move along that path. They were against any move to independence led by the Labor Party. At the same time, Ivor became the skillful political innovator. He manipulated both time and the politics to his party's advantage. Being the keen soldier that he was, Stevens thrived on the mistakes and omissions of the enemy—an elementary tactic to those trained in the art of war, as he was.

Despite some frustrations, the *Christena* years sharpened Stevens' oratorical skills; he was challenged to persist in his mission, and he brought an innovative aggression to his politics. Such factors ensured Stevens an important place in the history of Nevis politics and society. Further, despite the time it took, Mr. Stevens was able to keep the commitment he made to Nevisians. Ironically, that period also equipped Ivor for the more successful, less difficult years, that came after 1980. When the Labor government lost its commanding position in the election of February 1980, that outcome opened the door for an unprecedented coalition between the NRP on Nevis and the PAM on St. Kitts.

Coalition Politics

There is an adage, "A ship in harbor is safe, but that is not what ships are built for." (See Appendix C, for adages and Caribbean sayings, collected by Ivor Stevens.) While he served as an opposition member in the House of Assembly, from 1971 to 1980, Ivor Stevens seemed to have understood that saying. He was in the political fray and had performed well on the opposition bench, even beginning to accept that role as significant. However, Nevis needed help—water, roads, more economic activity, better education facilities, and more political autonomy. Was his politics then really delivering the change he promised?

Despite the lack of tangible achievements for Nevis up to that time, Nevisians continued to trust Ivor, and waited with him. They appreciated, applauded, and supported all his efforts on behalf of Nevis. They felt that his actions were on their behalf, exactly as he wanted the populace on Nevis to see his ongoing struggle. During legislative sessions, Nevisians kept close to their radios and soaked in his words. At each election, Stevens and Daniel could count on the people's vote of confidence. In return they spoke for their people, and only for their people, in the House of Assembly on St. Kitts. Ivor was their man of drama and style; Daniel, their less dramatic, but stubborn, faithful representative. He remained forever committed to secession for Nevis.

The *Christena* matter, along with 10 years of unfeeling, alienating politics toward Nevis, came back to haunt the Labor Party, particularly from 1975 and on to 1980. The Labor government experienced difficulties, as it nudged its way toward political independence, after 1975. The situation could partly be blamed on neglect of the persistent problems and lack of real change in Nevis, despite the concerted cry of Nevisians, through their politicians. The historical hatred and rivalry between the two islands were reinvented, dramatized, and cemented during those difficult political years. Few persons noted the role played by the British government in the ongoing drama. Too often, blame was directed at people such as Bradshaw, Southwell, and Moore who were themselves a product and victims of the British colonial system. Despite its position of dominance in the colonial arrangement, St. Kitts and its leaders were also colonized, and therefore limited by the very experience with which they were endeavoring to shackle Nevis and Nevisians.

In time, real change did come to Nevis, such that the island started to blossom socially, psychologically, and politically. In February 1980, there was a dramatic and unprecedented change of political fortune. Labor Party stalwarts Bradshaw and Southwell were both dead. An arrogant, less loved, and unsuspecting Lee L. Moore was the new Premier. He inherited the leadership of the islands, with all the prior independence arrangements by his predecessors. These included making arrangements and setting possible dates for independence, particularly after the December 1, 1975, general election. The Labor Party's campaign thrust then, led by Robert Bradshaw, was, "Independence for St. Kitts-Nevis, and no secession for Nevis."

With these two goals still in mind, Premier Moore sought to limit the strength of the opposition by keeping the PAM candidate, Dr. Kennedy Simmonds, from filling the vacancy after he won the by-election of January 25, 1979, to replace Mr. Bradshaw after his death in May 1978, and to represent Central Basseterre in the Assembly. It was a hard fought and close election between Dr. Simmonds for PAM, and Mr. A. T. Ribiero for the Labor Party. Dr. Simmonds received 1090 votes to Mr. Ribiero's 1067 votes. It was a close win and a surprise for PAM, but a clear loss by the Labor Party. However, during that time, the Labor Party dominated the House of Assembly. The Labor Party politicians were not ready to share the power. Accordingly, Premier Moore refused to allow Dr. Simmonds in the Assembly. He called no meeting of the Assembly for an unusually long period, and he did very little to show concern or alleviate the demand for secession from Nevis. Relations between the two islands deteriorated further under Premier Moore's leadership. His cronies on Nevis were asked to vet even the lyrics of calypsos to be sung during Culturama. Moore feared that the calypsonians on Nevis would be critical of his authoritarian leadership—and they were! However, the Premier's stance undermined the fundamental idea behind the calypso. Any topic is fair game for criticism, even arrogant and haughty politicians. Through his unfeeling vindictiveness, Moore had angered the electorate on St. Kitts and the people of Nevis. Notwithstanding, as 1980 dawned, Premier Moore was still bent on independence for St. Kitts-Nevis. He saw himself becoming the first Prime Minister of the new nation.

Consequently, for Moore, the election called in February 1980 was a critical move in his intent to consolidate and expand his political power. No one dreamed or expected the results from that historic election. There were already plans afoot for a grand, independence celebration in St. Kitts-Nevis, with Lee L. Moore as the first Prime Minister. The election of February 18, 1980 was intended to be a mere formality. The Labor Party leaders expected to perform the required formalities; then, the islands would make that grand leap to the anticipated political independence. The people of St. Kitts, Nevis, and Anguilla too, behind labor unionism, experienced a long and difficult, social, psychological, and political struggle, under colonialism and planter-class domination, throughout the early 1900s. But, by the late 1970s, political independence came within grasp. However, a haughty unassuming Premier Moore blundered. The party of the masses lost the 1980 election and its plans disintegrated. Suddenly there was a vibrancy and an ascendancy of the People's Action Movement—the political party instigated and supported by the planter-class, who had consistently decried the right to political empowerment for the working-class of St. Kitts, Nevis, and Anguilla. Their response to the promise of eventual political empowerment to the masses in 1937 is still shocking!

Meanwhile, the Nevis Reformation Party argued that the neglect and injustices directed toward Nevis were problematic for them to support political independence with St. Kitts. Its agenda became riveted on a position of secession and change for Nevis. The leaders of PAM argued that the islands were too small and unprepared for political independence. Accordingly, the *Democrat*, a newspaper then sympathetic to both the NRP and PAM's positions, expressed this hardline pro-Nevis stance, in September 1979:

> Where people are bound together by political ties against their will, the tensions which result are likely to impose a strain on their social and economic relationships. Consequently the people of St. Kitts and Nevis will be better friends when the ties that bind them have no political strings attached. The fact that Anguilla has severed its political ties with the State, and that Nevis has been clamoring so loudly for secession, proves that the political ties which bound us together have failed miserably to produce the unity, greatness and freedom, of which our National Song boasts so proudly. The key to social and economic solidarity between St. Kitts and Nevis is internal self-government, or free association with each other. Let us therefore open the door to a voluntary unity, a magnanimous greatness, and an unrestricted freedom with the key of self-determination within a confederation which is ours for the taking.

With the NRP taking advantage of the Labor Party's rigid uncompromising position, PAM's politicians were delighted. At the time, any anti-independence move that frustrated the Labor government on St. Kitts was welcomed by NRP and PAM. In that 1980 election, the Labor Party lost 3 of its 7 seats to the PAM on St. Kitts. In Nevis, Daniel and Stevens held their two seats. The two Labor Party candidates on Nevis lost big, getting a total of 441 votes vs. 2356 for the two NRP candidates. It was no contest. The large picture was that the Labor Party won 4 seats; the PAM won 3 seats; and the NRP won 2 seats. Whichever party on St. Kitts agreed to form a coalition with the NRP would become the next government.

Power Brokers

Suddenly, both parties on St. Kitts were reaching for power. They were willing to bargain with Nevisians. For the first time in recent memory, a political party on Nevis was poised to determine the direction for the islands' future economic, political, and social development. In desperation, Premier Moore talked of forming a minority government with the 4 seats he controlled. However, the political bitterness on the islands was too intense for Mr. Moore to get collaboration or any agreement for him to remain in power. Members of both St. Kitts parties, Labor and PAM, were soon across to Nevis, meeting with the NRP, asking its cooperation in forming a coalition government. Eventually, the new government came out of a coalition between the PAM and the NRP. Lee Moore and the Labor Party found themselves in the opposition and out in the cold. Any NRP linkage with the Labor Party would have been unacceptable to Nevisians in 1980. It would have been tantamount to "sleeping with the enemy."

The PAM party read the situation well and seized the opportunity. Its leadership approached the Nevisians, promising them honesty, respect, and a partnership of equality. Thus, they agreed to forge a closer bond between the islands. Consequently, the two groups of politicians displaced the Labor Party as the government and leaders of St. Kitts-Nevis. The new political leadership came together and agreed to form a PAM-NRP coalition government.

As far back as 1961, Nevis politicians had gone to the electorate and promised them secession. However, in 1980, when a real opportunity for secession came, they formed a coalition government instead. Many Nevisians felt betrayed and questioned the decision. Despite the loud cries for secession, Nevis leaders saw the situation as an unprecedented one. They also wanted to experience and taste revenge for all that Nevis had suffered at the hands of the Labor Party, up to that time. At the same time, the PAM was as excited as the NRP about the sudden good fortune and opportunity to dethrone the once all-powerful and haughty Labor Party. Even Daniel, the committed secessionist, understood that reality. He opted for coalition over secession. Even if it was meant to be only a temporary venture, they would join with the PAM, not the Labor Party.

The PAM's negotiators, led by, Dr. Kennedy Simmonds and Dr. William V Herbert Jr., began the negotiations in this manner: "We come to offer nothing. You all take. We will take what is left." However, the NRP politicians took a cautious stand and set some ground rules for their involvement in a coalition government. Swanston insisted that Daniel be made Minister of Finance. Herbert hesitated since, as he pointed out, the usual pattern in the Leeward Islands, except in Antigua, was for the political leader to be the Minister of Finance. As Swanston recalled, it was he who told Dr. Herbert that Daniel having the Ministry of Finance would be fair since "Nevisians have always been too far from the pot. It is time that they can see what's inside it." Stevens supported Swanston's suggestion.

An important decision was made to build the infrastructure on Nevis, whatever the cost. The team negotiating for Nevis (Uhral Swanston, Ivor Stevens, Sim Daniel, Levi Morton, Sonny Parris, Ralph Harris, and a few others) asked that the Ministry of Communications and Works also be assigned to Nevis, and given to Ivor Stevens. In return, the Nevis team gave up its push for secession. They accepted the two ministries and became part of the PAM-NRP coalition government. Nevisians were convinced that those two ministries could change the underdevelopment that plagued Nevis. Daniel, it is said, also refused an offer to become Premier of St. Kitts-Nevis.

Later, during the first term of the PAM-NRP coalition government, Daniel took a lackadaisical approach to managing the Ministry of Finance. Nevis barely benefited from the 4 years he spent managing the government's finances. There were times when Daniel even debated whether he should travel to St. Kitts to fulfill the duties of his office. Seemingly, such travel interfered with his thriving real estate business in Nevis, where he often had visitors to his office, intending to purchase land. There was a sense of ambivalence in Daniel's mood and attitude throughout his tenure with the coalition government. He was much more comfortable in his Nevis Island Government office. On Nevis he could see his off-island clients and sell land, or drive around Nevis to inspect new property to acquire. Reputedly both the late Suswin Mills, a Nevisian who then served as Permanent Secretary in the Ministry of Finance, and Mr. Stevens, did express their disgust to others about the nonchalant manner in which Mr. Daniel handled the Ministry of Finance. He could have used it to benefit the affairs of Nevis much more than he did.

For Ivor, the experience as a minister of government was different. He had spent from 1957 to 1980 in the political trenches battling for a chance to ascend to the inner circle of government. When it came in 1980, the opportunity came unexpectedly, but it did come. Mr. Stevens' yearning for meaningful political participation was finally being realized. Ivor used every opportunity that came to him to show that he was a knight in shining armor, a champion for the cause of Nevis. Within limits, he made political decisions and used the available resources in his Ministry to help undo those many years of neglect and underdevelopment in Nevis. For the rest of his political life, Mr. Stevens cherished the unique opportunity, and used his position in decisive, creative ways, to promote development and progress on both islands. While he enjoyed the position of authority and a high level of acceptance on Nevis, Ivor never forgot that he was from Sandy Point in St. Kitts.

Maybe heading a ministry with the PAM-NRP government was more an experience of conflict for Daniel than for Stevens. However, each man had to contend with a clear dilemma. It must have been a conflict for any Nevis leader at that time, agreeing to become part of a coalition government with St. Kitts after having promised secession repeatedly to Nevisians, whenever a real opportunity ever came. However, times had changed. Admittedly though, the matter is still debated by Nevisians, every now and then. How could their leaders for secession accept to become part of a coalition government with any party on St. Kitts? Ivor, Sim, and their advisers would probably still respond, "We saw what we thought was a good and worthwhile political opportunity that would benefit Nevis" In many ways, the coalition did benefit Nevis. Thanks to both Mr. Daniel and Mr. Stevens, but more to Mr. Stevens and his sincere commitment to the island.

There are many stories about how Mr. Stevens went out of his way and used the Ministry of Communications to help Nevis and Nevisians. At times the approach had to be unorthodox, but, Ivor liked an unorthodox approach to life when dealing with such matters. In time, however, his manner of dealing with getting things across to Nevis drew attention and criticisms from both Premier Daniel and Prime Minister Simmonds, but he did not give up. Ivor was always more concerned about the things that needed to be done on Nevis, than about the approach to getting them done.

The leader of the PAM-NRP coalition government, Dr. Kennedy Simmonds, recalled, "Ivor was not too concerned about protocol. He was more result oriented and did not mind short cuts. At times when Ivor skirted protocol, he had to be reigned in." One such time, a caterpillar machine was shipped from St. Kitts to Nevis without the normal governmental authority. "Ivor simply felt that Nevis had a greater need for the equipment than St. Kitts, at that time. So, he sent it across," Also, according to former Prime Minister Simmonds,

> Stevens was reprimanded at times when he was perceived to be wrong. The machine he sent to Nevis never came back, but it was accounted for. The Permanent Secretary, the late Mr. Haynes, was warned that in future he would be held responsible. But Ivor did get things done, even on St. Kitts.

Once Stevens arrived at the place where he could be a decision maker in government, he chose a practical approach as his constant motto in life. To Ivor, "The essence of who a person is cannot be based only on what the person has, but also on that person's commitment to improving the quality of life for others." Even before Ivor died, Nevisians could look back with appreciation at where Nevis is, and where it came from. Nevisians also appreciated the ongoing transformation in their time. Those who witnessed the changes recall them with pride and gratitude. They see notable differences between the islands before and after. By 1990 and the dawn of the 21st century, a marked shift in perception of things had taken over on Nevis. Things now taken for granted throughout the island include electricity, local government, paved roads, water, telephone, and the sixth-form college. Today, along with Culturama, there is so much more available to Nevisians to smile and be proud about, than back during the1950s and 1960s. Nevisians now agree that the road to change has been long, winding, at times treacherous, and always challenging. However, Ivor Stevens stayed the course, kept his commitment, and helped to implement changes that transformed Nevis. Many of his ideas and actions contributed to bringing the islands into modern times. Unlike certain other Nevis politicians, Stevens was never involved in schemes that hindered, blunted, or confused his commitment to do everything possible, so that life and society on Nevis could be enhanced. Ivor Stevens promised Nevisians change. He lived what he promised. Today, his very vibrant and unique legacy to Nevis shows that Ivor Stevens remained true to that promise.

CHAPTER 6

The Revival

Through the years, it became a multifaceted effort to encourage and foster a spirit of patriotism on Nevis. One of the chief architects of that awakening was Ivor Stevens. Along with his group of pioneers, Ivor went from village to village, speaking with Nevisians, one person at a time, or in small groups. He sought to create an organization, and at the same time build consensus that would make it work. All through the 1950s, 1960s, and 1970s, Ivor Stevens spoke hope to Nevisians, amid towering disillusionment and despair. So many Nevisians, then, saw hope only in escaping Nevis. In time, however, every Nevisian 18 years and older, had the option to choose support for the idea of a revitalized Nevis, under new leadership—leadership with a grander vision for the islands.

Daunting as the challenge was, thousands of Nevisians, young and old, at home and abroad, became inspired to join the march for change. For those who lived on Nevis then and shared the experience, it was a time of new beginnings and renewal. A band of committed Nevisians finally stood tall, and spoke to the existing power—the power of false consciousness, colonial manipulation, and misguided leadership. One challenge was against double exploitation designed first in Britain. It was accepted with minimal criticism, then later enforced from St. Kitts.

Through those years, there were Nevisians who became known political stalwarts, always in the fore, rallying the charge for a changed relationship with St. Kitts. Most of the pioneers are gone now, but one, Uhral Swanston, still keeps fighting for NRP and Nevis. There was also the group led by Calvin Howell. They sought change by focusing on the humanities. Through the arts, they challenged the psychology of despair and self-hate that had overtaken Nevisians. Along with the new politicians and their political messages, there were village leaders and certain academicians who served as messengers of hope to the island. Back then, leadership in the island was inspired by love commitment and a desire for change—not greed for money and status.

Today, political involvement and leadership on Nevis has lost the purity and altruism of the 1950s, 1960s, and 1970s. It has become corrupted. However, looking back, Nevisians can still remember the Stevens era as one that inspired hope in all on the island. The Nevis Reformation Party became the champion for all Nevisians, and every Nevisian knew that Nevis would win its battle for transformation. Many Nevisians still owe so very much to that determination, commitment, and foresight of a small band of men who dared. They envisioned change, held to their dream, then through a demonstration of self-confidence they made a great difference on the island. Ultimately it was not one man, but a group of men, and women too, who were desperate and committed to pursuing change. They rose up and acted in unison, as if they were one. They wanted to win back Nevis to the control of Nevisians. Maybe, as the island reaches a time of ease and complacency, those lessons from the 1950s, 1960s, and 1970s should not be forgotten. They should always be instructive to Nevisians and to other Caribbean people. Through time, the actors do change, but the dramas in the islands' history can continue, often with parallel scenes and depictions.

It was with an unusual determination and commitment that Nevisians challenged those politics of domination, false consciousness, and exclusion, being imposed from St. Kitts, at a time when Nevisians were experiencing a powerful ideological and cultural shift. The politicians, their ideas, and the politics imposed from St. Kitts were losing meaning to Nevisians. For them, a new view was coming into focus—they saw creativity, dynamism, confidence, and new expectations for Nevis. For thousands of Nevisians, only one thrust really mattered on the island then. It was the thrust of "Let's do it all for Nevis, and to secure better for our children!" Acting together as never before, Nevisians chose the practical and liberating psychology of self-actualization.

To Ivor's credit, his battle for the hearts and minds of Nevisians can be traced back to the early 1950s. During 1956, for example, after a severe storm had struck the island, Ivor mobilized a clean-up force in Charlestown. He used his two cane trucks to assist with the clean-up work throughout the island. Later, he led the way in helping Nevisians repair their houses and set them back in place on stabilizing nags. One of Stevens' legacies to Nevis is his visible, vibrant action, demonstrated during times of crisis, and during the process of physically making the island a better place.

Although Stevens was never named leader of the Nevis Reformation Party, there is agreement among many Nevisians that he gave the island as much as, and more than, many other members of the party, in service, in commitment, and in vision. Mr. Stevens was never daunted by obstacles, internal or external, as he moved to fashion and give momentum to the transformation of Nevis.

In his early assessment of the relationship between St. Kitts and Nevis, Stevens agreed with others that Nevis depended too heavily on St, Kitts. However, that was the nature of their colonial reality. Colonialism linked the two islands together, politically and economically. Meanwhile, the early attempts to lessen Nevis' dependence on St. Kitts threatened fundamental cultural and ideological assumptions inherent in colonialism. There were concerns about disrupting established patterns of behavior and relationships between the two islands. What existed was the accepted notion by the controlling politicians on St. Kitts, that the relations, the service, and the exchanges between the islands should be forever. They were viewed as eternal verities. Nothing was to change through time about the privileges or the power.

To Ivor, however, there were myriad of negative outcomes from that historical domination of Nevis by St. Kitts. They were noted everywhere: in the inefficient water supply system, the second-class education system, the need to travel to St. Kitts for everything, the unpaved roads throughout the island, the darkened villages, lit only by the moon, and more. Meanwhile, Nevis politicians were limited to the opposition bench, incapable of implementing any laws to benefit their island. Often, Nevisians had to accept job transfers to St. Kitts to receive promotions. Sixth-form students from Nevis had to travel to St. Kitts and virtually lived there, just to attend school. There was also psychological evidence that some Nevisians had started to imagine a future with no changed relationships between the islands. Some assumed airs of superiority after moving from Nevis to live on St. Kitts. Others went to visit St. Kitts for one day, but never returned to Nevis. Meanwhile, some Nevisians were quite mesmerized and taken in by the conflicts between the two islands. They became actively engaged in the war of attrition, ongoing between the islands. This was demonstrated in their words and actions, during cricket and netball competitions, or in other tit-tat exchanges, as they passed one another on the piers. The relationship between the islands was often less than expected for two islands called "sister islands"—a name that can often be associated more with the islands' proximity and shared history, rather than with their people's emotions and respect.

At times, the domination and control from St. Kitts was blatant, willful, and humiliating. For example, any suggestions originating on Nevis about how the central government could improve the island, were rebuffed unceremoniously. That was the case with an early plan by Stevens to boost agriculture production on the island. Bradshaw treated the plan with disdain. He also ridiculed the idea that Nevisians wanted to secede from St. Kitts. Further, during the period of the Anguillan revolt (1967-1980), soldiers and weapons were sent from St. Kitts to Nevis, used repeatedly in open displays of weapons, with the clear intent to harass and intimidate Nevisians. History and the colonial experience handed St. Kitts all the authority between the islands, and in such matters. That was very much the accepted thinking. Consequently, when Ivor started his early planning and strategizing to bring a new politics to Nevis, he was also designing a vision of the future, one that would liberate Nevisians from the colonial thinking which limited and trapped the people of both islands.

Ivor's Strategy

One of Ivor's best weapons against the dependency problem was the secession idea. It has a revolutionary thought for Nevisians since 1882. Even during the coalition government era between the Nevis Reformation Party and the People's Action Movement, secession was accepted as the brinksmanship strategy for Nevisians. Stevens and Daniel did all they could to champion that secession idea and keep it alive. They were able to do this because of assistance from the *Christena* tragedy, the coming of the NRP, and the mistrust that remained even after that coming together of PAM and NRP in 1980, to form the new government. These events were followed by the acceptance of Clause 113, as a part of the islands' independence constitution. Together, one or more of these factors impacted Nevis's call for secession, during the 1970s, the 1980s, and beyond. Ultimately, secession became Nevis' political trump card and super weapon. It has been an integral part of the islands' recent political development since 1961.

It appears, however, that even when Ivor operated alone, he managed to use what he later termed, his "divisionist" strategy, successfully, against the then powerful and usually unbending Bradshaw. Dr. Keith Archibald, one of the many Nevisians who lived and worked on St. Kitts, for many years, recalled that in 1966, even Bradshaw made some concessions to both Walwyn and Stevens, because they appeared set on breaking from the colonial union. Bradshaw needed at least an outward show of unity between the two islands as he moved toward statehood.

At that time, Walwyn agreed to present the Labor government with a shopping list of things needed on Nevis, including the need for a better agriculture program, government's ownership of a number of abandoned private estates, and the dire need for better roads. One benefit that came to Nevis, although temporary, was the transferring of the office, Director of Agriculture, to the island. The director, Mr. H. Croucher, went to work on Nevis. He was assisted by Mr. Abbott, based in St. Kitts.

However, when Walwyn agreed to accept the post of Attorney General, Ivor became very suspicious of him and his commitment to change on Nevis. In time, Walwyn used that position largely to help himself financially. Nevisians, as a people, received few benefits from Walwyn's promotion in the government. Later, Walwyn became more and more isolated and aloof from the people of Nevis. Relations also worsened between Walwyn and Stevens, making Stevens' efforts to improve Nevisians' sense of dignity and feelings of equality with Kittitians a much more difficult task. On more than one occasion the two men took different sides on what needed to be done to develop and improve Nevis. Soon, many Nevisians came to see Walwyn as a special agent for the St. Kitts government in his actions and some the things he said critical of Nevis. Both Sim and Ivor refused to work cooperatively with Walwyn or with the government. They persisted with that stance of defiance against St. Kitts leadership, until February 1980, when the two men accepted ministerial roles in the new, PAM-NRP coalition government.

During the 1980s, as Minister of Communications and Works, Ivor used many strategies, some unorthodox, to help build the infrastructure of Nevis. He scrounged in the bushes at Frigate Bay, a dumping ground for wrecked vehicles, to search for used tractor parts. He sent needed items to Nevis without following the established protocol. Some of Ivor's actions on behalf of Nevis also came close to being illegal, like sending tractors and other heavy equipment needed to build the infrastructure across from St. Kitts to Nevis without the proper permission. When Ivor was asked how he acquired some of the equipment, he would respond humorously, "I borrowed them." Theodore Hobson, then an ardent supporter of the Labor Party, once attacked Ivor, calling him a thief. Ivor's response was, "I stole it for Nevis, not for myself." Ironically, now that it is later in his life, Hobson does appear to have found some love for Nevis. But back then, Theodore Hobson was one of the Nevisians who chose the easy path and supported the Labor government. Despite the struggle for the soul and future of Nevis, such Nevisians saw Nevis as less satisfying. Their abandoning of hope in the island's future was more financially rewarding. Consequently, the easy path was the one some Nevisians chose to follow.

In another incident, Stevens used his office as Minister of Communications and Works in St. Kitts, and purchased a truck to help the local government on Nevis. However, Ivor did not consult with Premier Daniel, in advance, about that purchase for Nevis. As a result, Daniel refused to accept the truck; it did not matter that it was being sent by Mr. Stevens, his deputy leader of Nevis. Stevens was still from St. Kitts, and Premier Daniel was in charge of Nevis. Mr. Daniel later argued that Stevens was trying to undermine his authority on Nevis. Consequently, the truck sat on the island unused for a long time. Ironically, it was a time when Nevis could have really benefitted from the use of such a vehicle. Later, the matter was resolved amicably. However, the incident served as an illustration of some the subtleties that existed in NRP politics. It also points to the animosity that persisted between Mr. Daniel and Mr. Stevens. The matter was an early demonstration of the underlying conflict and emerging mistrust that challenged the two men. That incident also mirrored their contrary relationship, even when they worked together. There they were: two men working together, each striving to keep Nevis independent of St. Kitts; yet, there were times when each drew his line in the sand, daring the other to cross. At times they also engaged in verbal battles and other shenanigans, when one felt his personal political space had been invaded by the actions of the other.

A number of people, including Mrs. Stevens, Elmo Liburd, Rev. Bowers, and Dr. Kennedy Simmonds used the following story to illustrate Ivor's commitment to the common people on Nevis: Ivor once attended a cotton conference in Barbados with a local Nevis farmer who was not adept at eating with a knife and fork in a formal setting. When the conference group was asked to participate in a banquet, the bewildered farmer was at a loss as to the proper forms and etiquette. He simply looked on while the others ate. When Ivor noticed the farmer's dilemma, he acted quickly to resolve the problem. The attendant was asked to bring two sets of tablespoons, one for Ivor, the other for the farmer. The farmer then plunged into his meal with gusto. Mr. Stevens joined in too. When Stevens asked, "How are you doing?" The very pleased farmer responded, "Boss, eh taste good." The farmer could manage a spoon, but eating with a fork was an unpracticed skill.

On another occasion Stevens was going through immigration in Barbados when he spotted a fellow Nevisian in another line. He beckoned to the woman and calmly saw her through the process. There were also occasions when Stevens came to the aid of Nevisians who had traveled to St. Kitts on official business. Usually, no officials on St. Kitts arranged to meet Nevisians who came down on government business. There was no transportation arranged to their destination. While he served in St. Kitts as Minister of Communications and Works, Stevens ensured that such government persons from Nevis did not walk to their meetings. They were afforded the same courtesy extended on Nevis to visiting Kittitian members of government.

There was also the case of Ellen Skeritt-Watts, a native Montserratian who lived in Nevis since 1949. She resided at Bath Village and was well known to Ivor. Ellen's impulsive and erratic style left her with few friends. When he learned of the deplorable and squalid condition under which Ellen lived with her 2 dogs, 8 chickens, and 4 pigs, all inside the same dilapidated building, Ivor turned to one of his assistants, Phineas Griffin, ordering him to use resources from the government to build a house for Ellen at Bath Village. Phineas said, "The floor and the yard were one. There were dogs, pigs, chickens and filth, inside and outside the house. . . . Ivor usually did not leave room for arguments. He gave an order, then left." The house was built in 2 days. "The very condition and stench of the place forced us to work fast and get out," said Phineas. Eventually Ellen became a homeless person and lived at the infirmary next to the Alexandra Hospital, when she was not wandering around town in very dirty clothes. Despite her situation, in an interview with Ellen during the late 1990s, she remarked, "Ivor was a good man. He build me a house."

Ellen thanked Ivor often, and publicly. She wanted as many people as possible to see and know, Mr. Stevens was her friend.

One day, she met Ivor on Main Street in Charlestown, and with many people watching, threw her arms around him, hugged and kissed him. That was good politics for Ivor; he was being lauded by a "little" person. However, Sim Daniel's then father-in-law, Stanley Henville, a businessman in Charlestown, was quite annoyed. "Do you mean you allow the likes of Ellen to hug you up?" He asked. For Ivor, however, it was good drama and part of his campaign strategy. Ellen was a poor unfortunate person who needed help and he gave it. If she chose to thank him that way, so be it. Further, such public adulations were always good populist politics: the type Ivor thrived on to win elections.

Both Dr. Kennedy Simmonds and Arthur Evelyn agreed that Ivor was a major player in the government's decision to purchase and operate the ferry *Caribe Queen*, replacing the sail-boats that shuttled passengers between the islands, up until the 1980s. Even before the *Christena* incident, Ivor understood the danger. There was also the need for change to more efficient technology. He insisted that Nevisians should be given the opportunity to travel swiftly and safely between St. Kitts and Nevis. According to one observer, "Ivor was tired of seeing Nevisians traveling with cattle, pigs, and sheep, to St. Kitts. When Kittitians had to travel to Nevis, they did not have to travel like that."

Among the thousands of Nevisians with whom Ivor was ferried to and from St. Kitts, were sixth-form students. They travelled to St. Kitts on Monday mornings and spent the rest of the week there attending advanced classes. Quite often, the students had to live with unaccommodating relatives or friends. Ivor thought such classes could be held on Nevis, eliminating many inconveniences for the Nevis students and their parents. Accordingly, Ivor helped to initiate moves so that a sixth-form academic program could be added to the Charlestown Secondary School on Nevis. However, at the height of this educational innovation, the headmaster, Vance Amory, left the school unexpectedly, to work for the St. Kitts-Nevis National Bank. At that point, Wendell Huggins, who taught at the Basseterre High School in St. Kitts, was brought over to Nevis to head the Charlestown school. He worked there for one term. Alford

Thompson was brought in from Canada by Mr. Daniel to succeed Mr. Huggins as the headmaster of the Charlestown school. At that point, Huggins was transferred to the Gingerland High School. In his comments about Mr. Stevens, Huggins noted,

> When the school started in the Belle View Building, Ivor must have had added pleasure. The building once used to house the soldiers Bradshaw stationed on Nevis was converted to serve as a temporary venue for higher education on the island. Later a permanent building was added at the Charlestown High School for sixth-form students.

Nevis now provides better academic training for its citizens than at any time before. The benefits to the island, the nation, and the world have been enormous. Today, Nevisians are serving, in large numbers, as educators, doctors, social workers, architects, engineers, and lawyers, at home and abroad. Hundreds of them continue to give credit to time spent at the sixth-form college on Nevis. That experience is still remembered as a major rung in their academic climb. Meanwhile, the availability of such higher levels of training in academia continues to impact positively on the island. For an emerging nation such as St. Kitts-Nevis, the greatest promise of transformation is still in its human capital. Singapore has lived and now models this.

Ivor once recommended that the government purchase the Pinney's Estate, just beyond center city, Charlestown. It was going for a reasonable price then. Stevens also devised a financial plan through which the property could have been purchased when the price was about $8,000,000 Eastern Caribbean dollars (about $2,500,000, U.S.). By the time the government gave serious thought to the purchase, the price had escalated to $49,000,000 EC (about $17,000,000, U.S.). When Daniel became interested, Stevens secured a loan from the Social Security System for about EC$10 million. It was too late. The Nevis Island Administration was never again in a position to purchase the estate; the price became increasingly prohibitive.

Over the years, Stevens also became very concerned about growing impositions of foreign ideas and cultures in Nevis—particularly the Americanization of the island. He wanted to preserve traditional Nevis art forms, architecture, and cultural traditions. Ivor always felt that progress on the island should be managed and controlled carefully. He was partial to the fundamental culture forms and traditions of the island. He consistently advocated preservation of the beaches, the coconut groves, and local fishing. Today, a major part of the island's problem is related to massive culture shifts. This has led to criminal behavior, including gun use, rampant drug addiction, and growing involvement in gangs. These are not traditional Caribbean culture forms. There is also a growing trend to limit Caribbean youths' exposure to religious education, church attendance, and proper discipline. These were once critical aspects of Caribbean life for cultural transmission. Further, it must always be remembered by Caribbean youths that education is a disciplined journey. It is never a haphazard or frivolous experience.

According to a close family friend of Ivor, he was not excited about the Four Seasons Hotel project started in 1991. Mr. Stevens tended to prefer smaller hotels such as the Golden Rock. He saw the Four Seasons as too imposing, insensitive to the island's traditional architecture, and disruptive to the environment. It also detracts from the island's uniqueness and serenity. Ivor particularly appreciated the effort made by the owners of the Golden Rock Hotel to preserve the natural beauty of the island.

Unlike Ivor, other politicians loved the Four Seasons Hotel. Some seemed to line up frequently, hat in hand for favors. Meanwhile, the hotel was given carte blanche authority to operate on the island. There have been a number of cases when Nevisians working or visiting the hotel were treated unfairly. At one time, during the early 1990s, a group of people from the U. S. and the Virgin Islands visited Nevis and tried to visit and see the hotel: They were told no one, including native Nevisians, except workers, were allowed to visit the hotel. It appeared that a group of wealthy people visiting from New York had contracted the hotel for two weeks, and thus the ban. Not ordinary people, including native Nevisians were welcome to visit. A local newspaper published an article criticizing the incident as unacceptable and an illegal imposition on the island. The manager tried quickly to control such publicity. However, he did not promise the discriminatory policy would end. It is hoped that such archaic discriminatory practices are no longer allowed on Nevis, without appropriate challenges in 2013.

At one time, it was also common knowledge on Nevis that a number of politicians frequented the hotel in search of perks. Ivor was unhappy that some of his fellow politicians deliberately advertised themselves for sale to such institutions. When that happens, it is always at a cost to the dignity of Nevisians, and the well-being of Nevis. What would Ivor say now if he was to see the changes Four Seasons instigated, since it virtually appropriated part of the beach area next to Jessups Village? Nature has not been kind to the area either. Dr. Osmond Farrell was born at Jessups Village and spent many youthful days on the same beach. On recent visits from the U.S. where he works as a professor, Farrell has been surprised at how the entire beach area has changed since the Four Seasons' era began. Over time, Nevisians are beginning to understand, and appreciate the concern, the foresight, and the love for Nevis, expressed in the ideas and actions of Mr. Stevens, many years ago. Unlike a number of the other politicians on Nevis, Stevens understood that gifts can become vehicles for bribery and control, causing politicians to compromise their integrity, while undermining any commitment to Nevis. Unfortunately, despite those grand claims by Archibald (2010), Dr. Daniel lost sight of the original and shared NRP vision for the island. He became adept at trading Nevisians' dignity and land for personal profit. His wavering position on such matters created a divide between Mr. Daniel and the citizenry of Nevis, including his colleagues in the NRP. Just as Walwyn and Parris did earlier, Dr. Daniel drifted away from the citizens of Nevis and lost the common touch. Over time, as he accrued wealth, he forgot his earlier commitment to the island. Further, Daniel had been such a complex person that his secession argument might well have been a "red-herring," a classic case of cognitive dissonance, and a diversion from the real story behind his persistent anger toward St. Kitts and Kittitians.

By the time Ivor died in 1997, he had dedicated more than half his life's service to the betterment and well-being of Nevisians. Ultimately, Ivor's challenge remains a challenge to every Nevisian. Love of island must always be reflected in positive, egalitarian action, not selfish scheming for personal profit. Before he died, Ivor reasoned that he should have done even more for Nevis. He wrote in his White Paper: "Had I served my party as diligently as I served my leader (Mr. Daniel) Nevis would not now be in this predicament in which it finds itself" (see Appendix D). Ivor was concerned when, just before he died, the secession issue reemerged. He died leaving the matter still unresolved. Seemingly, even as he was dying, Ivor asked the questions, "Did I accomplish my mission for Nevis in the best way I could? Which did I serve the most, the NRP, Sim Daniel, or Nevis?" By 1983 and on into the 1990s, the NRP was losing ground with the people of Nevis. Stevens must have sensed the coming rejection by Nevisians, when he opted to retire from the party in 1987.

New Political Parties

By the early 1980s, Stevens and Daniel started to become concerned about the future of the Nevis Reformation Party. Daniel approached me. I was then a lecturer at the teachers' college on St. Kitts. He suggested that I prepare to take over the leadership of the NRP since he did not want it to fall in Uhral Swanston's hands. At the time, my intention was to return to Temple University in the U.S., to complete work started on a Ph.D., during the late 1970s. Mr. Daniel was asked whether there was the possibility for some level of financial sponsorship. However, there was never any commitment and nothing was resolved. The matter was never discussed again. However, my action a few months later incurred the wrath of both Stevens and Daniel. I aligned myself with Attorney Myrna Walwyn and her cousin Edread Walwyn, to form the Nevis

Independent Party, and opposed the NRP for the upcoming local election (1983). For me, my sudden entry into politics was to challenge NRP's haughtiness, its growing selfishness, along with the political and social naïveté being perpetrated on Nevisians. I also saw Nevisians' sovereignty as being at stake.

Unlike Ivor, by 1983 Sim was demonstrating a pattern of caring for himself first, his friends and family next, and Nevis some time later on. Daniel got to the point where in his greed for wealth, everything on Nevis, land, his influence, and the citizens' rights, were all for sale. At times, Mr. Daniel would stop cars with White visitors to Nevis, and without knowing with whom he was speaking, offered them land for sale. Once, a friend returned to the Virgin Islands from a brief visit to Nevis and complained about how land-sale pitches were made to her by Mr. Daniel. She was not amused at the way it was done.

Shortly after the Nevis Independent Party was formed, Myrna and I met with Vance Amory and asked that he campaign and run in the St. George's constituency against Levi Morton. The plan was to offer Nevisians an alternative political leadership by winning the majority seats. I was almost certain of a win in the St. James Parish. Vance Amory could challenge Morton for the St. George's seat, and probably win. We did not expect Myrna to beat Daniel. However, Amory leaked the NIP plans to Daniel and was awarded a permanent secretary's position with the NRP, since he was leaving the St. Kitts-Nevis National Bank. Because he was part of the NRP leadership team, Stevens, too, was unhappy that the NIP had been formed. He did not make complimentary statements about the members of the NIP during his campaign stints. But that was Stevens' campaign style: quite often he responded to opposition politicking with statements that reflected the arrogance of a dominant political party—some of it was meant to be demeaning and intimidating.

Joseph Parry remembers that the NIP plans were leaked, but observed, "Sim never revealed to me what he was told." However, everyone in Nevis was aware that Amory was given a cushy job with the NRP administration—it was a third victory for Amory. He had been awarded jobs such as headmaster of Charlestown High School and manager of the Nevis branch of the National Bank by the Labor Party government, because he was not a committed supporter of the NRP's pro-Nevis movement. Despite his talk with a forked tongue, Amory was allowed in the NRP, the winning Nevis party, in 1983. Reportedly, that was despite warnings to Mr. Daniel by a number of friends against accepting Amory into the NRP leadership. After a few years, Amory, too, became disillusioned with NRP politics and the perception of his future role in it. He left the NRP and Nevis to attend the University of the Virgin Islands, on St. Croix. Eventually, Amory's exile from Nevis, coupled with his disappointment with the NRP, then an exploitative association with Mr. Carlyle Jeffers, a Nevisian living in St. Croix, laid the foundation for a new Nevis based political party: The Concerned Citizens Movement.

When Amory returned to Nevis from St. Croix, he was still friendly with the Labor Party on St. Kitts. Amory reputedly accepted financial assistance and consulted with Lee Moore while he built the Concerned Citizens Movement opposition against the NRP. Soon, Amory was challenging NRP domination on Nevis, and the PAM-NRP government. It was only a matter of time until the fall of what had become an arrogant but declining NRP.

I left the Nevis Independent Party before the 1983 election, and Nevis in 1984. Vance's betrayal left me very disillusioned. Myrna persisted with her run against the NRP. As everyone anticipated, she was soundly beaten at the polls by Daniel. Those were the NRP glory days. As with the Labor Party on St. Kitts, the tide would soon turn in Nevis for the NRP. Despite its short existence, the NIP did sow seeds of resistance in the minds of many Nevisians, against the growing power and arrogance of the NRP, and to Daniel's unfocused leadership of Nevis. By the end of the 1980s, he had become a leader out of touch with those he led. But, instead of seeing reality, he saw conspiratorial mirages. Suddenly, everyone else in the NRP was conspiring against the leader. Meanwhile, other people on Nevis were beginning to see what the NIP saw, back in 1983. They were also finding the will to criticize, to resist, and to think of political change. The Concerned Citizens Movement was in place to capture the growing need for a politics that could fill the vacuum and betrayal, Nevisians were beginning to sense then.

Before he left the Nevis Reformation Party, Stevens did seek to recruit young Nevisians to be trained under NRP's tutelage, so that they can carry the baton of future leadership in the politics of Nevis. Two of Stevens' recruits and protégés were Franklin Brand and Victor Martin. Victor is now an attorney; Franklin still has politics in his blood, but, he became a reluctant businessman—quite successful too. Both men continue to speak glowingly about a wonderful and enlightening association with Ivor. At one time Franklin, too, opposed the NRP, but he still maintained a good relationship with Ivor.

In contrast, Sim wanted to exercise control over his underlings. He maintained a brittle and fragile relationship with Swanston, Stevens, and Parry. At one time Sim worked closely with Parry and he might have liked Victor Martin. The three men are from the same general area. But later, Sim appeared to have supported Vance Amory over both Parry and Martin. Until his death in May 2012, Mr. Daniel insisted that his drive for secession from St. Kitts failed because other members of the NRP conspired not to support his position on the secession issue. As a result, Daniel claimed that he stood alone on the matter from early in the 1980s.

Ironically, Vance Amory was brought into NRP by Sim Daniel, and given the position, Permanent Secretary of Finance in the government. Later, Amory left the NRP government in anger and disgust to form his own party. However, there was a special tie that bound Amory and Daniel together. Both men spent time growing up under the tutelage of White Anglican priests. Also, according to Ivor, Vance and Sim conspired together against him in the NRP, thus broadening the rift between Sim and Ivor.

From time to time Vance did express admiration for Sim and seemed to have maintained a friendship with him, as was convenient. According to Carlyle Jeffers, Vance had to be pushed to declare himself as being in opposition to Sim and the NRP. In time, however, Vance became Sim's most dangerous rival on Nevis, eventually engineering Sim's political demise through the Concerned Citizens

Movement. In 1992, the CCM overwhelmed the once invulnerable NRP. By then, however, the party had started to experience what Galbraith referred to as the "rotten door syndrome." The party was rotten inside. One simply needed to kick the door in. Amory did just that. Accordingly, the CCM took over the reins of Nevis Island Government, in 1992, and held it in consecutive elections, until it was lost to NRP, in 2006.

During all the time of the NRP's gradual decline, one of the lieutenants in the party who remained faithful to Daniel was Joseph Parry. Seemingly, he was as steadfast in his loyalty to Daniel as he could be. However, when Daniel lost his seat he blamed Parry, left politics, and at times even sought to undermine Parry's political aspirations. Consequently, Mr. Parry became the scapegoat for Daniel's election loss and political downfall. When the time came to choose a successor to the party's leadership, Ivor supported Parry, a quiet, mature, and seasoned campaigner with the party. Sim backed Victor Martin, more in the style of Ivor, but much less exposed to the dynamics of politics. Further, at that time, Victor did not seem as focused or as committed as Parry. The two men depicted different styles and visions about leadership. Eventually, Parry won the consent of the party faithful, got the leadership nod, and managed to hold the NRP together. He stopped the party's downward slide by winning the 2006 local election. He repeated the feat on July 11, 2011. However, the legality of that election result was challenged. The court sent it back to the voters, suggesting that a by-election be held. The court ruling on the matter came Monday, August 27, 2012, and it favored the CCM. Hensley Daniel had to vacate his seat. A new general election was held on January 22, 2013, instead of the proposed by-election in the St. John constituency. NRP lost the election. The CCM's candidate, Mark Brantley, won the disputed seat.

During the great secession debate of 1998, Sim Daniel surprised many observers by disassociating himself from members of his party, the NRP. Daniel campaigned in support of Amory's party, the CCM, and supported the position that Nevis secede from St. Kitts. Interestingly, during the 1970s, on into the early 1990s, both

Vance Amory and Theodore Hobson were closely aligned with the Labor Party of St. Kitts. Back then, the two men stood against the secession thrust on Nevis. In November 1991, for example, Amory published a memorable column in the *St. Kitts-Nevis Observer*, condemning the secession idea. Seemingly, some time during that period, Amory gave the Labor Party leadership hope that he could re-ignite pro-Labor Party sympathies on Nevis. However, by 1998, Amory's CCM party was championing secession, whereas the NRP argued loudly, "No secession!" When the two parties went at each other over the secession matter in 1998, the two roles were reversed. The CCM was for secession and the NRP against secession. Each party went at the other with the usual vim and vigor.

Shortly before he died in 1997, when the CCM had just begun its secession campaign, Stevens confided "I cannot support secession under its present leadership." It was well known in certain circles that Stevens was no admirer of Vance Amory, whom he saw as an unethical person, driven by opportunism—a position echoed loudly by Mr. Amory's one time friend and political ally Carlyle Jeffers.

CHAPTER 7

A Political Party for Nevis

It was not an accident that Ivor Stevens became one of the founding members of the Nevis Reformation Party. From as early as the 1960s Stevens worked aggressively with Uhral Swanston and other Nevisians to pioneer ideas about political reform and change for Nevis. They started an early effort to build political awareness and independent political thought throughout the island. The group labored tirelessly, and often quietly, to bring an acceptable form of political organization to Nevis, with which Nevisians could identify. It was as far back as the late 1950s, early 1960s, when it dawned on the leading politicians on Nevis that they needed to develop a political party of their own. It had to be Nevis-based, Nevis-centered, and with a political agenda designed by Nevisians. Without any doubt, Nevisians needed some semblance of independence. They needed freedom from the powerful and always threatening Labor Party on St. Kitts. One thing the Nevis leaders had in their favor was the fact that the plantation system that dominated production on St. Kitts was no longer a successful form of economic organization on Nevis and Anguilla. Consequently, labor unionism was weak in both Nevis and Anguilla. Unlike on St. Kitts, the labor union had limited political force on these islands.

After 1961 and following the increased duty placed on cotton export by the St. Kitts government, there was a concerted effort to rally Nevisians to a raised political consciousness, leading Nevisians to make verbal threats about seceding from St. Kitts. The United National Movement emerged from that first thrust for increased autonomy and independence for Nevisians. Robert J. Gordon, first elected as a Nevis representative in September 1943, also claimed that he had an even earlier political organization, probably earlier than 1961.

Real formally organized political parties started to appear in St. Kitts-Nevis elections in 1957. The first two were the Labor Party, derived from the Workers' League, representing the working-class, and the Democratic Party, derived from the Planters' Association, representing the ideals and wishes of a declining planter-class. Of the 6 candidates who ran in Nevis that year, 5 ran as independents and one as a Labor Party candidate. According to Mr. Gordon's granddaughter, Greta Gordon-Lake, he called his organization the Nevis Progressive Party Ltd. However, that organization seemed rudimentary, as no independent documentation about the party has been found. In both 1952 and 1957, Gordon was listed as an "Independent" candidate. However, a recently discovered source does support the claim that Mr. Gordon had some form of early political organization. Meanwhile, Eugene Walwyn, Fred Parris, Wilmoth Nicholls, and James Brooks, appeared to have collaborated to create the United National Movement party. Mr. Stevens, too, seemed to have had some short-lived contact with that early political organization. However, once he became aware of Walwyn's duplicity in dealing with the government on St. Kitts, Stevens moved in other directions, gravitating toward building a political relationship with other Nevisians, particularly Uhral Swanston. It was suggested by Swanston that quite early on, "By 1962, Stevens had become disappointed about Walwyn's lack of leadership in, or commitment to the Nevis struggle."

Also, during the early 1960s, Kittitians too, particularly those who were better educated, began to question what they perceived as the authoritarian leadership style of Robert Bradshaw. They, too, started to search for an alternative to the Labor Party. The People's Action Movement emerged on St. Kitts around 1965, and attracted both Swanston and Stevens from Nevis. Fred Parris was excited about the PAM too. However, while Parris seemed quite content with being an underdog in a St. Kitts party at that time, Stevens and Swanston were still focused on forming a Nevis-based party. Notwithstanding, during the 1960s, thousands of Nevisians accepted the PAM party as an attractive and viable alternative to the Labor Party. The citizens of both St. Kitts and Nevis were fascinated with the young, highly educated, and dynamic speaker that they saw in Dr. William "Billy" Herbert, who had recently graduated from London University with a Ph.D. in law. Further, since at that time the Labor Party was not sympathetic to the peculiar needs of Nevis, they were willing to try for alternative leadership. So it was, everyone saw St. Kitts as the culprit in the islands' tumultuous relationship. Few persons at the time talked about England, which also neglected Nevis and Anguilla on a consistent basis. Meanwhile, Bradshaw's vindictive attitude toward his detractors on Nevis kept him at the forefront of the colonial experience with England, to which he too was as much a victim. In time, however, despite some shared political interests, the People's Action Movement did not last long as the dominant political party for Nevisians.

Nevisians were attracted to the idea that they should create an independent politics for their island. However, during that era, such a journey was an uncertain and difficult road for Nevisians to travel. Yet, the dream mesmerized and enchanted them. Since they benefitted little from the labor revolution of the 1930s and 1940s, which transformed Caribbean politics and its leadership, they were new to the organized, aggressive politics that was emerging in the area. Accordingly, Nevis party politics experienced traumatic birth pangs during the 1960s and 1970s. By then, St. Kitts politics and its leadership had become an overpowering force, and an ever-present threat to the emerging political empowerment of Nevisians.

Accordingly, as new political leaders emerged on Nevis, the people were often suspicious that some of them would make selfish deals with the government in St. Kitts and betray the cause of Nevis. For example, Gordon and Liburd appeared to have been figureheads. They showed little independence. Later, Walwyn accused Wilmoth Nicholls of planning to betray Nevis, but it was Walwyn who betrayed Nevisians by joining the Labor Party. Actually, when Nevisians first encountered the Labor Party, it was arrogant and haughty, but bruised from its many battles that eventually ended in victories against the planter-class. Nevisians felt they were treated by St. Kitts as too naïve, too unprepared to launch out on their own, and too incompetent to lead themselves. But, that was the same comment the planters made about the working-class on St. Kitts in 1937, when they were offered a first opportunity at limited franchise. Reflecting on the historical relationship between the islands, Sir Probyn Innis, former governor of St. Kitts-Nevis, wrote in 1983,

> It has become fashionable in recent years to project St. Kitts and Nevis to the world as "The Sister Islands" of the Caribbean. However, a study of the history of relations between the two neighboring islands reveals that their differences are deep and long-standing and cannot be dismissed as merely sibling rivalries.

Two of the first persons to work closely with Ivor at creating some political organization and consciousness were his wife Dora and Uhral Swanston. By 1966 the two men knew each other better and became close friends. That was shortly after Ivor lost for a second time to Eugene Walwyn. Swanston reflected on that early working relationship this way: "During 1966, Ivor and I continued to struggle together and toyed around with the idea of forming a political party."

Meanwhile, friendly overtures to Nevis from the People's Action Movement were appreciated, because of its anti-Labor Party rhetoric. The PAM was also improving its following in Nevis and Anguilla. By the end of the 1960s. PAM's first political success came with victories at the polls by Adams in Anguilla and Parris on Nevis, 1966. However, dramatic events on St. Kitts and Anguilla in 1967, followed by the *Christena* disaster in 1970, undermined further development of the PAM on Nevis. Parris did win for PAM in 1971, but later crossed the legislative floor, gave up his loyalty to the PAM, and turned to the Labor Party.

Swanston claimed that when the Nevis Reformation Party emerged as a Nevis party, such an independent political move for Nevis was opposed by the PAM leadership. Also, since Fred Parris was the PAM's candidate on Nevis, he refused invitations to join the drive toward a Nevis-based political party. Some years later, Parris became frustrated with the PAM and turned to the Labor Party. That move, however, made Nevisians suspicious. It was not intended to help Nevis, but was for Parris' personal financial gain. After that move, Ivor and Uhral never invited Parris to work with them again. Just as was the case with Walwyn, Parris, too, lost the support and trust of Nevisians. Later, it was quite a slap in the face of Nevisians, in the late 1980s, when Sim Daniel nominated Fred Parris as Leader of the Opposition in the legislature of the Nevis Island Government, ahead of the elected member of the Concerned Citizens Movement, Vance Amory. However, such a high handed move at that time helped foster the idea that Sim Daniel had become the "monarch of all he surveyed." Daniel avoided doing what was right because he could do as he pleased. He simply nominated a member of his "good old boys' club" to the island's legislature.

In relating how he and Stevens worked together in the early years, Swanston explained how they began to build a new vision for Nevis, as they struggled and dreamed together in lonely political trenches. After some years, they were joined by other visionary Nevisians, who in time, numbered among Nevis political pioneers. The group included Ralph Harris, Horace Liburd, Rhoan Liburd, Carlton Parris, Joseph Browne, Rev. Hicks, and others. Some of the new friends were part of the political group who felt disillusioned and betrayed by Walwyn, when he joined the Labor Party. In time, however, they consoled themselves, held serious indoor meetings around Nevis, and tried hard to build an independent political party for Nevis.

During the gathering process, Nevis party pioneers held preliminary discussions at the home of Alvin Warner in Cotton Ground, Joseph Browne in Brick Kiln, and Rhoan Liburd at Stoney

Grove, Charlestown. Ivor also claimed that he held similar meetings in his home at Low Street, as early as 1967. During those early years, Sim Daniel was not involved in Nevis politics. He was invited in later, when the early organizers sensed trouble from Bradshaw and needed the advice of a lawyer. They did not have the money to pay one. Ironically, years later, Ivor lamented the inclusion of a lawyer as leader of Nevis politics. He also commented frequently and openly that if he could do it all over again, he would not involve any lawyers in Nevis politics. It was also noted, Ivor expressed disappointment when one of his protégés, Victor Martin, chose to study law.

Stevens indicated that it was quite a challenge to agree on a suitable name for the new Nevis party. As they debated, Swanston suggested that it would be seen as an act of rebellion by Bradshaw's government, and they could expect some retribution. The new party's name therefore had to be crafted carefully, so that Premier Bradshaw and his Labor Party stalwarts did not see it as too radical or too threatening a move by Nevisians. Eventually, the pioneers of the movement agreed on the name, Nevis Reformation Party. Levi Morton claimed that the name was his idea, and one of his quiet contributions to Nevis politics.

During that period of the 1970s, Bradshaw found himself leading in an increasingly complex period of Caribbean history and politics. The era was caught up in the dynamics of a rapidly changing world, in ideas, technology, and politics. Despite his fascination with the British accent and the consequent affectation of his speaking style, there was never a doubt that Bradshaw was conscious of himself as an African person, and aware of his Caribbean history. He boasted frequently about his Ashanti bloodline, demonstrated his knowledge of African culture, and was always very committed to his Caribbean-ness. At the turn of the 1970s, Bradshaw was very hurt over his loss of control in Anguilla, due to an internal political revolt. Many persons thought that the uprising in Anguilla was quietly supported by other Caribbean governments, and by the British government. At the same time, there was the Vietnam War, radical Black nationalist movements, and civil rights protests in the Caribbean and in other parts of the

Americas. There were also growing demands that European nations and America decolonize the Caribbean. Efforts were ongoing to spread Pan-African radicalism throughout the African Diaspora. None of those developments made Bradshaw very happy. There was also great consternation in the government on St. Kitts when it was revealed that foreign soldiers and PAM supporters participated in the failed Anguillan invasion of St. Kitts, June 10, 1967.

In time, frustration from the continuing Anguillan revolt was heightened by the *Christena* tragedy. All these events occurred at a time when the Labor government, under Bradshaw, was also striving to achieve independence from British rule for St. Kitts, Nevis, and Anguilla. This had become a major political thrust for Bradshaw, after the achievement of Statehood in 1967, and after Kittitians gave him a vote of confidence for independence, in the election of 1975. However, Bradshaw still had a complex problem on his hands: the stress of dealing with the Anguillan crisis, followed by the *Christena* disaster, and a frustrating delay in the move toward independence from Britain. These all overwhelmed Bradshaw. Eventually, the pressure appeared to have caused a recurrence of an earlier illness from lung cancer. Everything possible was done to help Bradshaw live on. His ultimate dream was to lead St. Kitts, Nevis, and Anguilla into political independence from Britain. However, Bradshaw died quietly on May 23, 1978, surrounded by family and political friends.[35] Bradshaw's lieutenant and deputy leader of the party took the leadership baton, however, Paul Southwell too, died suddenly almost one year later, causing sudden, unprecedented uncertainty and shifts in the Labor Party's leadership.

With the People's Action Movement, things were different. While the party had its leadership issues too, illness or death had not attacked the party then. Instead, by 1970, PAM had started to make inroads into the politics of both St. Kitts and Nevis. The party won the St. George's—St. James seat, in 1966, and was poised to win it again in 1971. Eventually, some political and ideological skirmishes

---

35 Browne, W. T. (1992). *From Commoner to King*. Lanham, MD: University of America Press.

did ensue among the ordinary citizens, before the NRP was allowed to supersede the PAM on Nevis. The process took longer on St. Kitts for an overthrow of the Labor Party, but it did happen during the 1980s, and on up to early in the 1990s.

The effort to set up a political party for Nevis did bear useful fruit. According to Swanston, "The NRP party was officially launched on October 20, 1970." Sim Daniel was selected Chairman; Ivor Stevens, Deputy Chairman; Uhral Swanston, Second Deputy Chairman; Rhoan Liburd, Secretary; Carlton Parris, Treasurer, and Levi Morton, Party Organizer. Morton was responsible for setting up street meetings. All the pioneers worked hard, not only to organize the party, but also to get the masses on the island excited about their new political party. However, once the organization started to fall into place, jealousy and suspicion began to surface among the founding members—the usual jealousies seen in Caribbean politics did occur.

Some of the men from Walwyn's former faction were not certain whether they could trust Ivor because of his prior pro-St. Kitts leanings. They were also convinced that he was pro Labor Party, in 1957, and that he was still aligned with the PAM, in 1970. Stevens had been one of their candidates on Nevis in 1966. Generally, Nevisians trusted Sim, and were welcoming to him. However, Stevens and Swanston were not certain that he shared their all-out commitment to Nevis. Both Sim and his father, Job Daniel, had shown strong commitments to Bradshaw and the Labor Party in the past. It was also widely known that Daniel had been invited home from England by Bradshaw, to work as a magistrate on St. Kitts.

Victory

By the time of the general election, in 1971, and the local council election of 1972, however, trust and camaraderie had been rebuilt in the Nevis Reformation Party camp. The NRP won big in both elections and was on its way to becoming the dominant political party in Nevis. Reflecting on Sim Daniel, as a lawyer, and as leader of the NRP, Swanston concluded bemusedly, "Daniel ran his office of Nevis Affairs like a clinic. He saw more patients than a doctor." As Daniel himself suggested, for many years the real vibrant, decisive leader and mind behind the NRP's stability and vision was Ivor Stevens. Quite often, Daniel was engaged in building his personal wealth and business relationships, particularly with people who visited the island, some opting to invest in houses and land. The real estate business became Premier Daniel's true interest. It was no longer Nevis politics. He found little time to nurture ideas, build friendships with the average Nevisian, or ensure the growth of the NRP. There was a void in active and creative leadership of the NRP. However, Ivor seized the moment and moved in to fill that leadership vacuum. Stevens saw his actions simply as remaining loyal to the movement he worked so hard to create. Meanwhile, it was heartbreaking and discomforting for Stevens, particularly when he saw Daniel turn his back on the NRP during the late 1990s. It was the NRP that did so much to make Sim Daniel an important Nevis lawyer and wealthy businessman, even if not a respected politician.

The historical evidence is clear. For many years, it was Ivor's commitment to Nevis, to the success of the NRP, combined with the vindictive, myopic politics of the Labor Party toward Nevis, that kept the NRP vibrant and successful. For example, when Ivor rose to elected office in Nevis, it was a position from which he saw the secession idea could be used to gain leverage with St. Kitts for the NRP and for Nevis. Thus, he resorted to that strategy again and again, during the 1970s. It was still a useful theme during the 1980s, when the NRP formed the coalition government with the PAM. For example, Ivor insisted on having the now famous, Clause 113, embedded into the islands' independence constitution, asserting that Nevisians can attain secession, at any point in the Federation's history, provided they choose to, and can win the votes needed to approve the move, as determined by the constitution. However, during 1997, when both Daniel and Amory were clamoring for a secession vote and an ultimate break with St. Kitts, in 1998, Stevens noted, "On the secession issue the island lacks leadership."

One of the ironic features of the NRP's politics was its switch from advocating secession to embracing independence in the early

1980s. During the 1975 election campaign, Ivor and Sim campaigned vehemently against the Labor Party's proposed move to independence for St. Kitts-Nevis. They agreed with the People's Action Movement that the State of St. Kitts and Nevis was not ready for the move to political independence from Britain, as had happened in Jamaica, Barbados, and Trinidad and Tobago. Meanwhile, as leaders of Nevis politics, the men of the NRP insisted that the only move Nevisians wanted to make was the one that would separate them from St. Kitts, once and for all. Despite all the other claims, Daniel could blame no one but himself for the failure to attain secession for Nevis. Nevisians wanted secession more than coalition in 1980. However, Daniel was leader of the NRP delegation, and they chose coalition over secession. Many Nevisians, including Mr. Daniel, until the day he died, remained uncertain as to whether by joining with the PAM in 1980, Nevis won a victory. In retrospect, the association moved Nevis, at least for a time, from its historical position of opposition politics to St. Kitts. It also laid the groundwork for more creative and pragmatic politics between the two islands.

Independence Talks

The Nevis position on secession was hardened further as Robert Bradshaw made his argument for independence, then dissolved the House of Assembly on November 7, 1975. There were three planks in his political platform:

> (1) I therefore invite each and all of you to declare with me, as plain Robert Llewellyn Bradshaw, and with the government of this State which you kindly and generously elected me in 1971 to lead, to say unequivocally and now (a) that the sugar lands of St. Kitts shall forever remain public property (b) that all we are concerned about is paying a reasonable price for the land and (c) that the former owners will stop wasting time and come to a settlement with government within the next 6 months.

> In addition, and at this time, I also invite you, in the light of present circumstances as you know them, to join with me and with our government to say (11) that there shall be no secession for Nevis from this unitary state of St. Kitts, Nevis and Anguilla; and (111) that this your government, is empowered to seek independence either in association with another CARICOM State, or on its own. I ask you to answer each and every one of these three questions on Monday 1st December 1975, when you'll go to the polls to vote in General Elections on that same day.

The People's Action Movement opposed independence on St. Kitts, claiming the islands were too small and too poor to become independent. In retrospect, the problem seemed to have been that independence would come with the Labor Party still at the controls. In Nevis, Anguilla, and among certain people on St. Kitts, there was real fear that Bradshaw would become the leader of an independent St. Kitts, Nevis, and Anguilla. On page 7, of the *Democrat* newspaper for November 22, 1975, the PAM ran this advertisement:

> People of St. Kitts, Bradshaw is wrong this time. Independence will ruin us. Do not vote for independence. Vote against Bradshaw and his mad desire to make this little speck of dust his little independent domain to do what he likes.

On November 29th, the PAM also ran this in the *Democrat*: "NO TO INDEPENDENCE. Vote for Freedom. Vote for PAM." Despite the subtle threats and promises by the PAM, the electorate on St. Kitts voted as Bradshaw asked. On Nevis, however, to no one's surprise, the electorate listened to the Nevis Reformation Party leaders and voted for secession. Reflecting on that 1975 election, the late Fitzroy Bryant wrote: "In the General Elections of December 1,

1975, the Labor Party won the 7 seats in St. Kitts and the NRP won the two seats in Nevis."

For the next 5 years, while the Labor government planned and moved toward independence, both the PAM and the NRP did everything they could to thwart the move. On Statehood Day, February 27, 1976, Premier Bradshaw said in part,

> To be independent means that you neither depend upon nor are subordinate to anyone. Thus, as we approach the independence which we have freely and deliberately decreed for ourselves, let us be in no doubt at all about that which we shall embark upon, for manna will not fall from heaven just like that. Let us face it knowing that it will demand of us hard work, objectivity, unity, and self-respect and we must continue to be seen actively to be helping ourselves. Therefore, on this propitious day, let us all as brothers and sisters link hands together and deliberately say "Out Statehood, In Independence!"

The first round of independence talks was held with the government of St. Kitts, Nevis, and Anguilla, in London, during March 1976. A proposal was made that September 16, 1976 (Bradshaw's birthday), be the set date for independence. At the next round of talks, in April 1976, Sim Daniel represented the NRP. However, Daniel was combative and uncooperative, presenting only the position Ivor, the other Nevisians, and himself had agreed on: "Independence No, Secession Yes!" Bradshaw wrote to Daniel in October of 1976, asking for his cooperation, as the State government endeavored to achieve political independence. However, as Bryant noted, "The correspondence quickly became very acrimonious and ended in December 1976."

When the third meeting for independence talks was held in London, March 1977, the leaders of the NRP still had one goal in mind for Nevis—secession! They were even willing to accept colonial status with Britain, to which Anguilla had reverted since 1967. Even such a backward political move was preferred to independence with St. Kitts. However, the British government was not interested in an Anguilla-type move for Nevis. They were willing to have one new British colony, not two. Britain did have another dilemma in the colonies, but the hope was that it would work itself out.

After the independence meeting, the NRP carried out a secession referendum on Nevis, August 18, 1977. The outcome was overwhelmingly in favor of secession. Of those who voted, 4,193 said *yes* and 14 said *no*. Thirteen ballots were spoiled. Then, a letter was sent to Premier Bradshaw and copied to Governor, Sir Probyn Innis and Dr. David Owen, the British Minister of Foreign and Commonwealth Affairs. The letter was signed by Levi Morton, Secretary to the NRP. It said in part,

> I have been directed by the Executive Committee of the NRP to invite you to take cognizance of the wishes of the people of Nevis and act in a statesmanlike manner so as to give to the people of Nevis the right of self-determination and as expressed on the 18th, instant.

Proposals for increasing the powers of the Nevis Local Council were sent to the NRP on May 5, 1978, by the Labor government, which also expressed the desire

> that we will successfully bridge the gap between our two Parties and our two groups and bring about the unity of purpose which is not only vital to the survival of this country but honestly expected by all right-thinking people in the State.

By May 1978, the Labor Party had become concerned and even desperate over the slow pace of the independence talks. Bradshaw had also become ill and the Labor Party was very concerned about his longevity. Soon there were rumors about his declining health and possible death. However, the Labor Party was still hoping Bradshaw would be the first Prime Minister of St. Kitts-Nevis, even if Anguilla was excluded. Every member of the Labor Party, and most Kittitians, wanted to see Bradshaw lead the islands into independence, and become the first Prime Minister of an independent St. Kitts-Nevis—even if he was in a wheel chair and served for one day! Like Bird of Antigua, Barrow of Barbados, and Gairy of Grenada, Bradshaw's pivotal role in St. Kitts-Nevis-Anguilla's formative, working-class politics, made him deserve that honor. But, it was not to be! He died quietly surrounded by family and political comrades, 1978.

Following Bradshaw's death, political events in St. Kitts-Nevis stalled briefly, due to some bickering over succession. Even as he lay dying, neither Bradshaw nor the Labor Party established any clear line of succession for leadership. Seemingly, there was more interest about future leadership into independence. Later, matters moved rapidly and dramatically. Paul Southwell, who succeeded Bradshaw, died suddenly in St. Lucia while on government business there. The death occurred almost one year after Bradshaw, on May 18, 1979. Probably, because of the known wrangling over leadership succession, there was a rumor that Lee Moore, who was also on the trip to St. Lucia, and was in line to lead the government, had killed Southwell, clandestinely, in St. Lucia. However, few people believed that story. It was quickly seen as a rumor started by members of the PAM party. A number of people in St. Kitts were aware that Southwell had numerous health problems, even as he led the government, and before he opted for that fatal trip to St. Lucia. According to Dr. Sebastian, the medical evidence suggested that Southwell died of natural causes. Southwell was succeeded by Lee L. Moore. It was a critical point in political ascendency on St. Kitts-Nevis, but as time demonstrated, Moore was not the best man for such an auspicious time in St. Kitts-Nevis, and Labor Party history.

Under Moore's leadership, there was a meeting in Antigua, December 1979. A tentative agreement was reached on the march toward independence. The meeting involved the British Minister of State at the Foreign and Commonwealth Office, Nicholas Ridley, a delegation from the St. Kitts-Nevis government, and a delegation from the Nevis Reformation Party, then considered the opposition in the legislature. In just about 2 months' time, in February 1980, the Labor government was more surprised than everyone else when it was voted out of power. Suddenly, the PAM and the NRP were thrust into power. They took the reins of government as the new coalition government.

Everything was virtually in place for St. Kitts-Nevis to achieve its long-fought independence from Britain. Following the 1979 talks, the government started special preparations with the hope of attaining independence early in 1980. A draft Independence Constitution had been prepared, and the Independence Celebrations Planning Committee, first set up in April 1977, was reactivated on December 21, 1979. Ironically, the Labor Party politicians could only look on as spectators at the real independence ceremony four years later, in 1983.

Meanwhile, the PAM and NRP politicians, who had vehemently opposed any talk of independence, for the last eight years, were at the helm of government, and poised to lead the islands, when Britain allowed them the very special political status. The unprecedented position that confronted NRP forced a change of heart. Neither the NRP nor the PAM could afford to turn back the hands of time and refuse to accept political independence, being gladly offered by Britain. The next level of political advancement for St. Kitts-Nevis was there on a platter, waiting to be taken. Britain was still anxious to wean its Caribbean colonies.[36] The PAM politicians laid aside their poverty and size objections. Meanwhile, following Ivor's skillful strategizing to build secession into the constitution, the NRP agreed to take a rain-check on the secession matter. Thus, the new government of St. Kitts-Nevis agreed to take the islands into independence. It would have been an irony, yet a great honor to the memory of Robert Bradshaw, if the PAM-NRP leaders chose September 16, Bradshaw's birthday, as St. Kitts-Nevis Independence

[36] Palmer, C. A. (2006). *Eric Williams and the Making of the Modern Caribbean.* Chapel Hill: University of North Carolina Press.

Day. But the bitterness in the politics was too great for PAM-NRP leaders to agree on giving such an honor to Bradshaw. September 19, 1983, was chosen as Independence Day instead. Later, when the Labor Party returned to power, they honored Bradshaw's memory by naming September 16, National Heroes' Day. The man deserved such a legacy to his pioneering politics in St. Kitts-Nevis.

No one commented on it then, but all through the secession years, the NRP devised varied strategies of procrastination, as it sought to frustrate the actions of the Labor government, especially in its move toward independence after 1975. That was coupled with certain twists of fate, such as the sudden deaths in the Labor camp, 1978 and 1979. Those were factors that hindered St. Kitts-Nevis from attaining independence under a Labor Party government. Ivor and the leaders of the NRP did not win great material or political success for Nevis during that period; but they were not wasted years. The actions of NRP leaders were critical in ensuring a delay in the Labor government's move toward independence—they deliberately frustrated the Labor Party's effort in that direction.

Despite their sudden, unexpected thrust into power, the two opposition parties, NRP and PAM, came into their own, organized a government, and moved the islands forward economically and politically. They managed the affairs of government creditably, as they worked to change the political and economic culture of the islands. While the PAM-NRP coalition government diversified the economy of St. Kitts-Nevis, it also oversaw the beginning of a social downward spiraling on the islands. There were frequent allegations of drug dealing and money laundering connected to some of PAM's well-placed leaders. Then, there was the sudden and mysterious disappearance of PAM's first leader, Dr. William "Billy" Herbert. He, along with some family and friends went fishing on Sunday morning, June 19, 1994. None of them has been seen since.

Three suggestions have been given as explanations of what happened. None has been positive. And no one thinks it was just a sudden mishap at sea that led to the disappearance. One possible explanation is that the event was a political hit. Another is that it was a drug-related matter. The third suggestion is that the sudden disappearance was related to Dr. Herbert's involvement with money laundering. It was also during the PAM-NRP watch that the infamous character, Cecil Connor (Little Nut) came to town and found government's accommodation allegedly with the PAM, then with the Labor Party. In time he became a feared character on St. Kitts. Only the eventual intervention of the U.S. government and their arrest of Little Nut saved the day for the government and people of St. Kitts-Nevis—prior to his arrest the people lived in fear. During the rest of the 1980s, and for part of the 1990s, the seasoned Labor Party was in opposition to the new, untried PAM-NRP government. However, the new government maintained power long enough to gain the people's trust. The coalition government dominated the next 13 years of St. Kitts-Nevis politics. Its promise of "better" did not come to everyone, but under that PAM-NRP leadership, social relations between the two islands improved. There was broader inclusion of the local population in economic success, and the move toward private enterprise in the islands changed profoundly. At times, however, the impact was negative for the citizens.

Meanwhile, the infrastructure on Nevis did improve dramatically. Kittitians and Nevisians continue to acknowledge Ivor's critical role in unprecedented infrastructural development on Nevis, during his tenure in the PAM-NRP government. Ivor also helped ensure more tolerance between the two islands, and fostered a more workable St. Kitts-Nevis politics. Many Nevisians, and some St. Kitts politicians, including former Prime Minister Simmonds, continue to speak fondly of Ivor, the maverick, and his contributions to St. Kitts and Nevis development during that era. For most of those years, both Ivor and Sim served as actors in the NRP, and in the coalition government.

In time, however, as with all other dominant political parties, NRP leaders became conscious of their influence. Some became arrogant, selfish, and complacent too. Stevens and Swanston continued their work to keep the party sensitive to, and reachable by, the common people, as they endeavored to keep the political commitments made to their constituents. However, the party continued to leave the people behind. That was a reality the then financially successful NRP leader, Sim Daniel, did not even appear to observe. However, Stevens felt responsible for the party's failings, and repeatedly spoke of his personal shortcomings in ensuring a strengthening of the party. Stevens also admitted that at times he had serious problems with some of the unilateral decisions made by the party's leader. A former close ally of Stevens commented, "Ivor never challenged Sim. He believed in Sim although he felt Sim was crooked."

In his suggestions about what to include in the constitution, if and when Nevis becomes a Republic, Ivor was subtle, but a number of his ideas were designed to control the activities of the political leader. For Ivor, two important areas that should be controlled are (a) limiting the length of time a leader can serve, (term limits) and (b) setting up some oversight of the person who controls the finances in government, usually the leader of the government.

Undoubtedly, the NRP came to the point of being the monarch of all it surveyed in Nevis, during the 1980s. Stevens and Daniel were virtually invulnerable, politically. They knew it and lived it. Generally, Ivor channeled his popularity to help the citizenry and to keep himself electable, especially by the poor masses. He kept himself accessible and useful to the people, by seeking to make their daily lives better. During that time, too, those who opposed or attacked the NRP were ridiculed and treated with disdain by Ivor, Sim, and their vast following. I still recall being danced around in Charlestown by one overly enthusiastic supporter of the NRP to the lyrics "Look at um, look at um, look at um! Saying he running against Mr. Daniel." It was all because I chose to challenge the NRP in 1983. Usually, Sim was quiet, but attacks on the NRP and his policies could, at times, push him out of control. He too, became angry and prone to personal attacks. Like the Labor Party of the 1960s and 1970s, the NRP treated their opposition with a negative style and a brash attitude. In time, the new coalition government came to adopt some of the very strategies of arrogance they once hated and criticized about the Labor Party.

The first real challenge to the NRP's political dominance on Nevis came in 1983, at the height of the party's popularity—a time when NRPs leadership appeared invincible and eternal. That early attack by the Nevis Independent Party was quite sudden and unexpected. The response of the NRP leadership and its stalwarts was mixed with fear and anger. However, in reality, Ivor and Sim had little to fear at that time. Their support on the island was still quite broad and very sound. Seemingly, since they weathered the *Christena* years together, most Nevisians felt an affinity to the NRP and its politicians. There was a strong symbiotic relationship between them. During the 1970s, the NRP was the party that felt their pain, and led the challenge of Nevisians to Bradshaw, the Labor Party, and St. Kitts. One aspect of the Nevis Independent Party's attack was the ease with which the NRPs leadership was trading the rights of the island's citizenry. It was a criticism Daniel appeared to misunderstand. In a conversation with an NRP stalwart during 2011, I was reminded that Daniel actually defended his naivety on that matter. He once boasted at a public meeting about his right to sell vast acreage of the small island to foreign visitors. There were also occasions when supporters of the NRP attacked supporters of the Nevis Independent Party openly for one reason. They dared to oppose the NRP, their favorite party. Others sought opportunities to spy on the new party and then carried back reports to NRP leaders, because, at that time, opposition to the NRP was unthinkable. The NRP was Nevis' party. Nevisians had watched it grow and blossom as it emerged from the *Christena* storm, survived Bradshaw, and won a place in government for Nevisians. Back in the early 1980s, most Nevisians supported the NRP, and like George Washington back in the 1790s, did not see the need for another political party. All Nevisians wanted, then, was the NRP.

It was the reality on Nevis, at the time, and probably it is still the case, that a person's job, lifestyle, and future, hinge on their political party affiliation. Consequently, for a number of Nevisians, supporting the NRP meant success. It was the party in power on Nevis, not the Nevis Independent Party. Supporting the NIP translated into ostracism, harassment, and a precarious existence.

Even one's job was in danger. Eventually, the NIP fell apart, almost as suddenly as it had emerged. Just short of 10 years after the NIP died, another party, the Concerned Citizens Movement, appeared on Nevis. Ironically, the person who emerged as leader of the CCM had been crucial in undermining the success of the NIP. He had also been rescued and rewarded by the NRP leader, after a political betrayal. Strange as it may seem, the leader of the CCM once served as the Permanent Secretary in Finance on Nevis, under NRP leadership.

A concerted attack against the NRP came from the CCM during the late 1980s, and on into the early 1990s. For part of that time, Ivor was retired from active politics. His nephew suggested Ivor had become "tired, disheartened, and disillusioned, because of what had been happening within his party. Further, as compared with the other Nevis politicians, Ivor had already exerted himself beyond the call of duty." While the NRP's battle with the NIP was short lived, that would not be the case with the CCM. The new party had the support of young Nevisians who detested the NRP and its disinterested leadership. The CCM also had financial backing from Carlisle Jeffers, a Nevisian living on St. Croix, the Labor Party on St. Kitts, and some other Nevisians living outside of Nevis. By the late 1980s, many Nevisians were becoming tired of the NRP's insensitivity to the needs of the masses. Calypsonian Dis and Dat captured that reality in his song, "*Its in the Pipeline.*" This situation was further underlined and exploited with the airport at New Castle. The project was envisioned and planned by the NRP leadership. It was completed later by the CCM. Ironically, it was named in honor of Vance Amory, not Sim Daniel, who really deserved the honor.

Vance Amory, leader of the CCM, cricketer, educator, banker, and permanent secretary, turned politician also became a rising political star. He lacked much in political experience, but he was young, good looking, and bent on leading Nevis at all costs. Right from the start, Amory had a loyal following, bold and desperate enough to break ranks with the NRP. In the Nevis local election of 1992, to the delight of many Nevisians, Daniel lost his seat to Malcolm Guishard of the CCM. Ralph Hutton, and other excited

Nevisians, were overjoyed at Mr. Daniel's defeat. Many Nevisians went around the island that night, honking their vehicles' horns, as they celebrated the loss by Daniel and the NRP to the CCM. In their enthusiasm some CCM supporters also went to Mr. Daniel's home that night and demanded the key for the government-owned vehicle he drove. That is a hand-down from British politics. Once the election results are announced, those who lose the count are out. Sometimes, the party rivalries that develop during election campaigns can inspire exaggerated and unnecessary hand-over demands by party extremists. That was the case in Nevis 1992.

Ironically, back in 1983, Mr. Hutton was very committed to the NRP party. Without hesitation, he refused to support his cousin in the NIP party because he was daring to oppose Mr. Daniel. Since 1983, Ralph has learned a lot about trusting politicians, and how politics can change over time. Today he would probably consider supporting his cousin and the NIP against both the CCM and the NRP. He has become disillusioned with their politics. The CCM took the reins of political power on Nevis from the NRP in 1992, relegating the NRP to opposition status on Nevis. It took a period of 14 years before the NRP could be returned to power in 2006, when Hensley Daniel won back the critical Guishard seat in St. John's Parish. Unfortunately, Guishard was embroiled in a land-sale scandal, and died suddenly about one year after losing his seat to Hensley Daniel.

Ivor did live to see the once indomitable NRP wilt and fall. The powerful and vibrant NRP that he helped to build, as the darling of Nevisians, during the 1970s and 1980s, lost the people's confidence by the early 1990s. Often, as Ivor and others worked to keep the NRP alive and well, they became disappointed with the leader's lackluster commitment. The coup de grace came at the turn of the century, when Mr. Daniel launched a stinging attack against his former colleagues in the NRP. He was angry that they opposed his unchanging position of secession from St. Kitts.

However, during the 2006 campaign, when Sim Daniel noted that one tax item the CCM was seeking to move into law was detrimental to his real estate business, he openly attacked the CCM leadership and supported his old party, the NRP, again. As the 2011 campaign emerged, Mr. Daniel seemed to be wavering again between his old party, the NRP, and the CCM, the party of his law partner and protégé, now turned politician, Mark Brantley. It was a fight to the finish the morning of July 12, 2011. Initially, the victory was awarded to Hensley Daniel of NRP, by 14 votes. However, Mark Brantley, took the matter to the court and his argument that people's right to vote was violated, won the nod of the judges. A by-election for that seat was anticipated in 90 days, but a general election was called instead. Now, the Nevis local election of July 11, 2011, with all its fanfare and drama, must go into the history books. It will be talked about for a long time. However, even as the islands surge into the 21st century, the Labor Party on St. Kitts still remains fair game and a scapegoat to some Nevisians, for the venom and ills in Nevis politics. Thus, the secession issue can become vibrant again in the near future.

As his final years slipped by, Stevens did reflect on, and commented frequently, about Nevis politics. He talked about the loyalty he showed to Mr. Daniel and the ridicule he got at times, as he worked to keep the NRP together. There were times when Daniel seemed disinterested in the party's success, and unconcerned about its future. Stevens was heard every now and then making negative comments about lawyers in politics. He noted that in his lifetime he had been involved with, and observed the actions of two lawyers in politics, Walwyn and Daniel. Stevens concluded he was deceived by one lawyer in the United National Movement, then turned around to relive that experience with another lawyer, in the Nevis Reformation Party. When Stevens left politics, he talked of weaknesses he had observed in the NRP, and of anticipating its fall. There is no evidence that he and Daniel met or spoke with each other during his final days, even while Stevens was dying at the hospital. Despite those many years the two men worked together, to build and lead the NRP, during the 1970s and 1980s, they could not find it within themselves to reach out to each other, even as Stevens lay dying. The vicissitudes and currents of time had pushed them so far apart, physically and ideologically, by the 1990s. On the other hand, despite their wrangling, from time to time, Southwell was standing at Bradshaw's bedside while he died. There was even the idea that Bradshaw passed the baton of leadership, symbolically, as he died, when he made the statement to the group of Labor Party comrades at his bedside, "Hold strain."

Today, the NRP is getting to the point of a change in leadership again. It is also a political party under fire, after the recent, almost bloody elections in 2011 and 2013. No political party holds the love and interests of a people forever—not even NRP. But, the NRP will always be remembered as the Nevis political party that transformed the island. It challenged the powerful Labor Party, along with its legendary leaders, including, Bradshaw, Southwell, France, Bryant, Moore, and Payne. At times the men on either side virtually stood toe to toe, fighting to the bitter end for what each believed was right for his island. In the process, the aspirations and dreams of Nevisians were changed. The island has been transformed between then and now. No one politician did, or could have brought about such comprehensive transformation on any island. It took organized politics and a determined, united people, caught up in a symbiotic relationship. During its heyday, the NRP brought all these requirements together on Nevis, as it worked to change the future of the island for Nevisians. However, while Sim Daniel, the Nevisian, bore the name "leader of the NRP," it was Ivor Stevens, the Kittitian, who steeled himself, defied the challenges, and kept his commitment to Nevisians. He worked faithfully, at times without the support of Daniel, as he led the way in changing the drudgery that strangled the lives of the people. In time, those who care to examine the annals of Nevis will conclude, Ivor Algernon Stevens, more than any other contemporary politician, left unique markings on the sands of time in Nevis. The NRP, to date is still the most successful political party on Nevis. It was a tool, and an instrument for Ivor's political and transformational success on the island.

CHAPTER 8

LOYALTY VS. SUSPICION, TWO MEN, ONE NEVIS

Ivor Stevens and Simeon Daniel were generally accepted as the legitimate political leaders of Nevis throughout most of the 1970s and 1980s. The two men struggled together, with the people of Nevis behind them, through very difficult political times. They heard the people, won their respect and loyalty. To the average Nevisian, while Daniel and Stevens were at the helm, arguing the case for Nevis and reaching out to direct the island's affairs, all was well. Few people questioned the actions of the two men, their loyalty to Nevisians, or their leadership style. And, there were no questions about how well they worked together, planned together, what vision they developed for Nevis, or how each man's personal style or personality was impacting politics and society on the island.

In public, Stevens and Daniel were usually cordial and friendly toward each other. Few Nevisians understood that by the early 1980s there was an increasingly strained relationship between them. Over time, that friendship deteriorated to the point where the two men started to avoid each other. When they had to meet each other, the meetings were strained, tainted with suspicion, and growing evidence that the camaraderie had died between them. Each ensuing year their relationship lost its glue. If there were ever love it had become drained, to the point that it barely existed. People close to the men saw evidence of animosity. They noted how the two men acted toward each other. Others who observed the new developments in the relationship made insightful comments about the twists and turns in the association between the two men on their journey through time.

Both Stevens and Daniel returned to Nevis at critical stages in the island's social and political development. Each had spent a number of years abroad, and on the way back to Nevis, spent an interim period working on St. Kitts. Ironically, as a result of experiences each man had on St. Kitts, they both came over to Nevis with politics on their minds. One returned as a lawyer, a cautious, quiet, and deliberate man. The other returned a veteran of WW II, a jack-of-all-trades, businessman, a very practical, and confident human being. Under normal circumstances, the two men might not have been drawn to each other. They were different in many ways: In energy, in style, in perception of self, and in view of the world, they were complete opposites. But there is that adage, "Politics makes strange bedfellows." Stevens and Daniel came together and worked with the other pioneers to create and manage the NRP. In Nevis politics they found common ground.

The two men were so different in style, background, and ideology, that only something as subtle, as enchanting, and as complex as politics, could have drawn the two men together, kept them stepping in time, and working with each other, for as long as they did. Toward the end of their political dance, they drifted apart conspicuously, and the cohesion between them snapped. However, their break-up might have started much earlier. It simply became more visible and evident toward the end of their political waltz. By then, Nevisians had also become more politically conscious and more critical of the trends in the islands' politics.

Not long after Daniel assumed leadership of the NRP, it became obvious to most Nevisians that he was neither a strong leader nor a natural politician. He would have to work hard at being successful in both capacities. Although he was reputedly a good thinker, and at times a man with good ideas, Daniel never had the charisma, the daring, the political know-how, or the natural warmth to keep him close to the people of Nevis, long term. Unlike Ivor, Sim did not have it in his being to be a populist politician—the type of politician

Nevis needed in the 1970s. Daniel confided in friends, repeatedly, that he did not really like politics. Insiders from the NRP recalled at least two times during his leadership tenure, and long before 1998, when Daniel threatened to leave the party and its struggle. Many Nevisians still remember that on more than one occasion, between elections, Daniel himself stated, "I do not think I will run again." Trick or not, each time he made that statement, it was an open expression of uncertainty about his future in Nevis politics.

Daniel always seemed haunted by some limiting social or psychological factor in his life. This appeared to have come to the fore, particularly at times when he dealt with persons of European descent, and those who were of a fairer complexion than himself. While that phenomenon might have been a very complex matter for Mr. Daniel, his behaviors also suggested that some form of psychosis existed in his reality, and in his being. Even at the height of the Nevis Reformation Party's power and dominance on Nevis, Daniel was reclusive, more engaged with his legal and real estate businesses than with the people's business. At times when he did reach out to the people, he was in a "Culturama" festive mood. During that time, Daniel would do things in public that were seen as unbecoming for a leader of the island. Further, Daniel frequently became suspicious of other people around him, including Stevens, Parry, and other members of the NRP. Notwithstanding, since Daniel was a lawyer at the forefront of Nevis politics, his pivotal position there, became a vehicle to personal wealth and success, through persons visiting the island and interested in purchasing land on the island. After some time, Mr. Daniel became increasingly aware that the leadership position he held poised him to increase his personal wealth and status. That appeared to have been a critical reason why Daniel held onto the leadership of NRP and did not give up politics as he often threatened to do. Politics also won him an honorary doctorate degree from the Marquis Guiseppe Scicluna International University Foundation, in 1987, plus awards from other foreign academic institutions.

In 1970, Daniel was a Nevis lawyer working in St. Kitts for the Labor government, but he did not appear happy working there. For intimate personal and other reasons, he was angry with certain other Kittitians in the Labor Party and the government. Thus, Daniel was seen as a better ally, with the possibility of being more loyal to Nevis than another Nevis lawyer, Ted Hobson, whom the NRP organizers also considered inviting to be leader. That call from the founders of the NRP rescued Sim from a difficult time, and what seemed to have been a depressing spell in his personal life. The experience of entering Nevis politics lifted Mr. Daniel, remade his world, and created new dreams to be pursued.

Stevens, in contrast to Daniel, came back to Nevis always with politics on his mind. His tenacity, disgust at the second-class treatment of Nevisians, and belief in the possibility for change, laid an ideological foundation for real involvement on Nevis. Stevens also saw an opportunity for St. Kitts-style populist politics on the island. That was why he probably thought it possible to become, "the Labor Party man" on Nevis, as noted by Mr. Harris. When his first attempts at election failed, Stevens tried hard to understand Nevisians, and began to fashion an approach to politics on the island. He moved from supporting the Labor Party on St. Kitts to building an independent and inclusive politics on Nevis. Even though Stevens did not know Daniel well, he, too, was convinced that Daniel could be a useful ally, in shaping the emerging, new politics of Nevis.

Here were two men with two very different perspectives on life. However, time and events placed them in the same political arena at the same time. One went the extra mile to be accepting and cordial; the other was cagey, untrusting, always seeing an enemy everywhere, and in everyone. Yet, the challenge before them was so great that each needed the other. The people of Nevis and their politics were about to change and move forward. Seemingly, both Daniel and Stevens understood they had come to a momentous time in St. Kitts-Nevis history. Despite their personal differences, they came together and worked on behalf of Nevis. They saw transformation as possible on the island and agreed to make it happen.

When the *Christena* tragedy occurred, Daniel and Stevens skillfully manipulated the moment and the citizens' emotions. They reshaped the politics on Nevis during that time. Eventually, the two men were selected by the people to lead and give direction to the island's emerging politics. The leaders of NRP saw an advantage in placing the loss of so many lives on Nevis in the wider context of the island's politics—a strategy also used by the People's Action Movement on St. Kitts. Some of its leaders openly befriended, wined and dined, then defended Captain Wynter of the ship *Hawthorne Enterprise*, accused of seeing and ignoring passengers of the ill-fated *Christena,* as they struggled and died in the water. On Nevis, the Nevis Reformation Party's message to Bradshaw and his Labor Party was aggressive, accusative, demanding, and promised no cooperation from the island. Nevisians were convinced the *Christena* sank because of the government's inefficiency, lack of caring, and its spitefulness toward Nevisians.

By their nature, the two Nevis political leaders, Stevens and Daniel, always approached matters differently. Sim was calm, deliberate, hesitating at times, but always calculating. Ivor was some of all that, but in addition he was fluent, often acting in an agitated, hyperactive manner, and seemed forever in motion. As a team, they attacked Bradshaw's government repeatedly for what they saw as a cover-up or collusion in the *Christena* matter.[37] The government was also criticized for its failure to address the issue of compensation to families for the deaths, and for other survival concerns shared by Nevisians. No one bothered to note that in 1970, St. Kitts-Nevis was but a poor British colony, incapable, on its own, of providing adequate financial compensation to everyone after such a devastating tragedy. Not even psychological counseling was available to a demolished and demoralized society. Rather, healing came from an immersion into the vibrant and growing anti-St. Kitts politics. It also came from migrations. During that period in the 1970s, however, it was easier to see Nevis as being neglected by St. Kitts, not by the colonial government in Britain. Further, that Nevis

[37] Browne, W. T. (1985). *The Christena Disaster in Retrospect.* Charlotte Amalie, St. Thomas: BL&E; Browne, W. T. (1992). *From Commoner to King.* Lanham, MD: University of America Press.

developed slowly, and existed as second-class to St. Kitts, was always a good point about which to criticize the government on St. Kitts, instead of the government in Britain, the real culprit.

Meanwhile, the drama and acrimony between the islands throughout the *Christena* period allowed for little display of the developing Ivor vs. Sim conflict. At that time they worked together smoothly. They determined when to attack the government, then did so. Each brought his particular style and flavor to the attack. Then, they were both supported and applauded by the people, who loved the experience. For many years Daniel and Stevens received only unanimous, loud approval of solidarity and acceptance from the people of Nevis. Each time they took a stand against St. Kitts, on behalf of Nevis, real or feigned, there was thunderous applause from Nevisians. For an angry, hurting, and expectant people, all their politicians had to do then was deliver impassioned messages of frustration and disgust; then express visions of a changed future, directed by a new politics for Nevis. On the other hand, the Labor Party government kept hoping time would wear down Nevisians, and force an acceptance of its agenda. The St. Kitts leadership should have been aware, but were oblivious to the change that was occurring on Nevis. The people's way of thinking was changing. They had also begun to see the world differently. Time was not on the side of St. Kitts in its role of under-colonizer. Over time, the government on St. Kitts lost most verbal and ideological confrontations with Nevis, and had to keep licking its wounds.

The politics of Mr. Stevens and of Mr. Daniel was further energized and propelled by the thrust for secession that had become so vibrant in Nevis during the 1960s, 1970s, and 1980s. There was a certain vibrancy in the political consciousness emerging on the island—a direct product of education, the new political party, its vision, and an uncompromising new Nevis politics. When the Nevis Reformation Party was formed, its founders held the view that Nevis should be completely separate from St. Kitts for government and administrative purposes. There was a resounding call for a return to the independent political relationship that existed between the islands prior to 1882. Consequently, while the secession thrust in Nevis was somewhat revolutionary, it was also a unifying ideological force and a dynamic political movement. The secession idea challenged and destabilized Nevis' relationship with St. Kitts. Meanwhile, the leaders of NRP called on all Nevisians to unite behind its home-bred political leadership, building a solid political base in the process. So, with the NRP serving as the vehicle, like-minded Nevisians came together and built a movement for a changed political, social, and economic relationship between the two islands. There was also growing insistence by some secessionists that the changed relationship between the islands should include a deliberate movement of Nevis away from a total control by St. Kitts, to absolute autonomy and independence for Nevisians.

At one time, Stevens and Daniel worked together as secession hardliners, but, time and experience eventually persuaded Stevens to shift his position on secession. He reasoned that as long as cooperation between the islands resulted in real and improved benefits for Nevis, outright secession should not be pursued. Daniel, however, was adamant that there could be no common ground between the two islands. For many Nevisians, it was not until the late 1980s, early 1990s, before the deepening disagreements among the men in the NRP came to full light. For example, when the party lost power to the CCM in 1992, a very angry Mr. Daniel blamed everyone else in the party but himself. Some of the comments he made about Mr. Parry and Mr. Stevens were simply unfair. Mr. Daniel should have looked at the mirror within himself. Further, by 1997, even before Mr. Stevens died, Mr. Daniel was campaigning for the CCM. That switch by Daniel to supporting the CCM, at a time when Mr. Stevens was dying, should probably be remembered on Nevis as the ultimate let-down and betrayal of the NRP.

Meanwhile, instead of blaming his growing rejection by the people on the other members of the party, Mr. Daniel should have done some personal soul searching. He had isolated himself from the voters and repeatedly stood against them in favor of his wealthy friends. At times, all that seemed to interest Mr. Daniel was land sales. There were failed promises and a growing disinterest in things for Nevis. Further, other than a few close friends and family, Daniel chose to be aloof from most other Nevisians. It was a bitter pill, but Ivor was still alive when Sim left the NRP and supported the Concerned Citizens Movement position on secession in 1997, leading to a second referendum on the matter in 1998. More than ever before, that St. Kitts-Nevis secession debate caught the attention of people throughout the Caribbean and elsewhere in the world. Kittitians and Nevisians everywhere were tuned in to the referendum vote of August 10, 1998. That time, unlike what happened in 1977, the secession vote lost—but barely! Throughout the debate, Daniel campaigned on the side of the CCM, arguing his long history as a secessionist. Ironically, in that secession confrontation, Daniel was teamed with Amory, a person who, at an earlier time, stood staunchly against the break-up of the islands. He wanted little to do with it. Actually, at the height of the Nevis secession drive in the 1970s and 1980s, Amory was quietly a go-to "Labor Party man" on Nevis. He was singled out and rewarded, on at least two occasions, given special positions (headmastership and bank manager) by the Labor Party, because of his noncommitment to the secession struggle on Nevis. By the 1990s, it was therefore easy for Amory to form the CCM, attack the NRP, and have CCM supporters parade with monkey-like dolls during political campaigns, as an affront to the then NRP leader—Mr. Sim Daniel. In retrospect, such a racist act should never have been condoned or tolerated on Nevis, at that time in the island's history. According to the established protocol for such an honor, it was also an insult to Mr. Daniel, Mr. Stevens, and those many others—the real heroes of Nevis' contemporary politics that the airport on the island has been named in honor of Vance Amory, not Simeon Daniel. Despite his flaws, a number of Nevisians now agree that the honor and memento were more deserved by Sim Daniel who led and championed the cause of Nevis during the 1970s and early 1980s. During that period Vance Amory was noticeably on the political fence, and missing from the vibrant action to change destiny for the people of Nevis.

Meanwhile, it has been suggested that probably Daniel's unwavering commitment to secession from St. Kitts was inspired by personal grudges against certain Kittitians. They crossed him in ways that were personal and intimate, while he worked in St. Kitts. Until he died, Sim held vendettas he never settled with persons such as "Scratch" Ward, Fitzroy Bryant, and Lee Moore. In time, that hatred was directed against St. Kitts and all Kittitians. However, Mr. Daniel's animosity against a number of Kittitians and in time St. Kitts, seemed to have been carefully couched in Nevis' drive for secession. There were also those times in the coalition government when Prime Minister Simmonds failed to stand and support Mr. Daniel's efforts to resolve some emerging problems on Nevis. Such lack of support from Dr. Simmonds did not assuage Mr. Daniel's feeling of anger against Kittitians. Quite often, when they had disagreements, Daniel reminded Stevens, that he, too, was "a St. Kitts-man." It seemed that Daniel expected some of his wealthy clients, along with his Nevisian friends abroad, would succor and support an independent Nevis. Maybe he also had dreams of a forever fiefdom for himself on the island, if he led and attained secession from St. Kitts.

Few members of Mr. Daniel's former party shared his views about conspiracies. Rather, certain members of the NRP still remember Daniel as being a very complex person who seemed to have had delusional interludes. Ironically, the very secession matter that made NRP the Nevis party for the 1970s and 1980s, returned in the 1990s and tore the party apart. The NRP has now changed to a more conservative position on that matter. Meanwhile, on the issue of her husband conspiring against Mr. Daniel, Mrs. Stevens concluded, "Sim was always suspicious of Ivor, that he was undermining him. But Ivor was always very loyal to Sim." At times it appeared that Sim was the one who behaved unfairly to other members of the NRP. Uhral Swanston, always a front-seat viewer of the NRP, noted that while Ivor first served as Minister of Communications and Works on St. Kitts, Sim did not allow him to have an office in Nevis.

During the early 1980s, Sally Sheldon, the U.S. Ambassador to the Eastern Caribbean, arranged for Daniel to spend a month in the U.S., meeting with developers. Mr. Daniel did not suggest that Ivor, his deputy leader of the NRP, be appointed to act in the Ministry of Nevis Affairs during his absence, as the law required. Rather, Daniel requested that Swanston be allowed to act in his place. Finally, Premier Simmonds assumed the duties of the office, with Swanston advising him on Nevis affairs. Thus, Daniel prevented Stevens from holding the reins of command in Nevis, even for one month. Ivor would have had legal authority had he challenged Sim on that matter, but there is no record of him doing so. Ivor seemed always cognizant of the fact that he was not born on Nevis. From time to time, he did express lack of interest in being the leader of the island, as long as there were capable Nevisians around to lead. Norman Jones supported that notion: "At times, [Ivor] probably thought he could have been a better leader than Sim. But Ivor preferred to walk behind Sim, in that matter." Meanwhile, it was also possible that sensitivity to the sociology of class and color on Nevis, and a good psychological sense of self, played a subtle role in Ivor's decision never to challenge Sim for the leadership of the island.

Al Thompson is still convinced that Ivor had no interest in challenging Sim for the premiership of Nevis. "Sim had no need to be afraid," he said. On one occasion when Simmonds was planning to be away from St. Kitts-Nevis, he offered to leave Sim in charge. Sim turned down the offer. It was reported that when Ivor heard about the matter he was disappointed that another representative from Nevis, himself, for example, had not also been considered to be the acting leader: "He might have accepted the position, because from that position Ivor felt he could have done more for Nevis." Further, it would have been quite an honor for Ivor to serve as leader of St. Kitts-Nevis.

There were also reports that at times Sim refused to cooperate with St. Kitts politicians, even when such cooperation could have benefited Nevis. Some members of the Nevis Reformation Party, for example, felt he did not perform creditably, when he was awarded the Ministry of Finance, with an office on St. Kitts. Although he was an actor within the People's Action Movement—Nevis Reformation Party coalition government, Mr. Daniel continued to display a combative, Nevis vs. St. Kitts attitude. And, often, the biases and shortsightedness of certain St. Kitts politicians in the PAM party, did not help the relationship.

On Ivor's part, however, he made an attitudinal, a social, and a political adjustment. He kept encouraging a more harmonious relationship with St. Kitts politicians, and between the people on the two islands. During those times, when Ivor's unorthodox tactics bothered Prime Minister Simmonds, strategies were considered to "rein him in." However, Ivor always made himself available, and was usually amenable to discussions, debates, and at times reprimands. It was widely reported that Dr. Simmonds would have preferred to deal with Sim, but Ivor was always the more approachable of the two. He demonstrated a willingness to solve problems and find common ground with Kittitians.

In contrast, there were times when Mr. Daniel had critical assignments on St. Kitts, but he chose not to visit the island. Former minister in the coalition government, Hugh Heyliger reflected: "Stevens and Daniel differed in how they dealt with the matter of St. Kitts vs. Nevis. Ivor was a more open person. Sim held back." On that issue, Uhral Swanston said: "If Sim had tried to get more by working with Simmonds, the Prime Minister just might have preferred working with him. But Daniel often stayed away."

The NRP rode a political high, from the early 1970s, on into the 1980s, the only direction left for the NRP to go by the 1990s was down. By the late 1980s, the party was being attacked from many sides. In defending the party and themselves, both Sim and Ivor responded from their political platform in haughty, sometimes vicious, nasty, and at times personal tones. They always meant to wound, not to cuddle the opposition. Attacks against political enemies were designed to inspire fear. In time, there was an observable decline in the popularity of the NRP. In time, as the party lost its popularity, it helped to instigate and foster that aggressive, vicious politics on the island. Increasingly, Nevis politics mirrored the politics that the planters' Democratic Party, and the workers' Labor Party on St. Kitts, instigated and encouraged, during the 1950s and 1960s. Each of the parties kept demonstrating deep anger and a certain vehemence against its political detractors. Suddenly, there was a very intense battle for the minds of Nevisians. However, as the NRP's years in leadership increased, its political message became stale. One time it was fresh, vibrant, visionary, and enchanting. But as the islands moved into the 1990s, there was little action from the then too comfortable and arrogant leader—Premier Daniel. Quite often, the lofty promises made to Nevisians, no longer became reality. It started to appear that some promises were made simply for the sake of keeping Nevisians contented with, and dependent on, the NRP. About that time, one popular joke on Nevis about the NRP, and regarding things that were to benefit Nevis was, "Wait, it is in the pipeline." When the opposition CCM was voted into power and its leader, Vance Amory, took on the island's leadership in 1992, he simply acted on the plans for road repair and other capital projects already in place. Amory activated the plans to rebuild the airport at New Castle. He later ensured that it was named Vance Amory Airport.

In dealing with opposition politicians, Ivor maintained some level of interpersonal relations with people known to have attacked NRP politics. He even continued to greet opposition politicians cordially. Sim, however, preferred to avoid such people. In some cases he treated them as clear enemies deserving of social alienation. There were times, too, when such people were made to experience periods of joblessness, because NRP leaders wanted it that way. Another difference between the two men was their attitude toward foreigners and their understanding about the role foreign influence should be allowed to play in Nevisians' lives. Daniel seemed convinced that Nevis' future survival rested on foreigners, particularly if they were White and wealthy. He was willing to sell land, his influence, and even the sovereignty of Nevisians to such people. At one time there was also concern on the island that Mr. Daniel was making deals to have foreign garbage shipped to Nevis and dumped there for a fee, as had been done in Haiti. In contrast, Stevens was concerned that too much foreign influence could cause tiny Nevis to lose its unique cultural features. He felt that things such as the island's quaintness, folklore, and those peculiar things that define Nevis, should be preserved and protected as sacred, and for our progeny. To Stevens, these included the island's architecture, folk traditions, and the nature-given gifts such as beaches, coconut groves, meandering hills, a fog-capped mountain, breadfruit trees, mango trees, and small villages close to the sea.

Stevens wanted Nevisians to preserve their independence from England, the U.S., and everywhere else. This they were to do, as much as they were committed to securing it from St. Kitts. He saw every form of dependency as dangerous and threatening to the autonomy and well-being of Nevisians. Mr. Stevens felt that if dependency takes hold in Nevis again, Nevisians can find themselves trading their ideas, their freedoms, their traditions, and their very way of life, for a return to varied forms of control. They may even find themselves being exploited again, as gardeners, maids, and prostitutes. They may even be restricted from the island's beaches again. Ultimately, the absence of those physical chains associated with captivity and slavery, does not alter the possibility for a return to exploitation through unequal relationships and varied kinds of oppression. Nevisians can again be overwhelmed, by cultural and other forms of imperialism.

In his comments on the differences he noted between Mr. Daniel and Mr. Stevens, Arthur Evelyn, a friend of both men, and a staunch supporter of the NRP, recalled:

> Generally, Stevens and Daniel got on, but there were times when they did not see eye to eye. Stevens was not as cautious as Daniel in his approach to getting things done. However, both men had been trained differently; one was a soldier, the other a lawyer. There were some clashes between them too, but Stevens always respected Daniel, even when he disagreed with him. "I never got the idea that Ivor wanted to take over from Mr. Daniel."

Franklyn Brand remembers Ivor saying to him:

> "If I served Nevis as well as I served Sim Daniel, Nevis would have been better off. . . . I would never again, in my lifetime, join any political party led

> by a lawyer. And, I will think twice if a lawyer is even in it." There were times when Ivor covered for Sim, and did not let the people know the truth. Yet, Sim was suspicious of Ivor and even suggested that Ivor wanted to harm him. At times, it was my father, who acted as mediator. He encouraged them to hold on in the party.

For Lee Moore, a critical moment between Sim and Ivor came during one of their visits to England, to determine whether St. Kitts-Nevis should become an independent nation. "Sim acted with a sense of nonchalance. It was Ivor who suggested that a mechanism be created to keep the PAM in power, but offer Nevis some future autonomy. Sim said very little. The result was the now infamous Clause 113."

"Never join a political party run by a lawyer." For Rev. Bowers, this one-liner from Ivor told everyone a whole lot about what went on between him and Sim Daniel. It also spoke to his experiences with Eugene Walwyn.

Dr. Keith Archibald saw things this way.

> Sim felt Ivor could help him start a party for self-determination. He knew of Ivor's position on self-determination for Nevis. . . . Ivor was not too much in favor of the party. He felt that a few people could run Nevis effectively and well.

Mrs. Stevens suggested a number of people she felt should be interviewed for the research project about her husband's life and politics. She thought of good friends and close associates. However, it was a surprise that Mr. Daniel's name was not on her list. When Mrs. Stevens was asked about his absence from the list, she responded hesitatingly. Eventually Mrs. Stevens agreed Mr. Daniel could be interviewed. As the research progressed, Mrs. Stevens' hesitancy was understood. On more than one occasion, appointments were set up to interview Mr. Daniel about his former colleague in politics.

On one occasion it was understood that I would travel from St. Thomas, USVI, to interview Mr. Daniel on Nevis. He was aware that a book was being written about his one-time political colleague, Ivor Stevens. However, no interview with Daniel ever took place, even after I got two attorneys to intervene. One time I arrived at Mr. Daniel's office and waited for hours to see him. His junior partner, Mark Brantley, was made aware of my mission and we chatted for a while. However, his senior partner never showed up. That Mr. Daniel spoke glowingly about Ivor Stevens the politician, and about his varied contributions to Nevis, was an interesting admission by him, in 2006. However, he was assisting the Nevis Reformation Party's campaign against the Concerned Citizens Movement, amid rumors that the CCM had plans to hike real estate taxes. Seemingly, Mr. Daniel was very concerned about the cost to him, if there was a tax increase. So he mended bridges with the NRP, at least for a time, and spoke glowingly of his one-time friend and partner in politics, Ivor Stevens.

A former permanent secretary to Mr. Stevens, Al Thompson, suggested, "a reasonably good working relationship existed between Ivor and Sim. They had their differences but Ivor respected the office of the Premier." However, according to Thompson, there were times when Stevens took the position, "It is my Ministry to run." Seemingly, he did not like having micromanaging interference from Sim. Usually, such intervention from Mr. Daniel was to allow some form of injustice to come to the common people of Nevis, and to allow an unfair advantage to some one of his wealthy friends. There were some noted cases;

During a dry spell on Nevis, Mr. Gaskel, at Montpelier Hotel, wanted to ensure that his hotel had water. Gaskel did not think the available water should be shared with the nearby villages Cox Village and Cole Hill. In the ensuing discussion, Mr. Daniel supported the hotel owner's position. Mr. Stevens did not. What Stevens did was to find an amicable way to share the water between the villages and the hotel. Mr. Stevens also took a stand against Nisbett's Plantation Hotel when the management wanted to prevent local citizens from passing through the property on their way to the beach—an issue

Bradshaw sought to resolve on Nevis as far back as the 1960s. At that time, Jones' Bay homeowners and Cliff Dwellers' Hotel, were the spoilers. It is still interesting and ironic that Mr. Daniel was willing to close his eyes to an issue of beach access for native Nevisians, in a more modern and better educated Nevis, some 30 years after Mr. Bradshaw took a stand against the same matter and had resolved it.

Joseph Parry a former Permanent Secretary to the Nevis Island Government, also served as Premier, from July 11, 2006, until January 22, 2013. Following are some of his comments on the relationship between Mr. Daniel and Mr. Stevens.

> Sim was afraid of Ivor. He could tell Sim anything and get him to change his mind. Ivor was more intellectually sound than Sim, who always seemed insecure and afraid of Ivor's background. Ivor also knew Sim was afraid of him. There were few open clashes because Sim backed down readily, and often.

Parry noted that it was Ivor, not Sim, who steered the NRP through the difficult years, after Sim almost capitulated to Bradshaw and the Labor Party. A close friend of Ivor was quite blunt on the Ivor vs. Sim matter, he said:

> Ivor and his family did not respect Sim. He was too Black. Ivor was also more of a visionary than Sim. At times, too, Ivor must have had hidden feelings that he could have made a better political leader for Nevis than Sim was. By that time it was obvious that Mr. Daniel was losing his way. His real estate business and his wealth were increasing. Those promises he made to the people back in the 1970s were being forgotten.

Al Thompson disagreed that Ivor ever contemplated being leader of Nevis. He argued, "Ivor never aspired to be the Premier of Nevis."

The matter of Sim's dark skin color seems to have been a complex issue, even for himself. By the 1950s the Stevens family was well known on both St. Kitts and Nevis. Through their academic and civil-service achievements, they had also gained admirable social status on the islands. Complexion was certainly a factor in social mobility then, but it was not the only factor shaping the relationship between Mr. Stevens and Mr. Daniel. Every member of the Stevens' family had managed to achieve better than an average level of education, respect in the society, and in time, personal confidence. For example, Ivor was very secure about who he was—a Stevens, Ma and Pa Stevens' son. Through education, members of the family had achieved a fair measure of social mobility and respect in St. Kitts, in Nevis, in the British Virgin Islands, and in New York. The subtleties of skin color must have been a factor in this matter too. In contrast, Daniel never appeared to be a very confident person. Neither his growing wealth nor being leader of an emerging vibrant NRP seemed to have made a difference in that aspect of his personality or life. Also, it did not appear that Mr. Daniel's shade of blackness helped his self-confidence. For him, that reality seemed to have become deeply psychological and much more than skin deep.

There were reports that Mr. Daniel usually seemed insecure and confused when dealing with matters related to color. Local Nevisians were ushered out of meetings with Mr. Daniel when his White clients came. His White friends and clients always had to win, even when they undermined the rights of Nevisians. Quite frequently, he was known to defer to White and near-White persons, even when his decision was unfair to local citizens, as in that access to the beach matter at Nisbett's Plantation. One classic example of how he managed such matters was noted in the case when a White supervisor at the Four Seasons Hotel struck a local Black woman from Bath Village, Nevis. He also called her humiliating racist names. There was never a court case on the matter. The woman was paid some money and her supervisor allowed to slip out of the island, with Mr. Daniel's knowledge. Probably, Daniel's willingness to accept second-class treatment and to assume that it was good enough for other Nevisians, had been learned from his association with a White Anglican priest, Fr. Thomas, during his early adulthood. Mr. Daniel's later experiences as a West Indian attending law school in Britain during the 1960s might not have helped such thinking either. Further, Mr. Daniel growing up in the Caribbean during limiting colonial times such as the 1940s and on, could have gone a long way toward helping to shape his perception of race, color, and place in the island's society.

Ivor's nephew Maurice Stevens reflected on the Sim vs. Ivor saga in very transparent language. Speaking about his uncle Ivor, Maurice said, "There were those who hated him, but none who did not respect him. At the end he could not cope with the double dealing in Nevis politics. That affected his decision to retire in 1987." Both Ivor's wife and his nephew claimed they saw Ivor's disillusionment with Nevis politics as the '80s were ending, so, they encouraged him to quit. Maurice concluded, "My uncle Ivor wanted to effect change; not to take Nevis from Sim."

The tribute Mr. Daniel presented at Ivor's funeral was simple, short, and vague, coming from a colleague with whom he worked and rallied Nevisians for almost 20 years. It reflected little emotion and little intimacy between the two men. However, Sim did remember Ivor's commitment to Nevis, and the contributions he made to ensure a positive difference came to the lives of common citizens on the island. Such an honest statement about Stevens, at the end of his life was important. However, it would have been a beautiful flower to him, if it was given while he still lived and during those last days when he met with his friends at the waterfront in Charlestown.

Ivor's final words on the relationship between himself and Mr. Daniel are embedded in the document he called his White Paper, written just before he died in 1997 (see Appendix D).

> There being no consultation, or should I say scant consultation, the founding fathers of the party have made little or no forward contribution. Not being a Nevisian by birth and considering myself to be one on account of my many years spent here,

> I consider it my home, but with it all, I always wanted to know that a person whose umbilical cord is buried in Nevis becomes the leader of the country. In which case, I always took a back seat in all endeavors, which leads me to now know that had I served my party as diligently as I served my leader, Nevis would not now be in this predicament in which it finds itself.

Such was Mr. Stevens' very sad parting comment about that relationship which was seen as meaningful, and as having brought so much hope for change to Nevisians. That was a glorious and transformational period on the island. Both Stevens and Daniel came to the point in time, when they were aware the high points in their politics and their collaboration were over. The politics on Nevis drew these two men together and inspired them. Once their political journey together came to an end by the mid-1980s, some of the glaring differences between Mr. Daniel and Mr. Stevens became pronounced. This also pushed them apart. Despite their once very close working relationship that helped to fashion a new politics for Nevis, that togetherness between the two men eventually came to an untimely end. Not even the memories of those glorious years when they led the NRP, changed the island's politics, created new visions and dreams for Nevisians, were powerful enough to bring the men together again. Mrs. Stevens too, as she grappled with Mr. Steven's death, understood the width and depth of the chasm time built between him and Mr. Daniel. The two men started that political journey on Nevis, side by side, hand in hand. They were excited about the possibilities as each envisioned the future for Nevis, beyond the 1970s. Then, long before Ivor died, the two men could look back and see a legacy of unique achievements for the island of Nevis—a place where they once stood together and led as valiant champions. But their worlds collided during the journey. The friendship shattered. And that political waltz they once danced together ended—forever!

CHAPTER 9

ENEMIES FOR LIFE

During the almost 40 years of his political involvement, there were four persons across St. Kitts and Nevis whom Mr. Stevens came to consider enemies for life. Despite the manner in which their journey together ended, Mr. Daniel was not one of them, even though he was a lawyer. Three of the men were Eugene Walwyn, Edread Walwyn, and Fitzroy Bryant, all dead now. The fourth man was Vance Amory, who is still very much alive and involved in Nevis politics. To Ivor, these four men offended him deeply and so painfully, that he could not find it in himself to forgive them. Rather, through the years, he kept remembering the misery each man brought to his life. For example, even as he was dying in 1997, Mr. Stevens was saying openly and unapologetically to anyone who paused and talk with him, "Although I respect the office of Premier, I have little regard for Vance Amory, the man who is Premier of Nevis." (Mr. Amory's party won the local election of January 22, 2013. After a brief respite, he has assumed the position of Premier again).

Stevens and Eugene Walwyn

According to numerous reports, Eugene and Ivor crossed each other's paths before they entered politics. Seemingly, their conflicts went back to issues stemming from boyhood, and later, probably even to matters of the heart. While there is some uncertainty about what happened before, the two men did face off directly when they both plunged into political careers on Nevis, at about the same time. At first, it appeared that they did discuss some level of cooperation and sought to avoid working against each other. Supposedly, it was agreed that Ivor would campaign in the St. Paul's, St. John's, and St. Thomas' constituency, while Eugene would campaign in the St. James' and St. George's constituency. According to the reports, Eugene reneged on the initial agreement, opting to run in the same constituency as Ivor. At that early stage of his politics, Stevens was the outsider. Mr. Walwyn was born and grew up on Nevis. His family was well known and climbing the social ladder. Eugene, therefore, was the more popular and better placed, of the two men. He also knew that he had the edge on Ivor. However, Walwyn's change from their earlier agreement angered Stevens, so he moved to establish some ground rules for his future relationship with Walwyn. Stevens also started to build a winning strategy for his politics. In time, despite the willingness of many Nevisians to show the young lawyer open preference, Walwyn and the other Nevisians soon learned to take Ivor seriously, and to treat him with respect.

The two men returned to Nevis at a critical time in the island's history and political development. Each man saw himself as destined to play an important role in changing the future direction of Nevis, particularly its society and politics. That was partly why Ivor collaborated with Eugene and was willing to support his leading Nevis' thrust toward secession in 1961. At the time, secession appeared not only to be different, but a best direction for the island's politics. However, as Stevens later concluded, as a political leader, Eugene was frequently duplicitous, and could not be trusted to lead such a move for Nevis. Consequently, from as early as 1961, the two men started to drift apart, ideologically, socially, and politically. Eventually, that relationship became an irritated open wound, and neither man wanted to heal what their one-time political friendship had become.

Their first matter of contention was the campaign and constituency issue in 1957. A second contention came about when Eugene reneged on his promise to present the secession resolution for Nevis in 1961, as he had promised and agreed to do. A third disagreement between the men emerged after the election of 1966. Stevens was convinced he won that election, but that Eugene Walwyn, and his cousin Edread Walwyn, colluded in one of their numerous clandestine exploits to defeat him. Accordingly, Stevens went to court intent on proving his point. The High Court ruled against Stevens; however, Stevens never completely accepted that political loss as fair. He simply thought that as a government representative and lawyer, Walwyn was better prepared and had more connections than he, Stevens, did.

There was another court case between the two men later on. It involved property including the sailboat, *Sakara*, which Ivor had purchased from the wife of Nevis businessman Henry Archibald. Mrs. Stevens is still certain her husband was honest and forthright in that matter. After the purchase arrangements, and after both of the Archibalds were dead, Eugene and Edread Walwyn brought a case against Ivor, accusing him of obtaining the property from the Archibalds by fraudulent means. Eugene therefore sought to prove that it was he, not Ivor, who had legal claim to the Archibalds' property. Interestingly, the Archibalds, at one time, well-known business people on Nevis, had no known living heirs. Seemingly the Walwyns were well aware of this fact and planned accordingly. That story is only one of the many, where the names of certain Nevis lawyers appeared mysteriously, on the ownership documents for other people's property.

To Ivor, Eugene's charge was unexpected and preposterous. The court case showed that Eugene and Edread were entitled to determine how the Archibalds' property should be probated, and Walwyn argued it could not be Ivor because his name was not on the documents. Mr. Stevens remained certain that his case was just and that he would prevail in court, since his attempt to purchase the boat took place before the Archibalds died. Even today, Stevens' family argues that some of the documents presented to the court by the Walwyns were forged and illegal. However, Ivor lost the case and also his financial investment in the Archibald's property.

Both court battles between Ivor Stevens and Eugene Walwyn were nasty. The aftertaste caused much pain. Accordingly, Ivor was forced to work hard, in order to preserve his reputation as a politician, businessman, and citizen of Nevis. Meanwhile, Eugene did all he could to present himself as an honest lawyer and citizen, with a worthy case. Unlike the prior political clashes, the second court case was more a personal matter between the two men. Seemingly, Walwyn's knowledge of the law and his political connections afforded him an advantage in the situation. However, the case and its related circumstances challenged both men's reputation and character. When it was all over, Ivor smarted about his loss to Eugene in court, more than at the ballot box—his character and reputation were at stake. Meanwhile, Walwyn, an astute attorney and politician found himself very much in his element inside the courtroom, while he dealt with that ownership of property case. Walwyn knew the tricks of the trade and appeared to have used them very well. Further, it was a time in Caribbean history when the legal brotherhood and the authority of the political leadership often manipulated outcomes in the court. Too often, the system of justice in the Caribbean islands has been skewed in the direction favored by political leaders and members of the masonic lodges. Also, from as early as back in the 1960s, a number of lawyers on Nevis have managed to claim ownership of land and other property for which they had no legal title. In a recent case, one family in the Barnes Ghaut, Cotton Ground, and Jessup's area, was shocked to find the name of the late Premier, Simeon Daniel, on the title to their land. The family was not amused and fought to have the name removed.

Edread (Dreddie) Walwyn was chief political strategist, consultant, and general advisor to Eugene—he was one of the greatest manipulators Nevis has known. It is well known that his scheming went beyond politics to impact and shatter the lives of others not associated with politics. Uhral Swanston suggested, "Dreddie was the political mastermind for Eugene and therefore he and Ivor would not have got on." To illustrate his point, Mr. Swanston referred to a situation that occurred in 1966. There was a contention between Edread and Eugene. Just before the election, Edread left Nevis and went to England on vacation. As the election date neared, Eugene contacted Edread to request his assistance in the election campaign. Edread was a hard bargainer, even with his cousin. He responded assuring Eugene that he would come home and work for him, but only after a specified amount of money had been deposited on his bank account, at Barclay's Bank. It was a close election and Eugene was desperate. He deposited the money suggested. Once Edread checked and made sure, he came home to manage the campaign. It was the last election Eugene Walwyn won on Nevis.

In that 1966 election, Ivor lost to Eugene by 42 votes. Ivor and his supporters campaigned hard and were confident they would win the election. However, Edread had come home, and was a factor in the election, being very skilled at manipulating paper-ballot elections. An angry Stevens' team responded to the results in disbelief. Of all places, Ivor lost votes in the St. Thomas area, the section of his constituency where he was very strong. Eugene was undaunted. He depended on the manipulative skills of Edread to keep his political effort alive and successful—he was Eugene's secret weapon and equalizer. Consequently, Edread was constantly monitoring, reporting on, and undermining Ivor's political moves in Nevis. Edread made it his duty to note, along with many other Nevisians, that Ivor ran on the People's Action Movement ticket in 1966. Even then, some Nevisians were convinced that a vote for PAM was still a vote for domination from St. Kitts. Meanwhile, Edread was always a committed, active agent of the Labor Party, on Nevis.

Stevens and Edread "Dreddie" Walwyn

Although Dreddie was never a political candidate, he was so intricately involved in Nevis politics that all who contested political seats saw him as a force to deal with, particularly if the candidates were not pro-Labor. He was the ultimate point-man, agent, and, "bag-man" for the Labor Party on Nevis. Dreddie shared money from his desk and made promises to potential voters on behalf of the Labor Party. Generally, whoever Dreddie supported on Nevis had the blessings of the Labor Party on St. Kitts. That fact was particularly true during the years when Ivor and Eugene went head to head against each other, and the Labor Party was trying to retain influence on the island. Further, since he served as Eugene's chief strategist and advisor, Edread and Ivor were often angry with, and suspicious of each other. Edread also played a conspicuously collaborative role with Eugene in Ivor's court case dealing with the Archibalds' property. That situation made the relationship between Stevens and Edread even more strained. Ivor was aware that Edread served as a paid performer and dangerous ally of the Labor Party on St. Kitts. Stevens knew, too, of the special friendship between Fitzroy Bryant and Edread Walwyn, and how that friendship was used to frustrate local political development and progress for the larger population on Nevis.

Through the years, Ivor also discovered two other important reasons to mistrust Edread and keep him at a distance. Edread appeared to work overtime to ensure the domination of Nevis by politicians on St. Kitts. He and other labor sympathizers on Nevis, worked hard to keep some semblance of organization for the Labor Party there. Accordingly, Edread made contacts, distributed the subsidies, and strategized to challenge and undermine the Nevis Reformation Party, with its secession politics. In retrospect, because Edread was also a major player in the Nevis Independent Party, that party, too, was probably designed to weaken NRP and support the Labor Party's policies. While we never discussed that topic, I was always conscious of the possible relationship. Little wonder, the NIP was soon labeled a friend of the Labor Party. I now agree that my entry into Nevis politics was exciting, but premature, and quite instructive about the intricacies of St. Kitts-Nevis politics. I was fired unceremoniously by the government and lost 20 plus years of service as an educator. Eventually, I chose to leave St. Kitts-Nevis to live and work elsewhere.

Since Edread Walwyn and Fitzroy Bryant were close friends, neither man was a friend of Ivor. Bryant and Stevens were constantly at war, verbally, politically, and philosophically. They challenged each other in the assembly, in the media, and elsewhere. To Fitzroy, despite Ivor's political success and populist style, he was an impostor—a bourgeois person, not deserving to inherit or benefit from the politics derived from the working-class struggles against the planters and their production system.

Stevens and Fitzroy Bryant

Stevens was from Sandy Point, on St. Kitts, but he held no doubt that he could make a difference in the lives of Nevisians. Meanwhile, Bryant, an Antiguan, had become comfortable and accepted in St. Kitts-Nevis. He also became an important figure and decision maker in St. Kitts-Nevis politics and society. On one occasion when Ivor reminded Bryant that he, Ivor, and not Bryant, had entitlement to St. Kitts-Nevis politics, Bryant's response was, "You are a Kittitian, but you are trying to speak as a Nevisian." Ironically, such a comment also spoke to Ivor's success at spreading a pro-Nevis message, and the extent to which Nevisians accepted and rallied around him as one of their champions.

In time, the quarrel between Stevens and Bryant became increasingly personal and punitive. Each accused the other of moral indiscretions. However, Stevens stood to lose the argument once it took on that sexual tone and became public. Bryant prided himself openly in being a macho man, and boasted of going through the trouble of keeping a careful count of all the virgins he deflowered—at times even boasting about the number. Mr. Bryant spoke unashamedly and repeatedly, about his love for "the joys of the flesh." Interestingly, many of those comments took place while Bryant was the government's Minister for Education.

Bryant's open boasts about his sexual exploits belied the fact that he was a leading man in the education system. Seemingly, his comments also found acceptance in his circle of friends, some of them members of government. Many of the others dared not move to condemn such poor modeling to young Kittitians and Nevisians inherent in such behavior. Not even Ivor Stevens, the supposedly moral purist, was able to protest such indiscretions by Bryant successfully. When he attempted to do so, Bryant responded by revealing criticisms of Stevens' own sexual indiscretion. That quickly humbled and, for a while, silenced Mr. Stevens. Something from his life, that he loathed, had been revealed to the public. Consequently, both he and his family must have cringed for some time, while they planned his comeback.

On Thursday, August 7, 1980, Ivor Stevens, then a minister with the new PAM-NRP government, made a scathing attack on Fitzroy Bryant, during a House of Assembly meeting that was broadcast live on the government-owned radio station, ZIZ. Stevens accused Bryant of immorality, sexual perversions, and more. Bryant was no longer in government, but he responded in kind. He published an editorial in the *Labor Spokesman* on August 9, 1980. It was captioned: "Ivor Stevens Is a Small Boy and a Coward." Bryant was deliberate in his attempt to hit Stevens where it would hurt. His response in the column began:

> Thousands of people in St. Kitts and Nevis and all over the Caribbean, listening to the live broadcast of the proceedings of the House of Assembly over Radio ZIZ last Thursday afternoon, would have heard Ivor Stevens, a minister in the "historic collision government" of St. Kitts-Nevis, launch a most vicious libel on me.

The rest of the article had Fitzroy claiming Ivor was not as principled as he wanted the citizenry to believe. His attack was deliberately launched in the House of Assembly because Stevens wanted to hide behind the immunity assured him as a member of the House, making an address in the Assembly. "That was cowardly," Fitzroy wrote. He also went on to suggest that he, Bryant, was not any more immoral than Stevens or his colleagues in government. Further, they were all married men while he, Fitzroy, was a single man. "All of us," he wrote, "are guilty of the joys of the flesh." When Fitzroy learned of Ivor's own sexual indiscretion, which produced a child out of wedlock, he spread the word and went after Ivor calling him a hypocrite. Seemingly, the two men got pleasure from challenging each other to verbal and moral duels.

Later, in a booklet, *The Road To Independence*, Fitzroy compiled a number of the speeches and articles presented by the Nevis Reformation Party and the People's Action Movement parties (1967-1983). They argued either the merits of secession, or the terrors of independence. That document stands as a classic testimony to the ironies in time, and in politics; particularly the manner in which time transformed and reshaped the politics of St. Kitts-Nevis in less than 10 years (1975-1983). Bryant endeavored to show that although the Labor Party and its leaders had a history of struggling to achieve independence for St. Kitts-Nevis, the leaders of the PAM and the NRP, including Ivor Stevens, had a history of laboring consistently to undermine workers' aspirations in that direction. Eventually, the PAM and the NRP agreed on a political contract, after pushing aside the Labor Party in 1980. They then led St. Kitts-Nevis to independence, September 19, 1983—a development that was one of the great ironies in Caribbean history and politics. It was also a classic illustration of how the twists and turns in politics and time can shape and reshape the destiny of people and nations.

Labor Party stalwart, the late St. John Payne, remembered Ivor and his politics fondly. He held no rancor against Ivor. Payne remembered Ivor as a difficult but competent and worthy political opponent. In contrast, for Fitzroy, the rivalry with Ivor went beyond politics, it seemed driven by disrespect and hatred. Accordingly, each man remained angry with the other, until death. They were both political strategists and idealists with active minds. Both men knew about the working-class experience on St. Kitts-Nevis, and wanted to alleviate the struggles of the common people there. However, Stevens and Bryant died as unrepentant, unreconciled enemies. Not even their shared desire for the people of St. Kitts-Nevis, could bring them to a place of common ground, in that tumultuous world of St. Kitts-Nevis politics. Ironically, both Bryant and Amory were quiet friends through the years. Over time, however, Mr. Stevens grew to hate both men, with unrelenting passion.

Stevens and Vance Amory

During Ivor's final months of life, in 1997, the campaign leading to the 1998 referendum vote to separate Nevis from St. Kitts, was at its height. The reality was strange to many people, but there was growing collusion between Mr. Amory of the CCM, and Mr. Daniel of the NRP, on the matter of secession. Meanwhile, Mr. Stevens kept speaking about his resentment for Premier Vance Amory and the regrets he had for agreeing to be led by a lawyer in the NRP. One incident demonstrating Ivor's disgust for Mr. Amory occurred the evening when Governor General Sebastian was officially introduced in Nevis. In the hustle and bustle of the evening, Ivor and Premier Vance Amory encountered each other and shook hands automatically, before Ivor realized what he had done. Afterwards, Ivor became so distraught that he left the ceremony immediately and went home, leaving his wife and sister at the affair. For Ivor, that encounter and virtually involuntary handshake, were very distasteful. He was so upset that he could not remain at the function. Being there and acting normal would have been impossible, because he shook hands with Vance Amory. Accordingly, Ivor chose to return home and brood there. Under normal circumstances, Ivor would never have left his wife and sister at a function.

What caused the two men to drift so far apart since they served the Nevis Reformation Party and the PAM-NRP coalition government together, at one time? According to reliable reports, the animosity grew from an issue involving Mr. Daniel, Mr. Amory, Mr. Stevens, and payment for electrical poles imported to Nevis, at the time when Ivor was working to improve the availability of electricity throughout Nevis. Some members of the NRP who knew about the matter felt that Vance Amory, at that time the Permanent Secretary of Finance in the Nevis local government, under the NRP, deliberately played Mr. Stevens and Mr. Daniel off against each other. He gave a false report to Mr. Daniel about Mr. Stevens' purchase of the needed poles. Seemingly, Daniel's penchant for conspiracies encouraged Amory's secret reports and accusations, against others in the government. When Stevens was made aware of the erroneous report, he became angry at both Daniel and Amory. Mr. Stevens also offered his resignation from the Nevis government.

Mr. Stevens found the problem he was being accused of setting up to be untenable and humiliating. That Mr. Amory wove him into such a false story to Mr. Daniel, shocked Stevens. Mr. Daniel's reaction also triggered a permanent mistrust on Ivor's part, toward both Amory and Premier Daniel. The actual story was that Daniel went away from Nevis, and that time, Ivor was left as acting Premier in Daniel's absence. Particularly during the early years, despite its thrust for independence from St. Kitts, the Nevis local government struggled to meet its monthly financial obligations. Admittedly, there were times too, when the difficulty in making the payments was worse than others. Interestingly, the People's Action Movement and its leadership on St. Kitts paid little attention and showed minimal interest in the fact that the Nevis local government struggled to pay salaries each month—a fact to which Premier Daniel and many other Nevisians were not oblivious. At the time in question, Stevens needed some electrical poles as part of his drive to improve electrification of the island. Accordingly, Mr. Stevens made certain that he consulted Mr. Amory about the island's financial standing. Amory assured the acting Premier that money was available to pay for the poles he needed. During the month of May, after discussions with Mr. Amory, a check for $111,000, was sent from the Nevis government to O. D. Brisbane, on St. Kitts, to pay for the poles. However, Mr. Brisbane did not cash the check immediately.

When Mr. Daniel returned to Nevis and it was time to pay salaries for June, there was a financial shortfall, after Mr. Brisbane cashed his check. Suddenly, the government's account was in the red. According to reliable reports, during a meeting between Sim and Ivor, Vance came to the room, whispered into Sim's ear, then left the room. Afterward, Sim turned to Ivor and said, "Ivor, you have done me that. I have heard all the time that you want to destroy my government." Daniel then started to cry as he spoke to Ivor. He continued, "Ivor, you knew it is coming to the end of the month." By that time Ivor realized he was being blamed for the financial problem the island must have been facing. Suddenly, Ivor understood what Vance had whispered about, to Sim. Mr. Stevens became irritated immediately and started to defend himself. He asserted that Amory was to be blamed for the shortfall and that he would prove it before the day was over. Mr. Alford Thompson, Mr. Stevens' Permanent Secretary, was assigned to review the documents on the transaction for the poles. Ivor wanted to point out a number of things from the documentation in his office. They were: (a) the check for the poles was handed over in May, not in June as was being suggested; (b) the Permanent Secretary of Finance, Vance Amory, had given him the go-ahead to pay that bill at the time he paid Mr. Brisbane; (c) the Permanent Secretary of Finance was the one who had erred in his calculations; and (d) Mr. Daniel was being ill-advised and misled.

Stevens went on to argue that if Amory had been efficient and thorough in his financial management, he should have noted that the check paid in May had not been cashed. Therefore, that amount, $111,000, should have been debited and incorporated into any calculation of the government's financial standing for June. Stevens also concluded that whatever Amory suggested to Daniel about him, Mr. Stevens, was malicious and evil. But Daniel listened, and without consultation, believed Amory, then pounced on Stevens.

Further, Daniel's eagerness to fall for the machinations of Vance, then his willingness to blame Ivor without hearing the other side, made Ivor very angry. After arguing and defending his innocence, Stevens offered to resign from his responsibilities in the Nevis Island government. According to Mrs. Stevens, "At that point, Ivor was very serious about leaving the Nevis government and politics." Reports from insiders claim it took the mediation skills of Arthur Evelyn, an NRP faithful, to prevent Ivor from actually resigning, and to maintain some sense of harmony in the party. As with the other people he considered long-term enemies, Ivor lived with that animosity toward Vance for the rest of his life. As a general principle, Ivor believed that a political leader should cherish and reflect characteristics of honesty and fair play. They should also hold a hatred for duplicity. To Mr. Stevens, Vance Amory failed to meet those standards, as a politician.

It was while Vance and the Concerned Citizens Movement party were seeking to build momentum for the second secession vote of 1998 that Ivor and I had a chance encounter at the waterfront on Nevis, during late 1996. We had not seen each other for a number of years. His frail appearance and the difficulty with which he spoke shocked me. When I inquired about his position on secession, he simply responded, "The wrong person is leading the move." Ivor's conclusion was based on his knowing about a stinging article Amory published in the *St. Kitts-Nevis Observer,* a few years before. In that column, Vance decried any move by Nevis to secede from St. Kitts. Stevens was also aware that money had been passed from the Labor Party to the CCM, during the early 1990s. Stevens' other concern about the secession movement and its leadership was probably related to what he saw as a problem with the leader's ethics. Stevens was not certain Mr. Amory could be a very ethical leader of Nevis.

By 1992, Amory and the CCM ensured that Daniel and the NRP were no longer at the helm in Nevis. At that time, all the retired Ivor Stevens could do was watch from the political sideline. Undoubtedly, he remembered the time when Amory and Daniel were supposedly friends, and Stevens made to appear the enemy. Nothing was discussed about Steven's thinking about Sim's fall to Vance, but Ivor must have had a quiet bemused smile of, "I could have told you so." Stevens must have been surprised when the two men came together again by 1996, to argue together "for secession," against the NRP's position of "no secession."

Later, during May 2000, I spoke with Premier Vance Amory at the University Center, in St. Kitts. I was about to present a paper on Ivor Stevens at a conference organized by the Continuing Studies Division of the University of the West Indies. We talked about Ivor and Vance had some very flattering things to say about him. However, Vance seemed to believe that he, Vance, was at times used as a scapegoat, in an ongoing situation of rivalry and mistrust between Sim and Ivor. Amory also suggested, "There were times when Stevens tried to undermine Daniel."

Few experiences in his political career seemed to have angered and hurt Ivor more than when Vance attempted to discredit him to Sim. Even though Vance later won the hearts of Nevisians and became the island's political leader, Ivor still remembered his inefficiency and duplicity. He just could not find it in his heart to respect Premier Amory. There were numerous occasions when Stevens spoke to friends and acquaintances about his respect for the office of Premier, however, he always added, "I hold only disdain for Vance Amory, the person who holds the office." Stevens commented further, "If you tell me the Premier calls me, I will dress appropriately and go. But if you tell me Vance Amory calls me, I would tell you to tell him go and [expletive . . .]."

When Ivor died there were friends who advised Mrs. Stevens that Ivor would not have wanted Vance to participate in his funeral ceremony. However, she was concerned over how the citizens of Nevis would have reacted to the Premier's exclusion from her husband's funeral, an official and island-wide funeral event on Nevis. It would have been almost impossible to exclude Premier Amory from participating in a big State funeral, on little Nevis. Further, Mrs. Stevens is a gentle soul who does not hold resentments, or grovel in the bitter politics of yesteryear. The matter between Vance Amory and Ivor Stevens was then, not now, and not something to hold on to during a time of mourning or beyond.

Many Nevisians still remember Ivor Stevens for his style, chivalry, gift of gab, and his standing tall for Nevis—always! Mr. Stevens had been a professional soldier. He understood the art of war and strategies for self-preservation. When he knew who his enemies were, Stevens fought to win, but also to protect himself against the enemy. It was very difficult for Mr. Stevens to hold an olive branch toward those marked, and known as his enemies. Instead, Ivor went all-out to defend his philosophical position and his dignity. He would fight an enemy to the bitter end. Ivor always gave as good as he got. Admittedly, this is not the way of the Christian. But Ivor did not claim to be a practitioner of the Christian faith. According to his friend, Pastor Bowers, Ivor was largely utilitarian in his religious life. He was a Mason and thought he got more meaning for his life from the masonic lodge than from the Christian church. Further, since he was a veteran of the Second World War, Ivor held that his best defense was always offence. When attacked, he gave no quarter. Once those wars were declared, Ivor allowed none of those four men into his inner circle. No white flag of peace was ever waved to them. They were enemies for the rest of his life!

CHAPTER 10

FROM SECESSIONIST TO DIVISIONIST

Ivor Stevens was persistent in his call for secession—the withdrawal of Nevis from its political unity with St. Kitts, during the 1960s and 1970s. However, by the mid-1980s, Stevens began to shift and was labeling himself a *divisionist* rather than a *secessionist.* Whereas a secessionist wants a complete break between St. Kitts and Nevis, each one governed separately. A divisionist, however, believes the two islands can remain as a common federal unit, St. Kitts-Nevis. But there should be two operating governments, separate and different, one on each island. There must be the acceptance of an inherent equality between the two people. This should be demonstrated by shared respect—Kittitians toward Nevisians, and Nevisians toward Kittitians. Accordingly, the politicians of Nevis must be empowered to control the day-to-day management of that island, while St. Kitts politicians do the same on their island. There should also be some federal system of assembly, not forever dominated from St. Kitts, but one in which there is shared leadership from each island.

During the early 1980s, one outcome from having the coalition government, was that the central government on St. Kitts became more sensitized and responsive to the affairs of Nevis. Since Stevens was part of that government's organization, he relented from his secessionist position, shifting his argument in the process. Meanwhile, an angry, uncompromising, Sim Daniel, remained a pure secessionist. Those times when Prime Minister Simmonds and the other PAM politicians left a cash-starved and struggling Nevis on its own to flounder, during the 1980s, could have been a factor that helped to cement Mr. Daniel's view on secession for Nevis. That was after he chose to trust the PAM to be the NRP's partner in the islands' new leadership and government.

That original secession argument on Nevis emerged as early as the 1880s, when the British Empire was the dominant economic and political force in the Caribbean. In an exercise of that authority, Britain forced Nevis into a common government with Anguilla and St. Kitts. It was against the will of most Nevisians, but they were allowed no voice, even as Britain acted only to ensure its imperial convenience. Caribbean colonies were becoming increasingly expensive to keep at a time when their productivity was declining. Therefore, Nevis with Anguilla and St. Kitts was financially more convenient for Britain. Meanwhile, over the years, the voices of protest had become silent, until events during 1961. The emerging politics on Nevis caused a revival of the arguments about governance and equity among the three islands. That secession matter exploded again after the *Christena* mishap in 1970. Ivor had observed the Labor politics on St. Kitts and understood the injustices of the plantation system, including how it impacted relationships among the islanders, on St. Kitts, Nevis, and Anguilla. However, after Ivor moved back to Nevis and saw the blatant neglect there, he became increasingly convinced that politics might be an avenue to transformation for the island. He also became aware that something radical would be necessary to bring a sense of equality, justice, and empowerment to the islanders on St. Kitts, Nevis, and Anguilla. The divisive colonial relations instituted by a powerful Britain, were being replicated by an increasingly powerful, labor-union driven government. Some of its expressions of authority included the deportation of even British preachers, who criticized the government's policies. Meanwhile, in dealing with the people on Nevis and Anguilla, the government in St. Kitts insisted on ensuring they remained dependent and disorganized.

At one point on both islands, political movements were largely concerned with pushing back against policies set in St. Kitts. The early leaders on Nevis and Anguilla, along with citizens on each island, became emotional, as they reacted to the frustration being experienced over development on their islands. Meanwhile, there was a disinterested Britain in Europe, and an unyielding Bradshaw on St. Kitts, implementing authoritarian strategies of control. These included coercion and retribution learned well from British colonizers. In the process, he increasingly forced Anguillans and Nevisians to seek radical political solutions to their ongoing backwardness, poverty, and disharmony on their islands. Meanwhile, Nevisians and Anguillans continued to experience a sense of alienation and powerlessness that haunted and suggested a lie to the relationship depicted in the islands' Statehood anthem, claiming it was a, "Great Trinity of Islands." Little wonder, Nevisians and Anguillans came to see one solution to the problem at hand: total separation from St. Kitts!

For most of the 1960s, and throughout the 1970s, secession became a divisive force, shifting and propelling the politics on Nevis, St. Kitts, and Anguilla. Ivor Stevens was among the men at the center of the politics on Nevis, as a band of novice politicians galvanized themselves and rode the tide of discontent on the island, spurred by increased education and growing political consciousness. Back then, almost all Nevisians supported secession, but none had really analyzed the true implications of a move toward secession. Nevisians became increasingly loud and emotional about the secession matter; however, there was no carefully considered structure or strategy to manage and provide direction for the secession process. Ultimately, that lack of real workable plans for the aftermath of secession was probably the biggest failure of the Nevis secession movement. Despite demonstrations, loud protests, and radical politics on Nevis throughout the 1960s and '70s, none of the leaders was really prepared ideologically, or with a workable strategy, to lead secession. Probably, such a realization factored into Stevens' progression to becoming a divisionist. He refused to remain a secessionist.

Even after the *Christena* incident, cries for secession on Nevis were largely directionless. It was more a political strategy for political leaders; no one had a real plan to deal with secession. However, the secession idea accommodated the evolution and expression of a radical politics on Nevis. Years later, Stevens claimed that those secession years were when he experienced some of his best politics. It was a time when Nevisians saw minimal legislative gains in the legislature, but that was a very dramatic and vibrant period in Nevis politics. Notwithstanding, the secession movement on Nevis never inspired the revolutionary daring that came to Anguilla, or the Anguillan financial commitment to fund the operations of their island, when that became necessary. On more than one occasion, a truck went around Nevis collecting money in the name of secession, and for travel to England. However, there is no record that anyone ever reported back to the citizens what was accomplished with the money collected in the villages. No one remembers that there was ever any serious accounting to the people on Nevis about that money. However, because of inter-island animosities, the secession idea did serve to unify Nevisians. It also gave force and meaning to the new politics emerging on the island. In an unprecedented manner, secession politics gave Nevis political leaders visibility, voice, venue, and acceptance. It also intensified enmity and mistrust between Kittitians and Nevisians, while Britain remained the dominant, but a disinterested and hesitant political partner—waiting to escape the reparation cost still owed to its Caribbean colonies.

None of the politicians on Nevis, Ivor included, could force Britain to help Nevisians realize fulfillment of their secession dream. Yet Britain was the ultimate colonizer, not St. Kitts. Further, until the Anguillans' unprecedented break away in 1967, Britain talked around the secession and increased autonomy debate, showing less and less interest in broadening its colonial relations in the Caribbean. Further, in light of the emerging relations between the Anguillan and British leadership today, questions are still being asked about the manner in which Britain resolved the Anguillan secession move that began in 1967. By the 1960s, the Caribbean islands had lost their former economic and strategic relevance to the British government. Islands such as St. Kitts and Nevis had become too poor to matter. Britain has little interest in mothering new colonies of poor and powerless Caribbean people. The islands it colonized and exploited for hundreds of years are now bereft of the economic resources it once needed for wealth and capital development. Unlike the French, British interest shifted to untangling itself from former Caribbean colonies. Consequently, during the 1960s and 1970s, the quarrels that divided St. Kitts and Anguilla, St. Kitts and Nevis, were mere distractions to Britain.

Theodore Hobson and Vance Amory were two prominent Nevisians who did not support the secession movement during its heyday. Rather, they pursued cozy relationships with the Labor Party government on St. Kitts. Their avoidance and insincerity about the early drive on Nevis for secession prevented Vance Amory and Theodore Hobson from being counted among true secessionists. However, since the mid 1990s, the two men have seized every opportunity to claim the secession issue. Questioning how and why the two men avoided association with the real secession movement may result in some interesting findings.

The demand for secession started to shift in 1980, after the People's Action Movement and the Nevis Reformation Party came together to form the first coalition government in St. Kitts-Nevis. After the set-up of that government, Nevisians started to make subtle but important shifts in their thinking about secession, and their island's popular politics. It came gradually, but during that period many Nevisians, including Ivor Stevens, switched from the pure secessionist position, to a more divisionist one. Stevens' real desire was a better deal for Nevisians and their island, from the St. Kitts leadership. In time, unlike Sim Daniel, Stevens refused to continue seeking a complete break from the historical unity, or for a total independent relationship between the two islands. For those Nevisians who did not want a clean break with St. Kitts, the view started to emerge that there could be an alternate way. For some, the ties with the other island were too long, too deep, and too intimate for a sudden drastic change. Accordingly, there was a noted hesitancy in the secession thrust, as the PAM-NRP government appeared to demonstrate a more sympathetic attitude toward progress, autonomy, and the fostering of success for Nevis.

Stevens indicated that, over time, he too moved away from the idea of an angry, clean break, secessionist way of thinking, to one of divisionism, as the political anger between St. Kitts and Nevis shifted and softened. Dr. Keith Archibald supported this suggestion. He pointed out that the early secession calls in Nevis were really attempts by the new and emerging politics to put pressure on Bradshaw's government for a fairer deal. There was also the hope that it would refocus attention on meeting the long-delayed needs of Nevisians. Dr. Archibald concluded that the strategy probably worked briefly, even during Bradshaw's tenure. He recalled that at one time Bradshaw did allow some concessions in agriculture on Nevis because of pressure from secessionists. The early secessionists were desperate and aggressive. They used the secession thrust as a last resort for Nevisians, when there was no sympathetic response from the government in St. Kitts about the ongoing problems in Nevis. So, through the years, secession remained a useful practical and brinksmanship political strategy for Nevisians. The secession idea has been used by the NRP and the CCM to galvanize voter interest against St. Kitts, or attract voter sympathy toward the party leading a particular secession protest, as in 1998. It does not matter the time of year, or how often the protests occur, Nevis politicians can always find a block of voters, old and young, ready to support secession moves against St. Kitts. Today, the determination and aggression may not be as dramatic as in the 1960s and 1970s; but there are always secessionists on Nevis, that politicians can inspire and reenergize.

An interesting and ironic story has been suggested, at times, to explain the intensity of the secession wish on Nevis. The proposition states that Nevisians on Nevis get upset with the changed attitudes of former friends, neighbors, and relatives, who moved from Nevis to live on St. Kitts. Some of those migrated Nevisians, have been known to collude with others and argue against the needs and well-being of Nevis. That situation was seen repeatedly, during the 1950s through the 1970s. Hundreds of Nevisians who migrated to St. Kitts, openly supported the Labor Party and Mr. Bradshaw against the desires of Nevisians for Nevis. And, whenever that situation was observed, Nevisians at home became very angry. They would push and argue for a total separation of the islands, reverting to separate and independent governments, as it was before 1882. Nevisians who migrated to St. Kitts were sometimes among the staunchest supporters of the labor movement and Mr. Bradshaw. Men such as James Halbert, Joseph N. France, and William F. Dore, could be counted among such Nevisians. Undoubtedly, their support for the leadership contributed to the development of Bradshaw's hard line toward Nevisians on Nevis, when they dared not to bow and adore him. Apparently, Bradshaw became so sure he could win the confidence of the other Nevisians and Anguillans that during the early 1960s, he seemed to have accepted blame for the setbacks and hierarchical relations on the islands, instead of shifting the responsibility to a stingy, crippling, and evil British colonialism.

Seemingly, despite Bradshaw's noted anticolonial stance, he too was a victim of the British colonial legacy to the Caribbean. Mr. Bradshaw depicted classic authoritarian leadership. He learned, very well, the alienating control strategies, along with the arrogant class attitudes of the colonizers. These were demonstrated repeatedly when Bradshaw dealt with Anguilla, Nevis, and those others who refused to support the Labor Party. The secession drive on Nevis was rooted in the Bradshaw government's demonstrated attitude of insensitivity and nonchalance to critical Nevis and Anguilla issues. The roles of leader and arbiter, and the idea of having power, were very attractive to Mr. Bradshaw. Ultimately, during that period, Anguillans and Nevisians were victims of a two-dimensional colonial system instituted first by Britain, then kept alive by St. Kitts. Nevisians and Anguillans responded by blaming the part of the system they saw and was within their physical reach. Over the years, the anger, bickering, and wrangling among the three islands have been momentous. Many Nevisians wonder how it happens that the two islands are still together as sister islands, and a political unit, all these years.

It was time and a shifting political perspective that brought Ivor to a more realistic, divisionist strategy, in dealing with the St. Kitts vs. Nevis matter. Even today it continues between the two islands.

Seemingly, Ivor's divisionist thinking does represent one model of the strategies that brought about an evolution of contemporary politics on Nevis. All along the way, Nevisians were determined to have more say in their own affairs. Bradshaw did not fully grasp the gravity or the implications of the Anguillan and Nevisian revolts. When he sued to obtain a compromise from Nevisians, it was to obtain an advancement of his personal status. Bradshaw was on the verge of becoming the first Prime Minister, and an even more autonomous leader of the islands. At the same time he was hesitating to give more political autonomy to the leadership on the other islands.

Even as he lay dying, Bradshaw and the masses in the Labor Party still hoped he could be revived from his illness to lead the islands into independence—if only for one day. Ironically, while he admired authoritarianism and British imperialism, Bradshaw was also deeply committed to Caribbean unity, and independence from Britain. He hated the idea that he lost control over Anguilla and that the authority was ceded to Britain again. Nevisians were also skeptical about the notion of a "trinity of islands," when only voices from one of the three islands had meaning. Under such controlling and tenuous circumstances, Nevis, too, was determined to leave the so-called, "trinity of islands." As was the case with the Anguillan break away, the very thought of Nevis trying to leave terrified Mr. Bradshaw—a stalwart of Caribbean leadership and politics was watching his fiefdom crumble before him. The hero was losing his crowd. But Bradshaw held on, defying the costs to the dogmatic colonial leadership policies he had seen and from which he had learned. Armed soldiers were therefore used as Bradshaw's political enforcers on Nevis. Nevisians were placed under siege for a number of years. It was difficult for the government on St. Kitts to listen. Nevisians were saying that the government should shift to more tolerable and humane policies that would work to involve and empower them on their island. Despite the threatening stance of the government, Nevisians stood their ground and did not budge, on the matter of secession vs. independence, under Bradshaw's rule. In the end, Bradshaw died while the islands haggled over an impasse related to independence. Nevisians remained focused on secession, not independence.

Later, Lee Moore and Fitzroy Bryant became so disgruntled with the cries and the blame from Nevis, that they were willing to let Nevis go its own way. Since the frustration on Nevis was hindering their move to independence, they too were willing to support the idea of a separate administration on Nevis. Secession for Nevis then, would have allowed the Labor Party to lead St. Kitts to independence. However, neither man had an opportunity to make it happen. Moore lost the government to the PAM-NRP coalition in 1980. By then, Bryant could only look on from the political sideline. Since he was born on Antigua, legislation was drawn-up by the PAM politicians to limit Bryant's future involvement in St. Kitts-Nevis politics. Despite his skills and aspirations, Bryant could no longer become a political leader in St. Kitts-Nevis. He was sidelined from politics permanently.

The 13 years of that NRP-PAM coalition government ushered in a general easing of the historic tension between the two islands. In retrospect, Dr. Simmonds, then Prime Minister of the country, gave much credit for the achievement to Mr. Stevens. According to former Prime Minister Dr. Simmonds, "Stevens, more than anyone else, worked to heal the pain and bridge the deep, historical gulf that separated Kittitians and Nevisians through the years." Uhral Swanston, Joseph Parry, Mrs. Dora Stevens, Pastor Lester Bowers, Hugh Heyliger, and Lee Moore, all concurred that there was some measure of healing during those years. Many other Kittitians and Nevisians who can remember the then and who observe the now, also agree on this matter.

A time did come when Stevens moved away openly from his radical secession argument to a more amicable and realistic position he called "divisionism." This position suggests that Nevisians and Kittitians can and must work together if they intend to survive into the future. The cost to St. Kitts is that Kittitians learn to accept the fact that Nevis is not a colony of St. Kitts, and that Nevisians deserve autonomy comparable to that enjoyed by Kittitians. On the other hand, the cost to Nevisians is that they learn to accept

Kittitians as fellow human beings—not as all devils. Both people stand to benefit from an adjusted perception, in their belief systems about each other. On the divisionism matter Pastor Bowers noted:

> Ivor felt there was too much in common to have an absolute separation of the islands, but that the St. Kitts administration should not have to approve everything for Nevis. Meanwhile, he thought that Nevis should maintain a healthy relationship with St. Kitts—not an absolute cut off with an "us" against "them" policy. This was not the same as how Sim, then Amory, came to envision the matter. Meanwhile, Ivor never hesitated when there was an opportunity. He brought Nevis' issues to the fore, and maintained an active, aggressive, opposition stance on certain matters, even though he was a part of the PAM-NRP government.

Lee Moore's reflection on the secession matter was very interesting. He suggested:

> Ivor never believed profoundly in secession. He was using secession as stratagem and cunning device. For Stevens, it was more to achieve the cause, which at that time was improved socioeconomic condition for Nevis. Ivor was one who used secession as a Damocles' sword. If secession did come, Ivor's mission would have been spent. It was also his tool to advance his political self and goals for Nevis.

Moore's conclusion also raised interesting questions about Stevens' shifting position on secession. He argued that Ivor's changed position was not a result of carefully laid plans, but a matter of political convenience and pragmatism. Accordingly, the suggestion that Stevens moved away from secession because it was a sensible strategy at the time still has merit. Historically the move made rational sense for his politics, and also for the future well-being of Nevis. He was poised to win at elections and the island was poised to win from his successes. It was classic political symbiosis.

After his leadership of the NRP ended, Mr. Daniel insisted that Stevens, Parry, Swanston and others in the NRP, betrayed him and Nevis. Through the years they never supported his push for complete secession from St. Kitts, neither during the 1980s nor the early 1990s. However, according to former Prime Minister Simmonds and former Minister of Economic Affairs for St. Kitts-Nevis, Hugh Heyliger, "Ivor was easier to speak with than Sim, even when the discussions were about moves to alleviate tensions between the islands."

Shortly before he died, Ivor opposed the new secession thrust, which came to consume the politics of Nevis, 1995-1998. It was an interesting position to many Nevisians, but Daniel disassociated himself from the conservative NRP's "no secession" position, and campaigned openly with the CCM leadership in support of radical "secession" from St. Kitts. However, even at that time there was still no workable secession plan in place on Nevis. Generally, the facts and figures presented to Nevisians to justify a move to secede from St. Kitts were crafted for that purpose, and in reality were little more than "smoke and mirrors." Their real strategy was still one of waiting to see how it all turns out—a lame and sad stance for any leadership to take in the 21st century. Probably it was a blessing to Nevisians, that the secession referendum failed and did not get the 66% of the votes the Nevis Island Administration needed to achieve the break from St. Kitts in 1998. Premier Vance Amory and his CCM Party must have been very happy, and sighed in relief the morning after. On the matter of effective leadership, who can forget his weak, "neutral" position when St. Kitts-Nevis needed strong leadership in 1993? Further, with global warming and all the impending crises about to overtake the world, including the Caribbean, neither the CCM nor the NRP is well prepared, presently to chart and lead a best survival strategy into the 21st century for Nevis. The political leadership in St. Kitts is not ready for the demands of the impending crises either. The recent performance on both islands in the managing of criminal activity is almost pathetic. And, that type of problem is miniscule when compared with the large complex problems about to overtake the islands in the near future. Despite its special place in recent St. Kitts and Nevis history, as was noted by Hastings Daniel, "The secession issue in Nevis can be compared to pulling a bulldozer in sand. The harder one pulls, the deeper it sinks." Finally, that reality has probably dawned on the leaders of the CCM, too. In their meeting on St. Thomas, October 28, 2012, when asked about their thinking on the secession matter, Mark Brantley, CCM's deputy leader, pointed out that any move toward secession must come from the people—a new and interesting position from a Nevis politician. From back in 1961, then the secession vote in 1977, and that in 1998, have always been driven by the politicians. They are who used the secession idea to rally the people and the politics. It has never been the other way around. Are Nevisians finally burying secession with Mr. Daniel, the forever secessionist, while keeping alive and vibrant, Ivor Stevens' idea of divisionism?

Although Lee Moore did not see Mr. Stevens as a person who prepared and planned in advance, Stevens did anticipate some of the emerging social and political scenarios well. Actually, it was probably Ivor's correct reading of the developing St. Kitts-Nevis situation that suggested the conservative and more realistic divisionist position would be more fruitful for Nevis politically, from the 1980s on, than the radical secessionist position of the 1970s.

Unlike Mr. Daniel, Stevens was willing to work with the government in St. Kitts, during the 1980s. Soon, everyone began to see positive results in the development of Nevis. At that time, too, Nevis politicians started to experience more political autonomy than at any time before in the island's recent history. Despite a few glaring setbacks that irritated both Daniel and Stevens, Some of the politicians on St. Kitts were actually becoming more sensitive to the needs in Nevis, and the desire of Nevisians to build the forgotten infrastructure on their island. For the first time since universal adult suffrage, in 1952, Nevis politicians were able to make promises to their constituents, then take direct action in an Assembly to deliver what they promised. They could pass their own laws on Nevis, then act to carry them out.

The divisionist position was an idea Ivor wanted preserved in the islands' future politics. It was the more creative approach to future St. Kitts-Nevis politics than secession, so he gave up on the radical secession position. Divisionism assured a better relationships between the two people, as it seeks to foster and integrate positive aspects of the politics. Further, since Nevisians and Kittitians share deep blood relationships, the divisionist position allows for and encourages the expression of the islands' shared history, culture, and ancestry in their coming together as one people at Christmas and Culturama time. Consequently, Stevens pushed to institutionalize the more creative relationship between the islands. His desire was cleverly hidden, when he managed to get the now infamous Clause 113, written into the St. Kitts-Nevis independence constitution. It preserves the possibility for secession, but it is to be used only as a last resort in Nevis's future political relationship with St. Kitts. However, knowing the special clause is embedded in the St. Kitts-Nevis Constitution does tempt Nevisians to experiment, as they did in 1998. It has also been suggested by some people close to Ivor, that he never intended Clause 113, to be a permanent fixture in the constitution. He intended that it be revisited as part of the islands' constitution document.

Ivor was the first politician who lived on Nevis on a day-to-day basis, but worked closely in the control and supervision of the total government. The evidence is there, all about, of how Mr. Stevens kept seeking special assistance for Nevis. According to former Prime Minister Simmonds, a good working relationship developed between them to the point that they came to respect and like each other genuinely. Gradually, the politicians and people in St. Kitts-Nevis came to a point where they no longer acted like strangers in combat. They paused and reflected on their animosities long enough to realize that in many situations, Kittitians and Nevisians share common goals, desires, and aspirations. Besides, many of them are really blood related—brothers and sisters, driven apart at an earlier time by the pressures of life, the escape-valve of migration, or the human inherent desire for adventure. Despite the stretch of water separating the two islands, in many ways, biologically and ideologically, Kittitians and Nevisians are essentially one people. Time has not changed those special encounters and thumpings of the heart; or that willingness to follow one's fortune, or love, to the other island. It has happened through the years—probably more so today, with heightened boating contact between the islands.

For example, Dr. Kennedy Simmonds, then Prime Minister, and Michael Powell, then Deputy Prime Minister, both have deep biological roots in Nevis. Meanwhile, there was Ivor Stevens, working directly on behalf of Nevis, but born a Kittitian from Sandy Point. Meanwhile, as if a follow-up to Stevens' divisionism, from July 2006 until 2013, there was a genuine and unprecedented effort at cooperation between Prime Minister Douglas and Premier Parry. Election politics of 2011 aside, Nevis and Nevisians benefitted in varied ways from the relationship. For example, the cooperation and common ground the two men found was a positive factor in Nevis' favor, particularly when the Four Seasons Hotel closed briefly. That cooperation was at a high level, and it appeared to be sincere.

Not even that earlier cooperation between the People's Action Movement and the Nevis Reformation Party compared to the level of working relationship between Dr. Douglas and Mr. Parry. Dr. Simmonds and others in the then coalition government spoke repeatedly about their concern about Mr. Daniel's aloofness. Meanwhile, Mr. Daniel never forgave Dr. Simmonds for those times he refused to make decisions that could have alleviated some of the financial distress in the early Nevis Island Government. Despite the changes, the present civility, and the growing hope for tomorrow, there are occasional glimpses of that old, angry, doom-and-gloom political strategizing, even today. There are some people who appear terrified, now that the era of secession politics has lost its vigor and attraction. However, this is a time when the global economic crisis is upon us, along with global warming and its discontents. They are expected to plunge the Caribbean area into unprecedented social and economic distress. It is only a matter of time before these calamities burst forth and strike hard at the soul of the Caribbean, wreaking havoc on the area. Secession is not a positive direction for Nevis in the foreseeable future. It still appears today that Stevens' move to being a divisionist was the more visionary and dynamic choice for Nevis. He was seeing for Nevis beyond the 20th and into the 21st century. Meanwhile, Daniel's uncompromising choice of secession continues to appear a dead-end for Nevis into the 21st century. The choices, those by Stevens and those by Daniel, also spoke to the ideological quality and vision of the two men. Stevens looked toward the others and the future. Daniel held on to the self and the now.

One drawback for the island is its population size—a few men can set up fiefdoms and do everything to preserve them, since the alternatives are limited. The education system on Nevis needs to move toward improving the teaching of science. All Caribbean islands need to have more homebred scientists. Caribbean politicians must learn to listen to the voices of the people. It is one of the challenges of contemporary Caribbean leadership. None of the political leaders has absolute knowledge, or lives forever. Further, as Nevisians contemplate their island's recent transformation, they can speak from a real experience and say with John Milton: "Peace hath her victories, no less renowned than war." Cooperation between St. Kitts and Nevis has certainly brought more positive benefits to each island, than secession can ever do.

Another matter that must have affected Ivor's perspective on St. Kitts and the relationship between St. Kitts and Nevis, was the fact that his wife and best friend, Dora, is Kittitian, too. Ivor, therefore, had deep commitments and loyalties to both islands and their people. He was born in one, but he lived on the other, enjoying its privileges, and the acceptance of its people. Meanwhile, at a time when the islands were experiencing a long, divisive disagreement, Ivor had to manage and control what must have become a personal conflict in loyalty, the best way he could. However, Ivor was an astute politician. It was hardly a surprise, that he rallied with Nevisians for secession from St. Kitts, at a time when it was politically astute and pragmatic to pressure Kittitians to allow change. Stevens' politics and commitment also endeared him to Nevisians, and heightened his political capital on the island. However, Ivor never forgot to remind everyone, from time to time, that he was born at Downing Street, in Sandy Point. In other words, he was always a Kittitian, living on Nevis, but a committed leader in the island's developmental and political thrusts.

Even if he thought about trying, it does not appear that Ivor could have found easy acceptance in Labor Party politics on St. Kitts. Maybe he did come to Nevis with Labor Party politics on his mind. However, Stevens soon became aware that there was more of an opportunity in Nevis, than in St. Kitts, to build an independent politics. At that time, however, the popular political thinking on Nevis was becoming too anti-St. Kitts and anti-Bradshaw for Ivor to take an open and successful stance as a Labor Party sympathizer. Consequently, even if Ivor was sympathetic to the St. Kitts Labor Party, at no time during his political life did he declare to Nevisians that he favored the Labor Party. Seemingly, Stevens managed his own political development. His style of deliberately courting the attention and interest of the ordinary citizens of Nevis, mirrored the political strategies of the Labor Party on St. Kitts—a matter that did not miss the attention of labor politicians, including Moore, Bryant, and Payne.

Despite the suspicion that Ralph Harris and other Nevisians sensed toward him, Ivor understood that it was foolish to show sympathy and support for St. Kitts and Bradshaw, while living on Nevis. Such an act could have easily resulted in his political extinction, early in the evolution of his political life. The review of such matters and the evolutionary stages in Stevens' political life and development do not belittle the man. Rather, it shows the caliber of the man, the complexity of his life, and his pragmatism, as politics evolved on the island. It also speaks to Stevens' capacity to understand the human need for change. Further, he demonstrated an ability to shift gears, accommodate change, and bring innovations to life on Nevis.

In retrospect, maybe Clause 113, was added to the islands' independence constitution because Ivor wanted it to register Nevisians' commitment to fair-play, accommodation, and change, not radical secession and all its possible discontents. According to Mrs. Dora Stevens, "Ivor saw Clause 113 of the constitution as a gentleman's agreement. He made the suggestion that the clause be revisited in 3 years' time." Moore noted that he was there in England when Ivor proposed the special clause in the constitution on behalf of Nevis. Mr. Moore died still convinced that Ivor was the chief architect of the measures taken to move Nevis away from secession, and toward accommodation. It was a crucial political strategy. Undoubtedly, that move to accommodation worked to bring about St. Kitts-Nevis independence in 1983. Further, it was achieved despite the fact that each island has its own leader. Thus, a classic case of "Divisionism" continues to exist between the islands, as it was conceived by Mr. Stevens. It is one of his critical legacies to St. Kitts-Nevis.

CHAPTER 11

Legacy

Everyone leaves some kind of legacy from his or her life and times. This is particularly true about politicians who become leaders and decision makers in the formerly colonized Caribbean islands. In time, the following questions are repeatedly asked of present and former leaders in these societies: What did they do? Whose lives did they touch? How do those who knew such people remember them? What legacy did they leave on the sands of that time? Since he died in 1997, these very questions are increasingly being asked about Ivor Algernon Stevens. Because of the life Mr. Stevens lived and the politics he helped to put in place on Nevis, one does not have to look too far in a search for the legacy of Ivor Algernon Stevens.

It is often through an examination of legacies that others can reconstruct lives and get meaningful glimpses of the stories, pictures, and lives hidden in them. Over time too, as can be noted in the case of President Bill Clinton, some people do become very conscious about the quality of their legacy. When this happens, the leaders endeavor to ensure their legacies are carefully designed, flattering where possible, and then preserved, to be shared in time. For example, Martin Luther King Jr. built a quality legacy, largely because he was challenged in his time to live altruistically. Frequently, the legacies left by such people, speak to their social consciousness, commitment to human dignity, and, at times, their unusual ethical sense. No wonder that our world today so bereft of ethical leadership, continues to find meaning in the unusual selfless lives of Mahatma Gandhi, Martin Luther King Jr., Mother Theresa, and Nelson Mandela.

In his life and his politics, Ivor Stevens often displayed unusual leadership for St. Kitts-Nevis and the Caribbean of his time. Quite often his life and actions demonstrated great altruism. Seemingly, Mr. Stevens could have lived successfully on St. Kitts or Nevis, whether or not he went into politics. However, he became convinced early that political life would be his best strategy to make a difference in the lives of ordinary Nevisians. Accordingly, he defied the dreams and fears of his family, and the early odds against his success. Two failed attempts at the polls, and disappointment about the politics of a colleague whom he trusted, did not deter Mr. Stevens from pushing toward his dream of an eventual transformation on Nevis. It took some 14 years and careful strategizing, but Ivor did achieve his goal of becoming a politician and decision maker for Nevis. A part of his life was spent making the political decisions he reasoned would work to better the lives of poor and powerless Nevisians. Quite often, some of those decisions benefitted Kittitians too. Since Ivor was very much a pragmatist, and had shared the islands' colonial experience, he saw all the people of Nevis as needing to experience empowerment, some success, more variety, and positive dynamic encounters in their monotonous lives.

Thus, in a spirit of understanding, coupled with his altruism, Ivor came to a point in his life where he did not argue for change simply because he wanted to be elected. Change was something he had come to believe in, and Ivor felt the people on the islands deserved to experience transformed lives. Quite often too, Mr. Stevens argued and fought for change, because he had been elected by common Nevisians and he wanted to impact their lives positively. Through the years he committed himself to sue for visible change to these people's lives. In turn, because of how his actions redirected their lives, the common people on Nevis did come to love and trust Ivor. They depended on him to champion new experiences for their communities, hoping these would bring change to their lives of drudgery and changelessness. At first, this probably seemed far-fetched, but, it was what Mr. Stevens, the dreamer and politician, promised to them. In time too, that was what he delivered.

No one else in Nevis politics, at that time, was as committed to change or did as much as Ivor Stevens to ensure change came to the life experiences of the citizens in Nevis. After a time, one saw in Nevis demonstrations of symbiotic politics: Ivor kept giving back to the lives of the people, while they reelected their champion to the legislature again and again.

Today, a high level of consensus exists among Nevisians that Ivor Stevens left a vibrant legacy from his time as a politician on Nevis. Even among the Kittitian politicians who worked closely with him and who got to know Ivor well, for example, Hugh Heyliger and Dr. Kennedy Simmonds, there remains a powerful and vivid consciousness of Ivor's legacy. Much of that legacy has also become familiar and well known to others. Its elements can be seen, touched, appreciated, and experienced in a variety of ways. Some are to provide special service for the people. Others are simply to be remembered. Few Nevisians can forget Ivor's confident and indomitable spirit. Today it is one of the things many people still talk about and remember. That was how he touched their lives.

Dozens of people from both Nevis and St. Kitts, were interviewed during the compilation of this book. All agreed that Ivor left a fruitful legacy on Nevis, for Nevisians. One of the strongest defenders of Mr. Stevens' legacy is Al Thompson, a person who served for a number of years as one of Mr. Stevens' permanent secretaries. Thompson easily recalled the hope, the discussions, the planning, and the untiring effort that helped to build Ivor's legacy. Because of his sincere, unwavering commitment to Nevis and its people, it is hardly a wonder that Ivor could leave such a vibrant legacy for the island and its people. While he did have dreams, Ivor could not have envisioned, in totality, how the things he did and stood for on Nevis would work to rebuild the infrastructure on the island and ultimately transform its society. Today, many people who watched the evolution and development of Nevis politics, and who understand the dynamics of social and economic changes, are aware that a large percentage of these came about under the leadership of the Nevis Reformation Party. Much of it was inspired by, and spoke to the untiring involvement and work of Ivor Stevens. Despite their mutual mistrust, and at times some disagreements, even Sim Daniel eventually agreed that Ivor Stevens played a pivotal role in the recent transformation of Nevis. At times, almost single handedly, and often fearlessly, Stevens worked for change in Nevis. He was also instrumental in fostering the integration of Nevis' politics that started to occur in 1970. Nevisians such as Uhral Swanston and Deputy Governor General John, cannot forget the commitment Stevens brought to changing that earlier, archaic infrastructure on Nevis.

Today, the ideas and actions of Ivor Stevens are embedded in many of the people-centered changes that came to the islands since the 1970s. His goal was to bring change to the island, inspire the lives of Nevisians, build their confidence, and give them hope as he helped them to grasp, and develop, a vision of change for their politics and total lives. Right from his return to the island, Stevens envisioned a new politics for Nevis. He intended that the change he envisioned would challenge and empower the lives of common people on the island. As much as was possible, Mr. Stevens wanted to ensure that Nevisians were afforded different experiences throughout the rest of their lives. Stevens also wanted to create and foster such a vibrant sense of hope, that it would pass to the children through education. His dream was never one where some live well while others experience only glimpses of hell, during their lifetime on Nevis. For too long, Nevisians had been deprived of electricity, water, and good educational opportunities for their children. They needed better roads, more meaningful employment opportunities, and comfortable houses to live in, as they raised their children and lived their own lives. In Al Thompson's words,

> Ivor was the politician I respected most because of his integrity. He was not for self. He did not look for gains in money or goods. Often those Ivor helped were really in dire need. They could benefit from the assistance because they were often people

> who could not help themselves. In one situation there was a lady who had some trees blown down in her yard after a hurricane. She tried everything to get them out but nothing worked. No one really bothered with her. Further, the tree trunks were probably deliberately overlooked, by government workers. As a last resort, the lady went to Mr. Stevens and reported her problem. Within quick time he saw to it that the trees were removed from the lady's yard. There was also that situation with Ellen at Bath Village. The woman lived in a filthy house, together with her dogs, fowls, pigs, and cats. Many people knew about her condition and realized it was unhealthy, but no one organized anything to help Ellen. Eventually Ivor heard about Ellen's condition and did something about it. Further, the urgency with which Ivor addressed the matter said that even a poor "nobody" like Ellen mattered to him. Such an attitude on Ivor's part gave hope to many Nevisians, young and old. One of his troubling concerns was that the advanced students on Nevis had to travel across to St. Kitts for a sixth-form education. Ivor led the charge to establish the Nevis sixth-form college, so that the advanced students on the island can be educated in Nevis, and have the choice of not traveling to St. Kitts. Mr. Stevens knew about the challenges the students experienced as they travelled to and from St. Kitts to get an education.

To date, the higher education experiment has been very successful on Nevis through the years. It has yielded a higher level of educational attainment than before, for a broader section of youths in Nevis. Back in the late 1970s and early 1980s, probably fewer than 20 Nevisians attended the sixth-form on St. Kitts, at any one time. However, in April, 2011, the Nevis Island Administration published a report which noted that some 137 students on the island attend the sixth-form. The establishment of the sixth-form college on Nevis significantly broadened access to higher education opportunities on the island. This dramatic change to education on Nevis must now be counted among the legacy of Ivor Stevens and his politics, as he worked for the transformation of the island.

Norman Jones served with Mr. Stevens as a civil servant. There was a time when he needed to have electricity connected to his house at Cotton Ground Village. However, the initial price Norman was quoted to secure the poles and complete the work was prohibitive. Accordingly, the matter lagged on, but no one seemed concerned enough to find a workable solution to the problem. In frustration, Norman turned to Ivor for help. He remembers that it came within a reasonable time. Mr. Stevens was able to work out a solution that Norman found to be both reasonable and cost-effective. Eventually his house was electrified. Almost singlehandedly, Ivor Stevens innovated to shorten the wait-time and increase the access of Nevisians to electricity.

Stevens' drive to help the underdog and promote a just society on Nevis made him a different type of politician. He often went beyond helping individuals to developing programs for whole communities. Ivor took on hotel-owner Gaskel, who suggested that having water for the guests at Montpelier Hotel was more important than having water for Nevisians living in the nearby villages—Cole Hill and Cox. Ironically, Gaskel's plan was supported by the island's political leader, Sim Daniel, whose ideas Stevens often challenged in defense of the common people. When roads needed repair at both Government Road, in Charlestown, and at Cox Village in the countryside, Ivor often saw to it that the road in the countryside was repaired first. He also insisted that the burden of electrical interruptions, via load-shedding, be shared throughout the island. Ivor was concerned that some people on the island had come to see themselves as forgotten underdogs, because the rest of society treated them in that manner. Stevens wanted a cultural change for them, too. He was interested in assuring such people that someone else understood their pain and disillusionment, and cared about their well-being.

Despite the claim of moving beyond the colonial era into political independence, it is still a time when governments in the Caribbean are cumbersome and bureaucratic. Very often, too, the leadership is selfish and too authoritarian. Quite frequently, movement toward people development is not comprehensive, and too slow. Also, decision making may not be integrated and meaningful because some officials have difficulty grasping the islands' changing reality. Many Nevisians still remember Ivor as a person who was always in motion, one who had things to get done and insisted that they were done. In matters where Ivor was involved, the government sprang into motion because time mattered to him. From time to time, Ivor seemed to peer into the future to see beyond his time. Younger Nevisians were brought under his tutelage in a sharing of ideas about the island and its future. Ivor understood that no one lives forever and that his time was running out. He was also concerned about mentoring future leaders for the island. Very few Caribbean leaders see this as necessary. Ivor Stevens practiced mentoring young leaders on Nevis back in the 1970s and 1980s. He was ahead of his time.

Electricity

Few people on Nevis disagree with the suggestion that Ivor was instrumental in making electricity accessible to Nevisians throughout the island. The Norman Jones case was one of many. Al Thompson recalled that when Ivor took over the Ministry of Communication and Works, scores of houses on Nevis were wired and waiting. Often the wait for electrification lasted an average of 4 years. There were people who used the limitations of the system to wield power or to extract special financial favors from those who could pay for the service. At that time, the electrical capacity on Nevis was always below what was needed.

According to Mr. Thompson,

> The connection mess changed because of Ivor. He also laid the groundwork and actually put in motion the movement to increase the electrical capacity in

> Nevis. Since there was no room for expansion in Charlestown, Ivor led the charge to have a new power station built at Prospect to provide greater electrical capacity.

Eventually, the increased electrical capacity was an important factor in the decision by the Four Seasons Hotel to locate on Nevis. Time has shown that the decision to improve the electric supply on the island, has also been a critical matter in the economic development of the island. Admittedly though, the Four Seasons project, was more a brainchild of Sim Daniel, than of Ivor Stevens.

Another electricity issue in which Ivor showed tenacity, leadership, and fairness, was how he resolved the frequent load-shedding situation on the island. The usual approach was to cut lights in the countryside whenever load-shedding was necessary. Consequently, there was always electricity in the town area, but quite frequently none in the countryside. After a time, Ivor established the principle: "Give electricity to everyone. When it is necessary to shed the load, the process must affect town and country alternately." That was a revolutionary idea on Nevis. In all aspects of life on the island, Nevisians knew about country vs. town wars, particularly in cricket, and in education. At one time this was part of the island's ideological and social culture. But that pattern of decision making was discriminatory. Ivor tried to change such institutionalized thinking on the island. It is hoped that this facet of the man's legacy will continue to have meaning on the island for a long time. Many Nevisians from the countryside can still recall and talk about wounds from that country-vs.-town war. In my case I took the entrance exam but was never invited to attend high school. I lived at Butler's Village, back then a place too far from town.

Water

The limitations of the water system on Nevis bordered on primitive when Ivor came to the political position where he could create some change. As Al Thompson remembers it,

> Probably the existing pipe system was over 70 years old. Only the older water-men, many of them already dead, knew the location of the pipe system on Nevis. Consequently, Ivor contracted an engineer to map the old, and create a new water-pipe system on Nevis. When Ivor started his crusade to improve the availability of water on Nevis, there were no pipes in the upper section of Bath Village. Frequent water problems occurred at Butler's, Brown Pasture, Brickkiln, Burden Pasture, Brown Hill, and in other areas on the island. Eventually, that whole water system was upgraded and improved, because of Ivor's dream, commitment, and guidance.

Today, social and economic progress on Nevis, make the demand for water much greater than it was back in the 1960s and 1970s. However, access to water on the island is no longer the great problem it once was for Nevisians. Ivor's initiatives did help. There is more water available on Nevis today than at any time before in the island's recent history. The only drawback to this system is its long-term impact on the island's underground water supply. It is not a limitless source of water. The wells can be depleted. The system of individual house cisterns, developed in the Virgin Islands, may also be worth copying. There are predictions that with the continued onset of global warming, into the future water will again become a very scarce natural resource around the world, including the Caribbean area. Thompson also noted and explained:

> In his drive to increase the availability of water on the island, Ivor sought financial and technical assistance from Canada and brought water technicians together in Nevis and St. Kitts. As a result of their advice, Ivor developed a system of wells on the island. Training in hydrogeology was arranged for well drillers on both islands. Wells were dug at Maddens, Butler's and in the

Government Road area on Nevis, some producing as many as 150 gallons of water per minute. New reservoirs for increased water storage capacity were also built at Stony Hill, Morning Star, Fothergills, Maddens, Hamilton, and Mt. Lily. Much of the technology used to build these reservoirs, using fiberglass and plastic, was adopted from England. Certain skills were taught, and in time adapted to Nevis. This approach proved a much cheaper way to build reservoirs than the traditional method of using local mortar and stones. Mr. Stevens' foresight also contributed to the improvement of the transportation system in the water department. He initiated a government-hire purchase program with the firm, TDC, to obtain vehicles. By using grants and other money for transportation, Ivor managed to settle the outstanding bills for those vehicles.

Telecommunications

St. Kitts and Nevis Telecommunications (SKANTEL) is now just a memory in St. Kitts-Nevis. But that was the organization that started the telecommunications revolution in these islands, during the 1980s. When the SKANTEL experiment began, no one understood how the idea would catch on, or where it would lead. Perhaps, with the available new technology, some people have forgotten or are unaware of Nevis' telecommunications story. Ivor Stevens was Minister of Communication and Works when the archaic telecommunication system in St. Kitts-Nevis was revamped, democratized, and made accessible to all who could afford the cost. Ivor reasoned that St. Kitts and Nevis deserved and could support a better, more efficient telephone system than the one in place. The new venture met with remarkable success. Today, the telecommunications system, is far beyond Ivor's time. However, the history is there; when tracing the modernization of communication on Nevis, Mr. Stevens was very much part of the process of revolutionizing telecommunication on the islands. That reality should not be readily forgotten, even at a time when new smart phones are king.

Waterfront Protection

The program to protect the coastline with a stone wall at the waterfront in Charlestown was started under Ivor's supervision. As the sea continues to wear and erode the island's coastline, there is growing need to have protective walls along more of the island's coast. Meanwhile, the idea is still a good one to be tried in other parts of the island, where cliffs have been beaten back and have fallen into the sea. Mr. Stevens' earlier model can still be instructive and useful today.

Education

Ivor has been credited with carrying the fight for the many students from Nevis who travelled to St. Kitts for a sixth-form education. He had travelled to and from St. Kitts with such students on many occasions. He knew of their plight, including the hardship of regular travel from Nevis to St. Kitts. Mr. Stevens was always interested in education, but it has also been suggested that his interest in education on Nevis was partly inspired by his long conflict with Fitzroy Bryant, the former Minister of Education. Mr. Stevens also travelled with some of those students on the boat. Whatever the case surrounding the sixth form start-up on Nevis, it was a project for Nevis students, which Mr. Stevens took very seriously. He followed through with the planning to ensure that a sixth-form-level education was set up and available on Nevis.

The first sixth-form classes were held at the barracks, long abandoned by the soldiers who were stationed on Nevis from St. Kitts during the tumultuous 1970s. These buildings that once accommodated an occupation force from St. Kitts were converted to a new and liberating function, to serve as a school, by the 1990s.

However, the setup of the sixth form at the barracks was temporary. But it was part of that search for a more dynamic and meaningful academic experience for all Nevisians interested in having one. Those barracks, once a symbol of repression and fear, became a place to share ideas, to liberate and expand minds, and as Plato once said of education: it is to bring about a turning of one's soul from ignorance. Today the sixth-form college on Nevis stands as a reminder of Mr. Stevens' determination, commitment, and vision—a vision that is still helping to transform the island, as souls are turned from ignorance.

Secession

A less tangible and more controversial legacy, partly attributed to Ivor, was the militancy of the movement to break from St. Kitts, during the 1970s. Some of the related drama is still remembered on Nevis. During the 1960s and 1970s, he helped to give value, vibrancy, and vision to the secession idea. Mr. Stevens' 3-day speech in the presence of the dominant and aggressive leader of government, Robert Bradshaw, and his Labor Party team, documented his determination and fervor for secession from St. Kitts, back then. Ivor was also credited with suggesting the inclusion of the now infamous, Clause 113, in the St. Kitts-Nevis Constitution. However, Ivor's political colleagues now conclude that a real break of Nevis from St. Kitts was never Ivor's goal—consequently, Clause 113. In the end, it was Sim Daniel, the born Nevisian, not Ivor Stevens the born Kittitian, who never changed from his argument for absolute secession.

Arthur "Buggy" Freeman recalled Ivor and his attitude to secession this way, "Ivor was a man that cared for Nevis and its success. He wanted to make it a better place. He was a secessionist but Nevis was not ready for secession yet." Ivor frequently said,

> Nevis has nothing. There are some things to be done first. We have to build the island first. Other people have to see we are ready. St. Kitts belongs

> to St. Kitts. Nevis has to be for Nevis, . . . I am fighting a cause, and Bradshaw is fighting a cause. He cannot treat Nevis like a village in St. Kitts.

While some people remember Ivor as a true secessionist, others disagree that he ever supported the idea of a radical break with St. Kitts. Just before he died, Ivor wrote the following statement among his final thoughts documented in his White Paper: "Let me end by stating that I took the resolution for secession for Nevis to the House of Assembly during Bradshaw's tenure as Premier." The resolution, introduced by Ivor on March 8, 1974, seconded by Uhral Swanston, was done deliberately. Apparently Mr. Stevens wanted Nevisians to remember him for, among other things, daring to stand up and challenge Bradshaw on, of all things, the matter of separating Nevis from St. Kitts. Because of the Anguillan revolt since 1967, and its impact on relations between St. Kitts and Nevis, such a challenge to Bradshaw, in 1974, was no mean feat, particularly since it came from a Kittitian in the role of a politician on Nevis. However, because Bradshaw refused to understand that the unitary State of St. Kitts, Nevis, and Anguilla, was crumbling, back in 1970, he alienated the people of Nevis, Anguilla, and many Kittitians too.

While it was a historic event, some of the words Ivor spoke on the occasion of that secession motion in the House of Assembly, 1974, did suggest an ambiguous position on the secession matter. Selected sections of the speech follow: "We must unite or perish, . . . We have to hang together or we will hang separately, . . . All for one, one for all, . . . Our only hope lies in working together."

The full text of the presentation was not located. However, Stevens was quite adept at speaking off-the-cuff, without prior preparation, and that was what he did with that historic address in the House of Assembly. However, when one is seeking secession at all costs, the sentences noted above do not seem to inspire a spirit of daring or the will to stand for a move toward secession from St. Kitts. Maybe, in 1974, as in 1970, when they formed the Nevis Reformation Party, the political leaders on Nevis, including Ivor Stevens, were still intimidated by the politics of Robert Bradshaw.

His use of terms such as, "unity," "hanging together," "hope," "working together," etc., when he was supposedly arguing about separating Nevis from St. Kitts, does appear to convey a sense of irony.

Model

It is not a normal characteristic of Caribbean politics that young people be pushed to the front of the political arena and groomed for eventual takeover of the islands' leadership. However, Ivor Stevens saw the future of Nevis in the young men associated with the NRP. Unlike other politicians on Nevis, Stevens met the younger men, from time to time, and talked politics. He also involved them in talking and thinking about the business of the party. Ivor was not afraid of them or their aspirations; rather, he instructed them to the point that he made the real involvement of young Nevisians a hallmark of his personal politics. Victor Martin and Franklyn Brand, both friends and protégés of Ivor, still speak glowingly of their meetings and relationships with Ivor, the politician and family man.

Without doubt, Ivor's populist political style brought him remarkable success. Throughout his years in politics, Ivor, who moved to the upper class and in complexion, close to being a White man, Ivor the born Kittitian, resorted to the skillful use of political stratagem and wooed the affection of Nevisians from all levels of society. Ivor's politics, his style, and commitment to the poor, are still inspirational monuments from his politics, left to Nevisians. Mr. Stevens' legacy remains very much a part of the recent social and political history of Nevis. Other politicians on the island can still turn to that legacy and find meaning about Nevis' political story, how to blend it with the socioeconomic life. Further, after Ivor had his fill of politics, unlike other Nevis politicians, he was sane, mature, and ethical enough to walk away from it all—a contented man returning to his family. He spoke of no anger or grudges against his former colleagues. Neither did Ivor act like a man caught up with the idea that everyone else on the island owed him something.

When he felt the time had come, Mr. Stevens performed an act that is still unknown among other Caribbean politicians. No one voted him out of office. Stevens simply walked away. Seemingly, he did not want to die there either. Ivor understood that it was time to leave, so he said goodbye to direct involvement in Nevis politics. He turned his back and walked away voluntarily. Like other settled and seasoned politicians, Ivor must have had misgivings. Politics had become his life. He could have won another election. However, Mr. Stevens left Nevis politics and did not have to blame anyone for a loss at the polls. Like the soldier in him, Ivor did it his way—he ended some 30 plus years of political life as a winner!

However, for men such as Lester Bowers, Maurice Stevens, Norman Jones, Al Thompson, Franklyn Brand, and Victor Martin, there are other more personal legacies to treasure from Ivor's life. They include successful family relationships, a love for politics, and a special understanding of the power in the organized masses. These men still speak readily about the many things they learned from Ivor about life. Pastor Bowers and Maurice Stevens reflected on how they listened to Ivor's advice about family. They admitted openly that they model his example. Mrs. Stevens, too, speaks glowingly of Ivor as an extraordinary human being, husband, and friend: "He was a perfect gentleman. There was mutual respect between us during our 47 years together. His politics hardly interfered with our marriage. Usually he would let off his steam outside the home." She said. Norman Jones remembers that Ivor was always willing to help solve big problems. Al Thompson was inspired by his commitment to the people of Nevis and by his deep philosophical thinking. There are some other things for which Ivor will be remembered. They include being a stickler for promptness. On numerous occasions those who had appointments with Mr. Stevens lost their audience with him or his attention, because they arrived for their appointment late and kept him waiting. One lesson such persons learned from Ivor is that being on time is always important.

Another monument to Ivor was established just one year before he died. The Social Security Board held a ceremony in Charlestown where a frail, but still gutsy Ivor was present. The Social Security

Building at the bottom of Chapel Street was named "The Ivor Stevens Building." At one time Ivor Stevens was the member of the Nevis government who oversaw the Social Security process on the island. Because of all that Ivor did for and gave to Nevis, his total legacy to the island and people of Nevis is as varied as it is complex. No single monument can be a comprehensive legacy to Ivor's life and politics on the island. However, having his name placed on the Social Security building is a fitting memorial and a relevant part of the rich legacy from him: his social consciousness and his politics; how they shaped the life and times on the island.

While Stevens lived, he gave of his best to the political, economic, and social life on Nevis. He respected Nevisians, championed openness and fair play, and made an honest effort on their behalf, to transform the island. Ivor's politics was sincere and in line with his promises to Nevisians. Now that Ivor is gone, there are legacies that all generations of Nevisians can know about, and should appreciate. Throughout his tenure in Nevis politics, Mr. Stevens demonstrated an uncommon commitment to changing the drudgery and monotony in the life of Nevisians, even his fishermen friends. He wanted change to be seen everywhere on Nevis, and to benefit all Nevisians. To reflect on what Nevis was like during the 1950s, when Ivor entered politics, and what Nevis became when he left politics during the 1980s, suggests a great transformation. Mr. Stevens did not and could not do it all by himself. However, he made unique and outstanding contributions to the politics that came and focused on changing Nevis—for the better. Mr. Stevens the Kittitian touched Nevis and the lives of its people in positive ways. Today, there is the newly designed waterfront; electricity and water are now available to even the poorer citizens on the island; the sixth-form students no longer have to travel to St. Kitts for classes; the social security system is still vibrant, and housed in a building named in Ivor's honor.

POSTSCRIPT—ON MODERN NEVIS

Despite the long history of the secession idea and its continued attraction to Nevisians today, a move to separate Nevis and St. Kitts can be both a political and an economic death-wish for both islands. Even now, when some Nevisians at home and abroad, are still set on secession, there is uncertainty and disinterest on the matter among other Nevisians and Kittitians. Secession is not in the best interest of either island.

In 1970, when Nevisians agitated to challenge their relationship and position with St. Kitts, they realized it was necessary to organize better, and gain more control over their own politics. However, they were still limited in opportunities to determine their larger destiny. Meanwhile, the seeds of dissention continued to frustrate the development of harmony and respect between the two islands for a very long time. Nevisians insisted on separate, Nevis-based political parties and more autonomy. The smaller population on Nevis kept Nevisians subjected to an unintended, almost permanently subservient relationship, and federal leadership from St. Kitts. None of the Nevis parties will ever be strong enough to form the federal government on its own. Either party on Nevis can attain federal leadership only through accommodation and at the behest of one of the political parties on St. Kitts. The closest Nevis came to that position, thus far, was with the PAM-NRP coalition back in 1980-1993. During 1993-1995, there was another occasion. However, instead of seizing the opportunity, Mr. Amory declared himself to be neutral on the matter of federal leadership.

A radical secession stance may no longer be a best way forward for Nevis or St. Kitts, politically, economically, socially, or demographically. Together, the islands form one of the smallest nations in the world. Further, they lack natural resources and no longer have the sugar industry. Meanwhile, they do need to build their human capital through education, scientific innovation, and entrepreneurship. Together, their population size is also just about right to make economic activity viable in the two islands. Meanwhile, the population size does allow for limits in the choice of politicians and allows for the creation of fiefdoms. The islands' election system is also being increasingly perverted from inside and from outside. There is too much power given to wealthy donors who pay for election campaigns. This allows for blatant forms of corruption. Even in the USA, that phenomenon of money-from-anywhere, to political parties, is undermining democracy. It is now a growing practice in the Caribbean islands. At election time, expatriates are rounded up from around the world and given free tickets to come home and vote. They then leave the local residents to live with what the visitors determined for them.

Presently, the whole Caribbean area is committed to tourism. St. Kitts and Nevis are competing with each other, and against the rest of the Caribbean, in their tourism endeavors. Caribbean islanders are again being forced into the throes of globalization with little recourse. Actually, very few Caribbean people are interpreting and understanding the strategies or the contemporary moves toward globalization in the area. This is all a new patterning of what Eric Williams captioned as, "Capitalism and Slavery." However, the factor most likely to undermine a move to secession is the blood-ties between the two islands. This history of blood relations goes back to the late 1600s and early 1700s. It remains a vibrant aspect of the islands' social history and politics today. For example, my mother's family, the Ottleys, are from St. Kitts. But my wife's father was from Nevis. Some of my children were born on St. Kitts, and some on Nevis. While I am a proud Nevisian, the evidence is there, many of us, on both islands, are blood relatives. How can I truly despise my family because they were born on Nevis, or on St.

Kitts, or indoctrinate them with messages of hate, one toward the other? This problem is also shared by Trinidad and Tobago, Antigua and Barbuda, Anguilla and St. Martin, St. Thomas, St. John, St. Croix, the British and U. S. Virgin Islands, and between other Caribbean islands. Further, how enlightening it can probably be to all across the Caribbean, if we can reconnect all those forgotten, but inseparable linkages, bound up in a common past, back in Africa. Maybe there should be an unrelenting search for all those records from slave ships, from Caribbean slave markets, and from the many Caribbean migrations. Then, some of the hate and that enduring sense of superiority and inferiority among Afro-Caribbean people can be replaced with humility and a knowing acceptance.

Through the years, it has been demonstrated repeatedly that no secessionist politics can keep the people of Nevis and St. Kitts from maintaining their deep family linkages. When there were labor strikes on St. Kitts during the 1940s, Nevisians living on St. Kitts simply went over to their families on Nevis for support. Also, during the 1980s, Ivor's divisionist politics served to nudge the people in both islands closer together. Travel between St. Kitts and Nevis is now more popular than at any time before. Usually, the travel is not forced, as was the case back in the 1960s, and 1970s, when Nevisians travelled to St. Kitts for everything. Today, the travel is usually a choice. Back in the 1970s, there were many adult Kittitians who had never visited Nevis, whereas most adult Nevisians would have gone to St. Kitts, at least once, for some reason. That scenario has now changed. People from St. Kitts travel to Nevis frequently, impacting the Nevis economy positively. Many are finding life partners there too, and are opting to live on Nevis, at a rate that never happened before. Kittitians are also visiting Nevis for Culturama, other festivals, and for sport events. Nevisians meanwhile have never stopped visiting St. Kitts. Admittedly, there is now the unfortunate downside of criminal activity, causing some concern about movement between the islands. Notwithstanding, some Nevisians are even contemplating that revolutionary, but persistent idea of a bridge joining the two islands—once a cherished dream of Robert Bradshaw. Meanwhile, the regular ferry service, and that special vehicular ferry called, "The Bridge," continue to keep the people linked, and business exchanges going at increased levels.

Among the Nevisians who continued to argue for secession are former Premiers Amory and the late Sim Daniel, Dr. Everson Hull, and some other Nevisians residing abroad. This is particularly the case when there is a closely fought election, as in July 2011. At such times, St. Kitts and St. Kitts politicians are often assigned the role of scapegoats by the politicians of one of the parties on Nevis. In the 2011 election, it was the Concerned Citizens Movement's turn to scapegoat. There is still an insistence that the islands be separated politically and administratively so that Nevis operates totally independent of St. Kitts. Despite all those efforts at strategizing by Ivor to ensure cooperation between the islands, the secession matter remains a nagging, critical, and unsettled issue between St. Kitts and Nevis. It just does not go away. Stevens worked to diffuse and divert Nevisians' desire for secession, but his effort was not totally successful. The secession matter, with all its complications, has survived Ivor. It certainly has not been buried with Mr. Daniel either.

However, along with the broadening impact of the world's economic downturn, there is the gathering specter of global warming and its gloomy foreboding for the entire Caribbean area. The secession of Nevis from St. Kitts may remain a good idea for politicians and certain other irrational thinkers, but it is not a very viable economic survival idea for the broader population of Nevis. Meanwhile, the notion that foreign investors to the island will stem the tide of the cost is only a sugar-coated myth that is for the now. There will be a dire after-cost to the people of Nevis. Both St. Kitts and Nevis need to look at education, science, and agriculture, as important areas for innovative development and research, as they move into the 21st century. The islands must also take a hard look at the matter of creative leadership and its role in their communities. There should be focus on helping communities become better educated, more innovative, and empowered to solve problems, as they deal with the oncoming change.

Seemingly, the 2013, political campaign on Nevis saw very angry opposition to the Labor Party on St. Kitts. After the calm on Nevis following the general election of 2010, there was the assumption that Nevisians were moving from their dismal past. The tendency now is to deemphasize the old natural animosity posture between Nevisians and Kittitians; something that Ivor sought to end. Honest citizens should be opposed to corrupt elections in St. Kitts-Nevis and elsewhere. The realities of the islands' politics should push the Prime Minister toward a more pragmatic people-centered politics and away from the myopic politics of the distant past. Recently he seemed genuinely engaged as he helped to deal with the matter of Nevis economic development and financial survival. But aspiration to forever leadership is from the distant past of Caribbean politics. Moving on, death, passing the baton are realities the Prime Minister must be prepared to face. If not, time will simply pass him by, making him irrelevant in St. Kitts-Nevis history. Further, as intelligent as Prime Minister Douglas is, he must learn from the past. There is still much to be learned and understood about dictatorships, false consciousness, and people empowerment for change. This is a time for transformational leadership on both sides of the channel, not the outdated authoritarian, dictatorial, and hero leadership inherited from colonial times in St. Kitts and Nevis. The election process must also be transparent. When this is not the case, it undermines the very idea of democracy in St. Kitts and Nevis, the Caribbean, and everywhere! Politicians should always bear in mind that any government that rules without authority from the people, or without the confidence of the people, is a dictatorship. It does not matter how many elections have been formalized and allowed to be counted.

Bradshaw's leadership of St. Kitts-Nevis was clearly authoritarian. However, that was another time in the islands' history. Many Kittitians and Nevisians can recall there were few positive moments between the islands. Now, in the 21st century, the challenge of St. Kitts-Nevis leaders is to carry that baton passed by Bradshaw, but with an enlightened vision. No political leader in the Caribbean today should look back to the 20th century to meet and grapple with the dynamism of change and expectancy in the 21st century. There is a need for new, enlightened, thinking, and transformational leadership. Caribbean leadership must become more ethical, less self-centered, more people empowering, and less materialistic. As we move into the 21st century, there must be a change of attitude, thinking, and dreams if St. Kitts-Nevis is to survive as a nation with its people. With these things in mind, how do we move to change and what should be changed?

- One of those changes must be a call by Nevisians for some arrangement for proportionate representation in the St. Kitts-Nevis government and its decision-making process, as long as there is a federal government. St. Kitts and Nevis should each be entitled to some form of local government—not Nevis alone. And, the idea of a co-Prime Minister arrangement should not be too far-fetched. Neither should be the idea of term limits for those who lead the islands.
- It is also about time that the women of St. Kitts-Nevis begin to play a more active role in the leadership of the islands. The idea of men being superior political leaders has always been a myth. Women have always been there supporting the leaders of St. Kitts and Nevis. Unfortunately, few have been pushed to the fore.
- Meanwhile, Nevisians are dissatisfied that their representatives sit on the opposition benches in the Assembly so often. Rather than being part of the decision-making process in the federal government, Nevis politicians usually come to the House in opposition to the government, simply because they are from Nevis. That political arrangement has not been working well for the islands. It must be adjusted to accommodate the peculiar situation with Nevis, since the present arrangement does not allow for regular Nevis involvement at the federal level of decision making. Despite experiencing some positive economic circumstances, at this time, an indefinite continuation with the present political

arrangement between St. Kitts and Nevis can push Nevisians back into the secession mode. One is also reminded of an important statement made by the late Fitzroy Bryant many years ago: "A Labor Party government and Nevis will never work together. Neither side can easily move beyond the bitter past between the two islands." However, that is not totally true. Human beings do have the capacity to change and move away from past, deep-seated and historical animosities. There was England vs. America, the U.S. North against the U.S. South, Germany vs. the rest of Europe, the U.S. vs. Japan, and the U.S. vs. Viet Nam. Today, they have all moved beyond the past animosities and hatred that drove them to war.

- The system of proportionate representation, now receiving review throughout the Caribbean area, may help to fashion a more perfect union between St. Kitts and Nevis during the 21st century. It is a challenge, but it can also be the mark of an intelligent people searching for enlightened, thoughtful leadership.
- Further, in the 21st century, good decision making cannot rely on any one person. Teams of people working together to solve problems do a more effective job than one thinker. Nevisians and Kittitians have to develop their capacity to think creatively and resolve the developmental problems they encounter. There should be more an emphasis on inclusion in decision making that impacts the islands' citizens. Those community and village councils still make sense.
- Meanwhile, there should always be suspicion by native people of the idea that the foreign, developed world, can, or will always do a better job than the indigenous people, of solving their local problems. Often, what the local citizens need to do is develop a proper perspective and then the ability to resolve their problems effectively. Unfortunately, many of the great tragedies in the Caribbean area have been related to foreign cultural impositions over time.

- Finally, the islands' history should be carefully documented so that there are accurate records available through time. Caribbean people must be actively involved in documenting their history!

By working together to resolve local problems, past or contemporary, Nevisians and Kittitians can become an innovative people, creating new paths to unity and respect, in a forever-changing world.

This is part of the challenge of two separate islands and their people committing themselves to being an independent nation, and no longer a British colony. Any reaching back to that older divisive style in St. Kitts and Nevis politics and history, during the 21st century, will be too simplistic and too regressive for enlightened leadership. Neither will such backward looking work well, after all the progress the islands have made in educating their people, since the 1980s. How can St. Kitts-Nevis or any other Caribbean nation today, continue to choose a hat-in-hand existence, bowing, begging, and accepting a forever dependency? This is a time for transformational leadership, and a continuous empowering of Caribbean people through education. Those who choose to contract with the people as politicians should be honest, competent, intelligent, and aware enough to make a positive difference in the lives of the citizens. As the philosopher, John Locke, once noted, when political leaders fail to live up to their contracts, and promises to the people, they do not deserve the loyalty of the people. Rather, through "any means necessary," such political leaders should be forced out of office. Their non-performance signals a failure to carry out and perform as was agreed to, in the political contract.

Meanwhile, one real problem that will haunt the islands and their politics for some time to come is the small population of St. Kitts-Nevis. This will certainly undermine the development of leadership on the islands. How many people on the islands are trained in leadership and can be competent political leaders? Why are a few Caribbean leaders so intent on dominating the leadership of the islands? Meanwhile, that strategy to bar Caribbean emigrants who return to the islands from participating as political leaders will have a negative impact on the development of leadership in the islands. It should never be forgotten that the labor revolution on St. Kitts was led by returning citizens of St. Kitts-Nevis, Wilkes, Fredericks, Nathan, Halbert, Challenger, Manchester, Solomon, and others, who made labor unionism the transformational force it became on St. Kitts. Further, in an era of globalization, both Nevis and St. Kitts will be encumbered by their size, their limited natural resources, and their long experience with dependency. It will be unwise for Nevis and St. Kitts to become engrossed in another open secession war during the 21st century. Instead, Nevisians and Kittitians are being challenged to demonstrate their growth in education and global understanding. The people must demonstrate tolerance, creativity, and increased levels of competence. These characteristics will be necessary from the people, as the islands face the future, with its myriad of challenges.

A secession war between St. Kitts and Nevis, today, may provide political drama for politicking politicians, but it will be a wasteful war of attrition for ordinary citizens. The people to benefit will be those poised to exploit the islands' poverty, lack of natural resources, and dependency, as they wave the banner of capitalism and globalization. It will be those others, gathering to benefit from divided nations, who will prosper from the fights between the islands. Meanwhile, as the two islands engage in an unwise war of attrition, the poor and seemingly powerless citizens remain in a forever search for a way forward. They still need affordable living, personal development, and some sanity in their lives. The, at times forgotten, people of St. Kitts-Nevis often find themselves, as if caught in mountain-like waves and vicious contrary currents, with no way forward.

If Mr. Stevens could come back and observe the politics of St. Kitts-Nevis, what would he see? If it's a return to the politics of the 1960s and 70s, that would be viewed as a weak, hopeless, uncreative endeavor, and a burden to the islands' future. A reflective Stevens would also conclude his political legacy has not been instructive to the evolving politics in the islands. Those 30 plus years of striving for a better relationship between St. Kitts and Nevis, he could therefore see as almost wasted years. Today, the real challenge for St. Kitts and Nevis politics seems to be the acceptance of their physical and symbiotic reality. They depend on each other, and need to forge a carefully thought out, workable, and lasting relationship into the future. The groundwork for "divisionism" is inherent in Clause 113. It is a part of the islands' independence constitution, and the section was proposed by Ivor Stevens. He was first a secessionist. Later, by the mid-1980s or early 1990s, Mr. Stevens turned to divisionism. He wanted that clause in the constitutional document to be temporary, but also dynamic. It was to encourage a revolutionary relationship between Nevisians and Kittitians. It is still a practical and positive approach with which the islands can experiment, as the nation surges into the 21st century, with all its unknown promises and challenges. The political leaders must do more for the people of St. Kitts and Nevis. Wealth, prosperity, and the sense of a better life, must come to them too, not just to the politicians—there should be balance! The people of St. Kitts-Nevis need paths in life that promise more than blind curves and dead ends. Political leaders must offer the citizens real, not false hope. As was demonstrated by Ivor Algernon Stevens, St. Kitts and Nevis can change and grow from humane, creative, and transformational leadership. These offer a real path to change and a grander vision for the islands' future. The legacy of Mr. Stevens challenges both Nevisians and Kittitians. Maybe none of us will change the 21st. century. However, each Kittitian and Nevisian can become an innovator, rising to the myriad of challenges, as the future unfolds.

Pictures of The Times, People, Places, and The Politics

AFTER 1882, LOCAL GOVERNMENT RETURNS TO NEVIS 1983:
POLICE WITH MACE

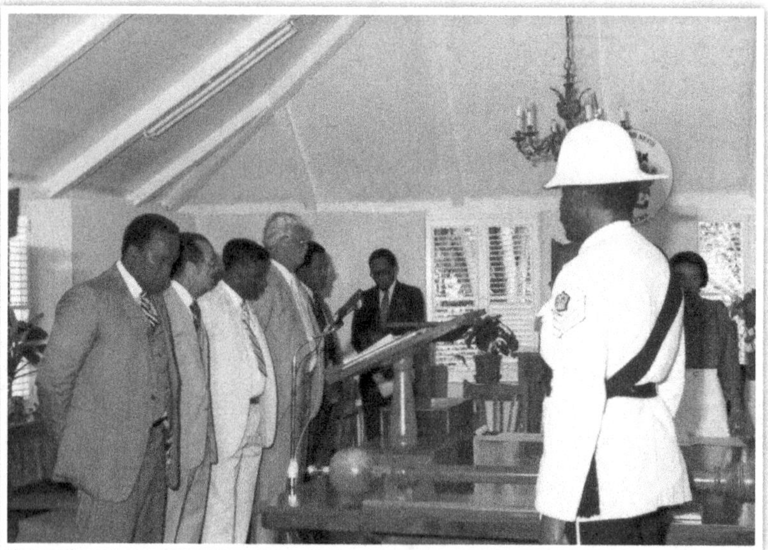

PRIME MINISTER, DR. KENNEDY SIMMONDS:
INDEPENDENCE CEREMONY, NEVIS (1983).

PRIME MINISTER, DR. KENNEDY SIMMONDS:
INDEPENDENCE CEREMONY, NEVIS (1983).

IVOR STEVENS ADDRESSING NEVIS ISLAND ASSEMBLY, 1983.

PM SIMMONDS ADDRESSING NEVIS ISLAND ASSEMBLY

NEVIS ISLAND ASSEMBLY, 1983.

UHRAL SWANSTON ADDRESSING ISLAND ASSEMBLY

NEVIS ISLAND ASSEMBLY (1983).

INDEPENDENCE CEREMONY, NEVIS, SEPT., 1983.

P.O.BOX 24.
Charlestown
Nevis, West Indies
19th December 1970

The Right Honourable Joseph Godber
Secretary of State for Commonwealth Affairs
Foreign and Commonwealth Office
London. S.W.1

Sir,

" Request to Her Majesty's Government of the United Kingdom to consider similar Constitutional Status for Nevis as Anguilla as a result of the present Constitutional crisis affecting the State of St.Christopher Nevis and Anguilla. "

Please find enclosed a petition on the above subject from Officers of the Nevis Reformation Party.

We humbly beg that you will consider the same petition in the light of the crisis affecting the State of St. Christopher Nevis and Anguilla and in particular the cause of Nevis.

We shall be willing if required so to do, to supply you with any further relevant information that you may require and also to meet you for discussions if you shall so desire.

We have the honour, to be Sir,

Yours faithfully,

S. Daniel
President, Nevis Reformation Party.

Ivor Stevens
Vice President.

Swanston
Secretary.

NRP LETTER TO BRITISH GOVERNMENT (1974).

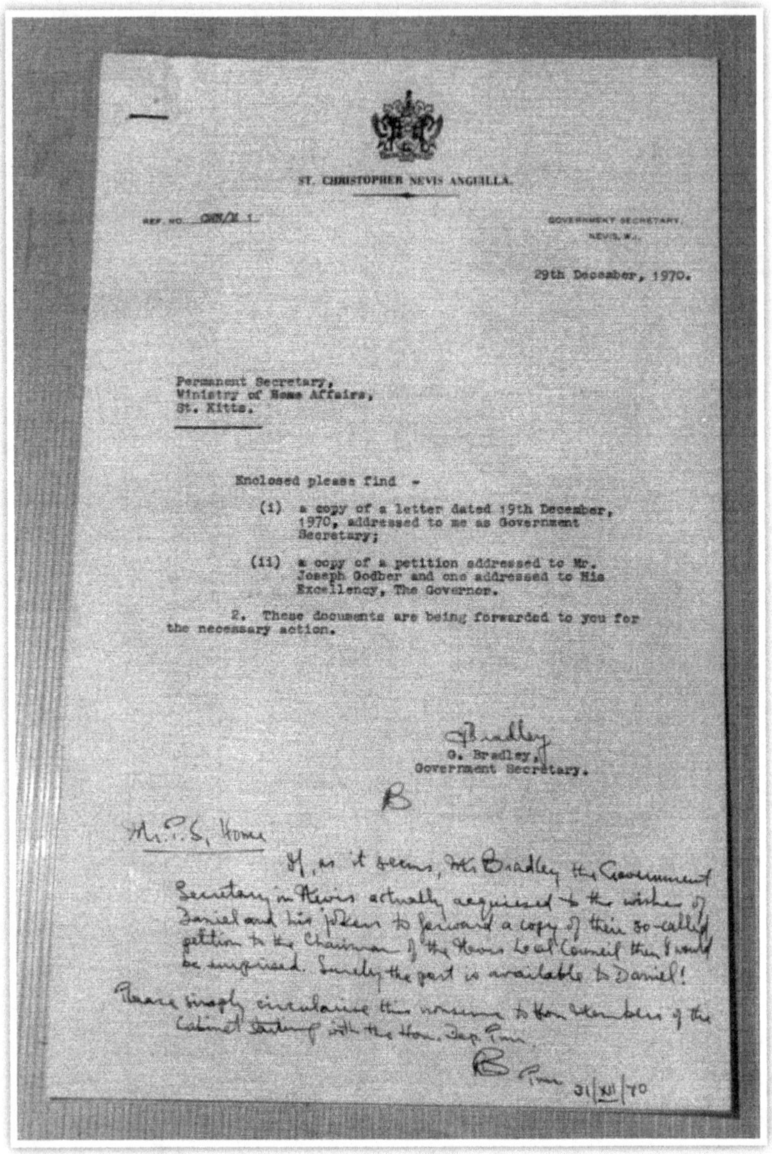

ST. CHRISTOPHER NEVIS ANGUILLA.

REF. NO. [illegible]

GOVERNMENT SECRETARY,
NEVIS, W.I.

29th December, 1970.

Permanent Secretary,
Ministry of Home Affairs,
St. Kitts.

Enclosed please find -

(i) a copy of a letter dated 19th December, 1970, addressed to me as Government Secretary;

(ii) a copy of a petition addressed to Mr. Joseph Godber and one addressed to His Excellency, The Governor.

2. These documents are being forwarded to you for the necessary action.

G. Bradley
G. Bradley,
Government Secretary.

B

Mr. P.S. Home

If, as it seems, Mr. Bradley the Government Secretary in Nevis actually acquiesced to the wishes of Daniel and his jokers to forward a copy of their so-called petition to the Chairman of the Nevis Local Council then I would be surprised. Surely the post is available to Daniel!

Please simply circularise this nonsense to Hon. Members of the Cabinet starting with the Hon. Dep. Prem.

RB Prem 31/XII/70

EXAMPLE OF BRADSHAW'S DISDAIN FOR
OPPOSITION ON NEVIS (1970)

A SAIL-BOAT FROM YESTER-YEAR

UHRAL SWANSTON: A TRUE CHAMPION FOR NEVIS

CAPTAIN ARTHUR ANSLYN

DEPT. GOV. GENERAL, EUSTACE JOHN

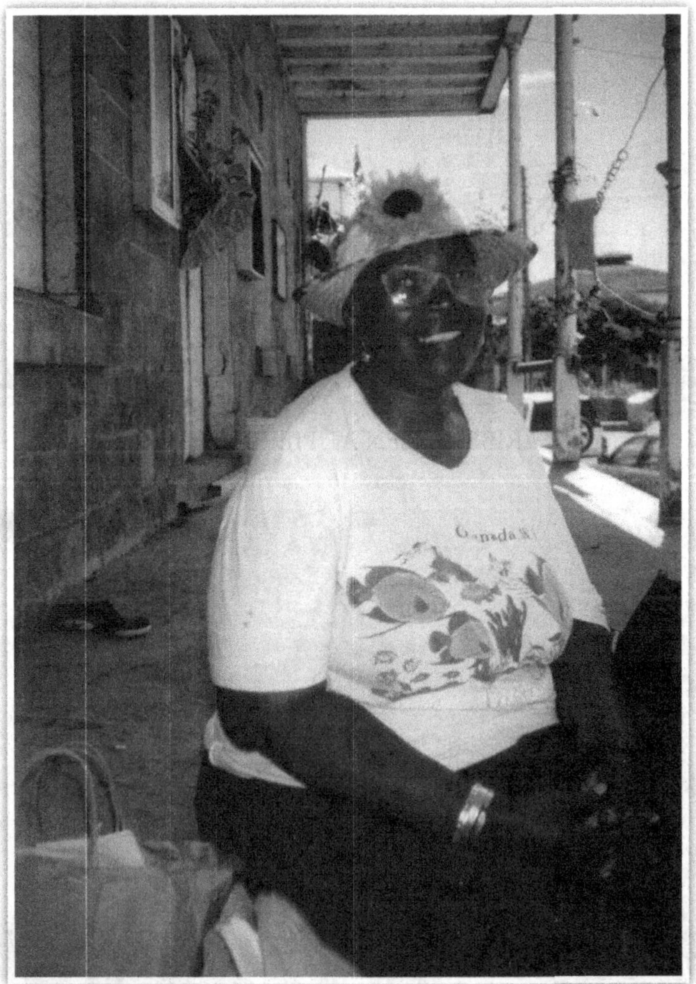

EULALIE FRANCIS: A FRIEND OF THE STEVENS

CARIBE QUEEN AT PIER IN NEVIS

SERVED AS MILITARY BARRACKS AND SIXTH FORM (SCHOOL)

THE ABANDONED HOME OF NEVIS OBEAHMAN

REMEMBERING THE CHRISTENA SPOT

A WELL SET UP BY STEVENS IN BUTLER'S AREA

IVOR STEVENS BUILDING AND THEN SS STAFF.

NEW SIXTH FORM CLASSROOM

NEW POWER PLANT ON NEVIS

BACK IN THE DAYS OF SAIL BOATS

ROCKS TO PROTECT THE WATERFRONT

ROCKS GIVING A NEW LOOK TO NEVIS WATERFRONT

WHEN SUGAR WAS KING ON ST. KITTS

THE STEVENS' HOME ON NEVIS

MS. MAY STEVENS & MRS. DORA STEVENS

APPENDIX A

ARGUMENTS IN FAVOR OF SECESSION

ARGUMENTS IN FAVOUR OF SECESSION

1. The party executive must be fully briefed by the Premier.

2. Immediately after the Executive Brief the Hon Prime Minister must be informed.

3. Simultaneously with 2 above the Hon Premier will advise His Honour the Deputy Governor General.

4. Action programme implemented.

5. Conditions regarding secession:

    (a) PAM to be advised of programme
    (b) Full and frank discussions invited
    (c) Friendship Treaty drawn up containing such provisions as say:-

        1. absolute freedom of movement

        2. freedom to own property in either or both islands

        3. in movement of goods, services or people, no passports, bills of lading, manifests, passes or other documents from either country

        4. as far as is possible all laws are applicable to both islands in other words a joint Judiciary similar to the OECS Appeals Court shall exist between both islands - the Legal Department will provide the necessary instruments.

6. Each island stands ready to come to the assistance of the other when requested or deemed necessary even if not invited.

7. There shall be no interference in the domestic affairs of the other provided that such domestic affairs are not directed to disturb the peace and good government of the other in any way.

8. Inter marriage -

FROM MEMORY

On the 18th January, 1980 the Big A Operator contacted me by phone saying that he was looking for news concerning the upcoming elections. Among other questions he asked were"

(a) Which party I was backing in St. Kitts

(b) If Labour should win would I favour NRP joining with them or

(c) Should PAM win would I favour NRP joining with them and

(d) Last but by no means least which party I thought would win in St. Kitts.

My reply was short and simple "I was neither concerned nor interested in the outcome in St. Kitts.

While this conversation was taking place that operator was taping and broadcasting it unknowing to me. Not that I cared in the least who heard or interpreted as they wished but I thought it was a bit cheap of the Big A Operator at the time.

My party in the 1980 General Election published widely a one paragraph manifesto, quote:

"The NRP will fight for Secession of Nevis from the State of St. Kitts and Nevis at all costs"

However since no one could predict the result of the 1980 elections the NRP meant to breakaway Nevis from St. Kitts no matter the cost (be the cost in lives or money).

The scene changed so dramatically since the 1980 elections that to proceed on the secession course at this time demands extreme caution on both sides of the channel. Of course this decision has to be made by the Nevisians and no other people.

No doubt the Hon Premier, Leader of the country's governing party NRP will present his promised paper in such manner as to give the "man-on-the-street" sufficient facts, figures and assurances as will:

(a) give him a 2/3 majority of the elected members of the House of Assembly (Nevis) and

(b) a 2/3 majority of the Nevisians living in Nevis and whose names appear on the voters list when the Referendum is taken in Nevis.

I am concerned about the draft constitution - considerable thought is necessary in framing same. Above all things I would desire to see entrenched, "No one individual shall be Head of the country for more that two consecutive terms.

Call it what you like e.g.
1. Johnnie come lately
2. A flash in the dark
3. He is a was-a
4. It is an after thought or Intelligent after the occasion

To Continue

Its a privilege to forget the past but it could easily return to face us again.
I happen to know that once Brad had a majority in the house he did not care one iota what happened to either Nevis or Anguilla. He would go abroad and beg in the name of St. Kitts Navis and Anguilla and having got assistance to spend all on St. Kitts. The time came however that the two colonies of St. Kitts (Navis and Anguilla) could stand it no longer thus a state of eruption began to grow. Time for a change therefore is long overdue.

In 1976 the NAP presented the bill for separation of Navis from the State of St. Kitts and Navis and Anguilla at which time the bill was not voted upon in the usual manner. Thus it remains inconclusive until this day and RLB is dead over ten years.

Since that time Southwell and Moore were Premiers of the State. Since 1980 Moore put forward a green paper "In Place of Strife" had he put forward the enclosed points in 1973 the Bradshaw Government would have fallen thus things would have been different today. But for all that has happened had Lee Moore presented the Green Paper in 1979 when he was Premier it would have had a different effect from what it now has and after presentation of a similar letter to Sim in 1995/1996.

Bearing in mind that I spoke with Moore in the UK on the subject on which occasion I gave him my view which he has now passed on as they were his original.

SHOULD NEVIS SEEK FOR AN ALTERNATIVE TO SECESSION

The only alternative to me appear to be a Federal Structure having:

(a) Each Island having its own House of Assembly and running its own affairs.

(b) St. Kitts House of Assembly.

(c) Navis House of Assembly.

(d) Federal top with equal representation.

(e) The Prime Minister to alternate from St. Kitts and from Nevis after each Federal Election.

(f) Consideration be given to having the Federal House of Assembly fixed in either St. Kitts or Nevis or alternate elections planned in St. Kitts and Nevis.

Considering that such an alternative is a new ball-game suggests very very strongly serious consideration, thought, planning and care to be exercised.

No fly by night hasty or trivial decision can be made.

Above all things the Nevis Government must be seen to have acted maturely in every step of the way.

MEMO ONLY TO MY PARTY (NRP) POLITICAL COLLEAGUES

Secession of Nevis from St. Kitts

1. The Hon Premier has promised a paper on this subject for our guidance and study.

2. I propose the following action be taken on the paper if and when circulated:

   (a) Discussion by members of Government be held in the five (5) constituencies.

   (b) Invitation be sent to all denominations, schools, other organizations and prominent citizens to discuss the paper.

   (c) Comments written and oral be invited.

   (d) All questions asked in one form or another be recorded **verbatim.**

   (e) All comments be recorded

   (f) All answers made to questions or comments be recorded.

   (g) A VON Radio and TV programme be instituted so as to give every person an opportunity of hearing and understanding the paper.

   (h) At least two (2) persons must do the explaining over Radio and TV taking two or three parts at a time.

3. Since all persons may not be able to fully grasp the content of the paper at once then Government must leave no stone un-turned to have fullest publicity made on the subject.

4. A minimum of eight to ten weeks be given so that Government be not accused of stifling this all important subject and a mere presentation would not be enough.

Thanks

Ivor Stevens
July 10, 1989

APPENDIX B

Bradshaw's Written Comment, December 1970

ST. CHRISTOPHER NEVIS ANGUILLA.

REF. NO. CMN/M 1

GOVERNMENT SECRETARY,
NEVIS, W.I.

29th December, 1970.

Permanent Secretary,
Ministry of Home Affairs,
St. Kitts.

Enclosed please find -

(i) a copy of a letter dated 19th December, 1970, addressed to me as Government Secretary;

(ii) a copy of a petition addressed to Mr. Joseph Godber and one addressed to His Excellency, The Governor.

2. These documents are being forwarded to you for the necessary action.

G Bradley
G. Bradley,
Government Secretary.

B

Mr. P.S., Home

If, as it seems, Mr Bradley the Government Secretary in Nevis actually acquiesced to the wishes of Daniel and his jokers to forward a copy of their so-called petition to the Chairman of the Nevis Local Council then I would be surprised. Surely the post is available to Daniel!

Please simply circularise this nonsense to Hon Members of the Cabinet ~~starting~~ with the Hon. Dep. Pm.

RB Pm 31/XII/70

APPENDIX C

CARIBBEAN SAYINGS, COLLECTED BY IVOR STEVENS

Who carn hear, feel

Is hard nacks and dry fall.

Donkey no go a horse race

Ah wha fu u fu u

Foot no walk, mouth no eat

Darg ded wid e

Who in de kitchen feel de heat

All skin-teeth no laugh

If u do good, good mit u

If u spit up in de air e will fall back in u face

Too much company mek crab no ha no head

No fisherman karl he fish stink

Moonlight run til daylight ketch um

U could carry de harse to de watering but u carn mek um drink

John drunk, John no stupit

Time longer dan twine

Do so no lub so

Na dig stick in raw sore

Fallaw fashion kill mangy darg

When u ded u dun

Trouble mek de monkey eat pepper

If u lie wid de darg u git up wid de flea

Monkey see fine salt and tek um fu white sugar

Na hang u hat wey u han carn reach um

Darg sleep a u fire place, craupaud smoke u pipe

You never see fowl bottom till win blow

Hard knack an dry fall

Long run fu marga goat

Mouth open twory jump out

Never dam de bridge u cross

No tongue cattle no gat wa mek e carn talk

Look for black sheep before e dark

Time so hard, darg an arl a look wok

Time longer than twine

Too much company mek crab no gat no head

Warl an Bush gat ears, long grass carry news

Play wid puppy, puppy lick u mouth

Play wid bull darg , bull e bite you

Fine thief, fine watchman

Wha sweet ah goat mouth bitter in he behine

Trouble pan tap a badaration

New broom sweep clean but ole broom know wey de dut dey

Monkey no wha lim fu jump pan

U never miss de water till de well run dry.

Who de cap fit draw de string

When ginney bud wing bruk e walk wid fowl

Lub so no hab so

Buds of a fedder flock together

Morticians live through death

Gel shut u shop door

Every cat climb wid e own claw

One one full dung basket

Better the debel u know than the one u na no

Na ball fu the bas who a go, barl fu de one who a come

Only he who wear de shu feel de pinch

U carn mek blood out a stone

Ebry fren gat a fren

Cockroach na gat no room in fowl ruse

One han carn clap

No throw way ole fren fu new

Look out for when cock crow 3 time, stranger a come

When u neighbour house a bun wet u own

No do wha a do, do as a say

Queeze e eye Queeze e eye

Cattle minor no cattle temper

Moon run till daylight ketch um

Go sofly fu ketch darg flea

Only he who feel it know it

Mouth open tory jump out

Two wrong no mek one rite, wa bout 3

wha start wrong mus en wrong

Mountain goat promis e self fu bul a hut fu shelter when rein a fall, after sun a shine e fuget e promis

Ef e no bang me e no lub me

Arl grin teeth no laugh

Na count u chicken before de egg dem hatch

U a play mumu wid u head arn

Drizzle rain kil Sarm Crook

No change horse in mid stream

One from ten lef nart

Ef 1 from 10 lef 0, 1 from 11 mus lef 1

De morse majarity

Chicken age hen lay a egg

When ram goat merry e pe a governor front door

Cleanliness nex to Godliness

Blue fly no so farse

No get mess up between de grin teeth an de smile

If Jamaica can lef the W. I. Federation wha mek Nevis carn lef dis

Time fu change de change

Power currupt but absolute power currupt absolutely

Ebry no ball aint a no ball

Ebry day no Christmas Day

Once a man twice a child

Shark belly never full

Little ting absorb little mind

De tail a wag de darg

Hurry darg yet raw meat

Ef you kill me darg a kill u cat

Play wid puppy puppy lick you mout

Dat dat is,is

Nutten new under de sun

Ef Mahammed no go to de mountain den the mountain mus go to Mohammed

Sly mongoose darg no u way

Some can read by karn understan

O Gard O Gard dem went fu write pan, dem write PHD

Neba carl name, ef u do u put uself in trouble

Jumbe fraid salt

ge he san fu sugar

Me no warn stale money

No fisherman say e stinking fish stink

Ebry shadda is a man

Ebry cloud a shower a rain

Kip a dry seat

Ah wet seat an a hungry gut

Ebry day a fishin day but ebry day no katchin day

Grass greena pan de ader side a de fens

Jus as big de fish in de sea as wah dun ketck

Action speak louder than word

Stick and stone can break bones but words can do no harm

When u are big u large

When u are small u little

Knock a drum, Knock a drum

Wa hut eye mek nose run water

Darde bouy marme gell

Wa go roun kum roun

Wa run arf a hars back gadda under e belly

So u lib so u ded

Man apoint man disapointed

A proud ginney bud proud mek e kip e tail dung

How it start no so e en

A man canvinve against e will, can easily be of the same opinion still

Me na no

Today fu me tomorrow fu u

Fus larf no larf

One man meat kan be anada man poison

Compiled by Ivor A. Stevens

APPENDIX D

STEVENS' WHITE PAPER

WHITE PAPER
by
Ivor Stevens

<u>BRIGHTER DAYS LAY AHEAD FOR NEVIS</u>

To begin with the contents of this White Paper are those of Ivor Stevens solely.

The fact that we have returned the same government to power indicates:
1. A state of confusion and the fact that the population has not been directed secession wise. First of all I wish it known that I am a firm believer in Nevisians directing their own affairs and not be directed by a St. Kitts/or Federal Government.

2. If the above constitutes secession then I am in all accord with it. In fact I am forced to consider myself a "Divisionist" which in my opinion is the same as above. From now on therefore all references shall be those of a Divisionist.

Let us examine as closely as possible the results of the last election. The effect of which took root in the result of the last Federal Election.

There have been many ups and downs in the political arena which resulted negatively for Nevis. I have always felt and still do that NRP based on secession was adequately prepared and able to take Nevis into secession. I have been wrong up to now. I can recall having called on Parry advising him to immediately go in search of Amory on which occasion he would use all powers of persuasion to have him come along with NRP. If however that failed then he should seriously consider joining with CCM. After all to the onlooker Nevis feeling should take precedence over the partisan.

Let us look even casually at a few points which of necessity will affect Divisionism.

Since there is so much in common with both countries, serious discussion and dialogue must necessarily involve both Federal and Nevis Governments that is (a)

Prime Minister and Premier (b) Transportation and Communication (c) Health and Police and above all (d) Finance.

Until both peoples - St. Kitts and Nevis - fully understand the implications there shall be constant confusion and distrust.

It is my conviction that the powers that be must travel to the highways, byways and hedges inviting and encouraging one and all to save some little portion of their earnings on a very regular basis with no intention of making withdrawals (time limit being prescribed by them). At the same time consideration must be given to the fact that there remains only two indigenous financial houses in Nevis namely:- Bank of Nevis and the Nevis Credit Union. Move now so that its benefits shall be seen sooner than later.

It is further considered that no Government can run a country without money (if wasted or well spent) therefore I look to the above named institutions to adequately finance the various projects in Nevis for Nevis. It is therefore suggested that (a) Government through discussion with the Prime Minister get hold of its correct shares in National Bank and Social Security.

With the use of these two indigenous institutions Government will have all payments and withdrawals made through them. This can be done on a six monthly basis or in whatever way the financial experts shall advise.

It is for the Bank, Credit Union and Government to handle the fiscal matters of the country so skillfully that other Governments and Countries will sooner than later seek our assistance.

It is for the Government of Nevis to keep its sight directed down the road for the next hundred years so that the politicians in sixty years hence shall be able to look back and say well done old forgotten servants of Nevis. Nevis at this time is suffering from four diseases, Love of freeness, Lack of Education, Too little attention to the Youths and Elderly and not enough attention to the Economy and Infrastructure.

Enough attention is not paid to the cultural upliftment of the society.

NRP was born in 1967 in Low Street as a result of Eugene Walwyn having promised that he would carry the resolution for the Secession of Nevis from St. Kitts. However the reverse took place in that he neither intended to push nor produce secession in the house of assembly where constitutionally it should have been first debated; so that when he and his party arrived in England the question was posed if he had taken it to the house. Having decided in the negative, he was told by the British Government that nothing could be done. This was well known to Eugene from the start.

This left entrenched in the minds of the people that Eugene accepted the post of Attorney General instead of pursuing the Nevis issue. In other words he became Labour and cemented his position by stating in public that he would sink his ankles in blood so as to keep Basseterre the capital of Nevis and St. Kitts. This was in 1966/67.

To further refer to NRP it has been dubbed the New NRP which caused and is causing untold confusion in that the original organizers assume that they no longer exist politically nor can contribute to modern thought and tendencies.

There being no consultation or should I say scant consultation the founding fathers of the party have made little or no forward contribution. Not being a Nevisian by birth and considering myself to be one on account of my many years spend here, I consider it my home but with it all I always wanted to know that a person whose umbilical cord is buried in Nevis becomes the leader of the country. In which case I always took a back seat in all endeavours which leads me to now know that had I served my party as diligently as I served my leader, Nevis would not now be in this predicament in which it finds itself.

I now refer to my allegation concerning the four diseases from which Nevis is suffering in the hope that correct solutions will be found and implemented in the course of time by the powers that be.

1. **Freeness** - Nevis, unlike the bigger countries such as the U.K. and the U.S.A. has not produced in order to pay taxes thus taxation is not acceptable to the people. However, since the country cannot be run without money, taxation becomes very necessary. While there are different types of taxation it has been established that income tax is in the past, so that the Government will of necessity bring about indirect taxation which has to be paid.

2. **Education** - It has been said that an educated nation is a wealthy nation.

3. **Youth & The Aged** - The indications are that one third of the population is of school age one third elderly, one third working. In consequence one third of the population has to maintain the entire population and with it all the Government's needs finance to carry out the various projects which it either has to borrow from foreign agencies, at exorbitant rates of interest or tax the population accordingly. (Be it clearly understood that Nevisians dislike taxation)

It is necessary for Government to find sources of revenue but it is understood that the lending Financial sources of the world have started reducing the amount of loans they had previously made and in some instances have refused.

This brings me to the point where the people of the country have to be trained and educated along fiscal lines. It is therefore necessary for the powers that be or Government of the day to go out in the byways and highways and hedges and encourage the inhabitants to go to a bank where they will deposit small amounts (minimum directed by bank) with no intention of making withdrawals whereby when one looks down the road he will find that he is carrying a three in one programme.

In this programme the bank will have ready cash for its performance; a young relative will be assured of stability and above all the economic structure will be reinforced.

In looking down the road I see Nevis appearing as the hub of Caribbean Unity which, in my considered opinion, leaves me to feel that she can set a proper pace for places like Barbuda, The Grenadines, Tobago.

Only after the dependencies become equal with the present membership of CARICOM will there ever be stability. Before going further I should refer to a few instances, though simple, as follows:

I was born on 23rd August, 1911 in Downing Street Sandy Point, of the Methodist Faith. My family moved to Nevis where I had the joy of attending the Charlestown Primary Boys' School, which was held at the Methodist Church Hall downstairs. The late Mr. J.E. Cross was Headmaster and disciplinarian of no mean order.

To indicate how long ago this took place he taught men like "Johnny Floop", "Cutcorn" Smith, W. T. Hanley and others too numerous to mention. All of the above named have long departed this life.

I then transferred to the Excelsior School the first, and only, Secondary School in Nevis at that time and privately owned by Ms Helen Bridgewater. From there I went to St. Kitts Nevis Grammar School. On leaving school I went to work at S. L. Horsford & Co Ltd. I left Horsfords and joined the Canadian Army where I served for six years overseas.

At this point I have to stop with this disorganization and will end by saying the Caribbean sea is the face basin of both Americas North and South and deserves better care and affection from both - in that our climatic conditions affect the Americas in like manner.

It is therefore for America's protection to build up the economy, education and infrastructure so as to adequately take care of the drug scourge, while looking down the road with every hope of mastering the approach of tropical storms within the next ten centuries.

I beg pardon for unnecessary repetition, poor construction and any disorderly putting together. Old age does not permit me to be more orderly for which I apologise.

It is amazing to consider how little things attract and interest little minds! I remember about 80/70 years ago there were two elderly men in Bath Village namely Mr. Benjamin Jones and Mr. Thomas Hanley. I will give a brief outline of who and what was Mr. Jones. He was famous for communication in that he kept the flow of goods and services between St. Kitts and Nevis.

During his time Mr. Jones kept a cart, four donkeys and a mule for conveying goods and services from all parts of the country to the pier in Charlestown so as to catch the lighter before they left for St. Kitts, which was usually at an early hour. He worked so hard in transportation that his one and only willing mule died during transporting goods hence Mr. Jones became known as "Kill-mule".

Even though my father and I lived under the same roof he chose to send a message to me by the same Kill-mule Jones. It was as follows: "Always get up from your table feeling that you can eat more because having eaten all that you have, a stranger might knock at your front door saying that he was hungry and sought something to eat, which you could not provide because you had eaten all. In other words do not be greedy always get up from your table feeling you can eat more.

On another occasion I was on my way to church on a Sunday morning when I saw someone else obviously coming to worship. It was Mr. Thomas Montgomery Hanley garbed in a black-double breasted coat, bell-bottomed pants, black umbrella and a black-topper hat, black tie and white shirt. Not having seen a costume of this type before, I rolled with laughter on the ground. Mr. Hanley got furious over my conduct and complained me to my father where-upon I got a lashing. I was born and raised in a Christian home of the Methodist faith and I can recall the time when I was a choir member under Miss Helen Bridgewater and a Sunday School pupil under the late Mr. Charles Byron.

I also recall the days when we would be sent upstairs at school for a five minute devotion. One day per week the school would be given a five minute lecture on human behavior.

This environmental effect on good conduct was intended by the powers that be to take you through life as a cultured human being. Respect for elders was constantly taught. Religious knowledge, good conduct and moral instruction are sadly missing. I find from the school curriculum the emphasis being placed on the academic.

While at the Grammer School a pupil could be easily identified on the street by virtue of a chip hat with school band and tie and was not permitted to pass an ex-school boy, an elderly person or a person of prominence without raising his hat, as in those days a mere complaint led to a caning at school. This eventually gave authority to a member of the public in whose opinion your action deserved a whipping, gave you one on the spot. Another was administered at home for having behaved in such a manner in public.

What I have written before still does not make me feel or accept that the modern day youth must. Sufficient to say the modern generation has never been taught, therefore does not know the merits or demerits of the old time system. It is time that the parents be taught how to raise a family along refined and decent ways as parental control does not exist today.

One Parent Home: A woman being the parent - more of this later. I do not blame the home entirely for short-comings as they were never given the necessary cultural exposure. You see!! if a woman has a child that is fatherless, more than one conclusion may be drawn:-

1. That she has the child by choice knowing that she can adequately take care of its future needs.
2. Having a child while not having to give an account to anyone for its existence or
3. The result of one night's pleasurable outing.

On the other hand a woman might have a child, a job limited income and at the same time having to face up to inflation - which leaves one to feel that she cannot pay the necessary attention to the child's upbringing therefore, viewing it from both sides the child suffers and eventually the Nation. Who am I to think otherwise when facts are facts and will always remain stubborn.

From the Christian stand point the community has always been based on Christianity. However we must not overlook the fact that a small percentage of the community has at one time or another, accepted negromancy (Devil's device) which leads me to believe that there are more good people than bad in our midst. There was a time when people of different persuasion had an altercation over a sheep or a goat and invariably a pastor from either church would patiently listen to the cause and effect of the matter and amicably settle the case, rather than going before the court.

I can recall that this was the method in force prior to the influx of Nevis Lawyers. Allow me to refer to the question of economic and social affairs for the future of Nevis. There were the days when cane and cotton held their own. Unfortunately they faded out when Nevis became the bread basket of St. Kitts. I can recall standing on the water front in Basseterre along with others anxiously awaiting the arrival of the Nevis lighters which would be laden with chickens, eggs, cattle, sheep, goats, pigs, charcoal and items too numerous to mention.

Today the reverse is the case because the building industry is at its peak leaving little or no room for agricultural development in which case the building industry must supply $40 - 50,000,000 to the Treasury in order to keep the infrastructure at a high standard while bearing in mind that the modern generation cannot allow

itself to produce the bare necessities of life by dirty fingers.
It therefore remains that the building industry must be carefully guarded by the powers that be as to enable it to both build up a cash reserve in the country thus providing for the next generation until another industry can be developed to replace it.

Constitutional - In 1985 it was clear to me that the constitution no longer served the purpose and should be re-hashed in the light of changing events. I had been convinced and still am, that the people of Nevis can carry the country where they want and at the same time be disliked by the Federal Government of St. Kitts. No government selected by the Kittitians will ever like Nevis.

1. I would like to see Nevis a Republic.

2. That the head of state be elected and not be partisan and who could be presented as a role model to its people.

3. Be debarred from serving as head of state for more than two consecutive terms.

4. Should be adequately paid so as to prevent him/her from accepting gifts in return for favours.

5. Include all freedoms

6. The legal system to be an independent department of Government which shall serve all its people alike. The Governor General (President) shall undertake decisions which cannot be taken before any court by any person.

To digress somewhat, let me at this point vigorously suggest that the Minister of Finance be guided by a select committee in the spending of tax payers hard earned dollars and a final Court of Appeal of one man be set up to investigate and decide on certain specified finances.

If the Minister of Finance is found wanting then not only he but his advisers, will be accountable for and if found guilty as charged, on summary conviction be fined $10,000.00 each or six months in prison with or without hard labour or both.

The Minister of Finance must openly declare to the public his plan of expenditure at regular periods. He well knowing how the people of Nevis detest taxation. Too much emphasis cannot be placed concerning the spending of the tax payers money.

I would also like it entrenched in the constitution that a disciplinary committee of five members be set up specifically to deal with complaints from or against Civil Servants above the rank of Assistant Permanent Secretary. It is vital for the people to be educated about secessionism or rather independence, so that the majority (simple or great) may understand what the country is in for. Therefore much time and understanding will have to be spent in the field by the powers that be, so the majority will get some semblance of what will be involved in secession/independence.

Phase 2

Nevis and Secession

Nevis is an island of 32 square miles with approximately 9,000 people and is situated in the Eastern Caribbean N.W. and about 40 miles S.W. of St. John's Antigua - 40 miles north of Montserrat, 2 miles N.W. of St. Kitts.

One hundred years ago it produced cane and cotton for the European Market but in time these industries ceased, thus leaving tourism and the building industry upon which the economy depends - both being very fickle industries, so that the economy remains unstable along with the lives of its people.

There used to be a regular sea transportation of Canadian origin connecting Canada, Boston and the Caribbean - the means by which a thriving tomato and onion industry existed. Through man made adverse activity this industry was short lived

Secession

Put briefly secession is the complete separation of two countries be it political or otherwise. In the case of Nevis it is an instance where the people of Nevis object to and will no longer permit a St. Kitts based Government to decide its every movement so that Section 113 of the constitution shall be implemented.

At this phase the thinking people of Nevis have recognised the fact that the majority has not yet understood the meaning of the term secession. Therefore the responsibility rests on the shoulders of the powers that be to go out into the country and teach the people so that eventually there will be a knowledgeable people going to the polls in order to finalize the matter of secession in a mature way. More on secession at a later date.

The situation in St. Kitts was so maneuvered as to bring further hardship on Nevis so that immigration became the order of the day for Nevisians who in some cases nearly gave away their property so as to get enough money to pay their passages to England which is affecting the country up to now.

The former estate owners left their properties in the hands of locals who very naturally assumed the ownership which was in the early twenties and thirties. It is from this standpoint that:

(a) An independent mentality plus land ownership caused Nevis to want or wish to handle its own affairs today.

(b) While secession is nothing new to Nevis, I am still amazed that total absorption has not yet been exhibited but hopes to be table talk in every home in the near future.

Barclays Bank

Barclays Bank has taught Nevisians that "one one full dung basket" thus my call on all Nevisians to draw the belt a notch tighter saving, through sacrifice, every cent for a rainy day, while assuring generations to come of a more suitable society.

This banking company opened its doors in the thirties/forties simply by sending a junior member of the staff to Nevis every Tuesday morning with a cash box. This person was met on the pier by the Porter Pemberton of Craddock Road and taken to Slack's Hotel where money was accepted from customers for banking in St. Kitts.

This system continued for sometime after which they opened their own office on Chapel Street where they dealt with all aspects of banking.
The Bank did exceptionally well in business to the point where it abandoned its

place of business and is now safely housed in H & F Henville's building, known as "The Popular" in the center of the town and no longer wishes to accept small accounts as these prove very costly to maintain.

Today it caters to the more wealthy. It is therefore necessary for the small man to save from his limited revenue - no matter how small - using an indigenous bank.

To refer once more to the drug crime wave which America, United Kingdom and France are so expensively attempting to get under control. Should the above named countries build up the infrastructure of the Caribbean at a much less price, we will soon find that the drug trade in the Caribbean will soon diminish. It must never be forgotten that the Caribbean sea washes the Americas both north and south to the point where the Caribbean sea is referred to as the - face basin of the Americas.

I understand, rightly or wrongly, that the Marijuana plant is growing into a powerful industry in both North and South Carolina and in short order the blame for trafficking will be shifted from the Caribbean and the drug industry in America will be legalized, thus leaving the Caribbean further exposed to exploitation.

Tuesday March 25, 1997

The NRP was created in 1967 at Old Hospital Road near the Roman Catholic Church by Ural Swanston, Ivor Stevens and his wife Dora. The name of the party was diligently sought and urgently found, this of course, was very time absorbing. It was felt that Eugene betrayed the trust placed in him by the people when he not only deserted us and joined the Labour Union but stated openly that even if he went down in blood to the ankles he would always want Basseterre to be the capital of St. Kitts-Nevis. As a result his followers started to shed their allegiance to him.

In the light of all this the people of Nevis needed a leader of quality and so those who followed Eugene turned to Dr. Simeon Daniel for leadership for which he was not prepared.

Roan Liburd, Horace Liburd, Ralph Harris, Carlton Parris and Simeon Daniel organised for a private meeting to be held in Brick Kiln. This meeting took us no further as some people who were present left the meeting at the height of discussion. We finally ended the night at Roan's home and it was there after midnight that I presented the draft constitution, the name of the party and probable directors.

We then started the life of the party in full. I won the St. Paul's seat at elections in 1971 while the late Fred Parris won the Gingerland seat. Let me end by stating that I took the resolution for the secession for Nevis to the House of Assembly during Bradshaw's tenure as Premier. The resolution has never been voted upon and is considered inconclusive.

I have been of the opinion and still am that if a conscious vote could have been made by the elected members of the house the response would have been favourable to the resolution thus bringing down the house which could not be tolerated.

I must express very many thanks to the varied and many persons who assisted me in one way or another in getting these notes together. I list below the names of some people:

1. Mrs. Roan Liburd - First Secretary of the Party in whose home the party was formed
2. Dr. Simeon Daniel - First President
3. Mr. Ural Swanston - Party Organizer
4. Mr. Horace Liburd)
5. Mrs Roan Liburd) ----Party Executive Members
6. Mr. Carlton Parris)
7. Mrs Dora Stevens who assisted me in the ground work
8. Ms. Y. M. Stevens
9. Mr. Alford Thompson
10. Mr. Browne
11. Mr. Cedric Harper

The popular opinion at the moment is that "the young become younger and the old become older" be this true or false is left to be seen. It is useless telling a young person of an incident that took place in my youthful days (70-75 years ago) because this would be of no interest to them. The young people of today and the university grads in particular are of the opinion that what they now learn is new whereas it was learnt in a university from books or records written by men long dead. I will just make on reference that is non existent today which was prevalent in my boyhood days - religious and cultural subjects were on the schools curriculum because old man James E Crosse saw to it that every Wednesday morning at 9 o'clock children of varied and many denominations were sent to church and every Friday morning some senior citizen visited the school and lectured to us on some moral aspect of life. I will go further and say that if my father and a colleagues father were at variance over an incident which brought about a breakdown in the social status of these two men, the children of these men could not pass one of the men in the street without raising his hat in deference to the gentleman otherwise he would be told that what happened between the two fathers was between men and boys have no business in that. This takes me further down the road when I say that an elderly man finding that you were rude in some way could hold you and give you a licking for such mis-behaviour.

Today teachers and elders are totally ignored by the youth particularly the school children. About 30 years ago I personally know of an incident where a boy was sent home by the school master having received a lashing complained to his father of the lashing the following morning the boy and his father called upon the school master, the father being enraged over the incident told the boy, "he knock you, well tek up the stone and stone the headmaster back, which the boy promptly did, the headmaster there and then dismissed the boy from the school. Up to this day the boy can neither read nor write.

Of all the disciplined known to me the most important one deals with the grand children of today's child bearing women, that is, youthful respect. When the youth of today can put a value to himself in this regard he automatically respects himself, others, property, government and his country. We meaning the elders and the government will recognise our responsibility to the youth and act accordingly, government included.

Having those under control the country has to see to it that the pre-natal, natal and post-natal care must be considered and take care of by the government, in other words, I feel that the great grand children to whom I refer gets the maximum care and protection bearing in mind that whereas a woman have very much control over the child in her womb but less after it is born. To be more explicit the mothers to be have to be taken care of by the government in similar manner all leading up to a future generation of substance

It is my opinion that the island is richer than most people accept. I come to this conclusion based upon the fact that Barclays Bank PLC started business in Nevis some years ago (say 15) when my nephew Louis used to come to Nevis with a little cash pan and was met by Barba Ranzo (Pemberton of Craddock Road) who took him to Slack's Hotel and he opened on the side walk sitting to a little white table collecting cash from persons who traded in St. Kitts in the afternoon. This took place once per week as a start then twice.

In his time the Bank was opened to business. In this short while has become so rich that it is no longer interested in small account as it is a waste of their time and money operating same. This brings me to the point that everybody in Nevis (I say with respect) every person in Nevis needs to operate a savings account at one of the indigenous banks here without the intention of drawing from it so that when the time comes for Government to need cash to carry out important work for the good of the country, cash will be in the local banks.

At the moment there are:

Bank of Nevis	)	
Nevis Co-operative Bank	)	- **Indigenous Banks**
Nevis Co-op Credit Union	)	
St. Kitts Nevis Anguilla National Bank	)	
Bank of Nova Scotia	)	- **Foreign Banks**
Barclays Bank PLC	)	
Development Bank of St. Kitts Nevis	)	

Suggested Readings

Archibald, W. (2010). *The legacy of Dr. Simeon Daniel.* Basseterre, St. Kitts: The St. Kitts Business College.

Blackburne, K. (1976). *Lasting legacy: A Story of British Colonialism.* London, UK: Johnson.

Bolland, O. N. (2001). *The Politics of Labour in the British Caribbean: The Social Origins of Authoritarianism and Democracy in the Labour Movement.* Kingston, Jamaica: Ian Randle.

Borg-O'Flaherty, V. M. (2004). *20th Century Election Results: St. Kitts-Nevis.* Basseterre, St. Kitts: Author.

Browne, W. T (1985). *The Christena Disaster in Retrospect.* Charlotte Amalie, St. Thomas: BL&E.

Browne, W. T. (2001). *The Christena Disaster Revisited.* Charlotte Amalie, St. Thomas, VI: BL&E Enterprise.

Browne, W. T. (1992). *From Commoner to King.* Lanham, MD: University of America Press.

Frucht, R. (1967). *Community and Context in a Colonial Society: Social and Economic Change in Nevis British West Indies.* Ann Arbor, MI: Ann Arbor University Microfilm.

Horne, G. (2007). *Cold War in a Hot Zone: The United States Confronts Labor and Independence Struggles in the British West Indies.* Philadelphia, PA: Temple University Press.

Innis, P. (1983). *Whither Bound St. Kitts-Nevis.* St. John's, Antigua: Antigua.

Manley, M. (1982). *Jamaica: Struggle in the Periphery.* London, UK: Third World Media.

Mills, F. L., Jones-Hendrickson, S. B. & Eugene, B. (1984). *Christmas Sports in St. Kitts-Nevis: Our Neglected Cultural Tradition.* U.S. Virgin Islands: Authors.

Mitchell, J. (2006). *Beyond the Islands.* Oxford, UK: Macmillan Education.

Naipaul, V. S. (1969). *The Mimic Men.* Harmondsworth, UK: Penguin.

Palmer, C. A. (2006). *Eric Williams and the Making of the Modern Caribbean.* Chapel Hill: University of North Carolina Press.

Richardson, B. C. (1983). *Caribbean Migrants: Environment and Human Survival on St. Kitts and Nevis.* Knoxville: University of Tennessee Press.

Robinson, A. (2008). *The Shaping of an Abolitionist: James Stephen 1758-1832 Exploring the Scottish and Caribbean Influences on Abolition's Chief Strategist.* Liverpool, UK: The Society for Caribbean Studies.

Wardle, H (1999), Jamaican Adventures; Simmel, subjectivity and extraterritoriality in the Caribbean. *Journal of the Royal Anthropology Institute,* 5, 523-539.

INDEX

E

F

G

H

M

N

O